THE
FOLLY
AND THE
GLORY

THE
FOLLY
AND THE
GLORY

AMERICA, RUSSIA, AND
POLITICAL WARFARE
1945–2020

TIM WEINER

HENRY HOLT AND COMPANY
NEW YORK

Henry Holt and Company
Publishers since 1866
120 Broadway
New York, NY 10271
www.henryholt.com

Library of Congress Cataloging-in-Publication Data

Names: Weiner, Tim, author.
Title: The folly and the glory : America, Russia, and political warfare,
1945–2020 / Tim Weiner.
Other titles: America, Russia, and political warfare, 1945–2020
Description: First edition. | New York, New York : Henry Holt and Company,
2020. | Includes bibliographical references and index.
Identifiers: LCCN 2019057823 (print) | LCCN 2019057824 (ebook) |
ISBN 9781627790857 (hardcover) | ISBN 9781627790864 (ebook)
Subjects: LCSH: United States—Foreign relations—Russia (Federation) |
Russia (Federation)—Foreign relations—United States. | Cold War. |
Intelligence service—United States—History. | Intelligence
service—Soviet Union—History. | Intelligence service—Russia
(Federation)—History. | Presidents—United States—Election—2016. |
Elections—Corrupt practices—United States. | Trump, Donald, 1946-|
Putin, Vladimir Vladimirovich, 1952-
Classification: LCC E183.8.R9 W428 2020 (print) | LCC E183.8.R9 (ebook) |
DDC 327.73047086—dc23
LC record available at https://lccn.loc.gov/2019057823
LC ebook record available at https://lccn.loc.gov/2019057824

First Edition 2020

Designed by Meryl Sussman Levavi

Printed in the United States of America

1   3   5   7   9   10   8   6   4   2

To Gene Roberts and Joe Lelyveld
And for Kate, Emma, and Ruby Doyle

Among the calamities of war may be jointly numbered the diminution of the love of truth, by the falsehoods which interest dictates and credulity encourages.

—Samuel Johnson, *The Idler*, 1758

CONTENTS

CHAPTER 1

THE SEEDS
OF FUTURE STRUGGLE

For seventy-five years, America and Russia have fought for dominion over the earth. In the twentieth century, America won the long cold war, and it seemed for a time that its triumph might endure, and freedom would flourish everywhere. The moment vanished. In the twenty-first century, Russia has fought back against America and its allies with stealth and subversion. Its stratagems have undermined American democracy, a political architecture that withstood a civil war and two world wars over the course of a quarter of a millennium. The outcome may determine if America will endure, and whether democrats or autocrats will rule the world. Great armies and navies and arsenals bristling with nuclear weapons have proved useless in this struggle. The battle depends on political warfare.

Political warfare is the way in which nations project their power and work their will against an enemy, short of launching missiles or sending in the marines. Its conduct requires the full spectrum of intelligence and diplomacy, from covert operations to coercive persuasion, and the skillful orchestration of these instruments by the president. The United States built a powerful machine for political warfare after World War II, and it sped the collapse of the Soviet Union, but the American engine sputtered at the turn of the century, and today it has all but died. The Russians have been using political warfare with skill and cunning ever since Vladimir Putin came to power twenty years ago. From 2014 onward, they have struck blows against the American political system, and in 2016 they helped elect a president in thrall to Putin, plunging democracy into danger. In 2020, they strengthened their powers of disinformation and deception and took aim at America again. We need to know how political warfare works before the next attack strikes. It is coming.

War is the state of nature in the world we have made. More than two hundred million combatants and civilians have been killed in the past century. The smoldering ruins of the First World War ignited the long fuse for the second, and out of the ashes of the second rose the toxic cloud of the cold war. Among the ideals shattered by these conflicts were the noble-minded rules codified early in the twentieth century: wars were fought between uniformed combatants, they began on one day with a formal declaration of hostilities, and they ended on another with the dignified signing of a peace treaty. Nations did not intervene in the internal conflicts of others. These proved to be empty promises for the thousands of American troops sent to Siberia to fight against the Red Army from August 1918 to June 1920, nineteen months after the Armistice; cold comfort to thirteen million Poles who woke up in September 1939 to discover that they were captives of the Russians, seized under a secret clause of the pact Stalin signed with Hitler.

Two laws of war still held in August 1945, after President Harry S. Truman dropped the bomb on Japan. One was fighting power—the will of a nation to sacrifice the lives of its soldiers. The second was firepower—the killing force of a nation's arsenal. For the moment, though not for long, the United States had sole possession of the ultimate weapon. The destruction of cities reduced to radioactive rubble left the living to wonder what the Third World War would look like if Stalin had the secret of the weapon. In truth, he had it in hand, though no one in Washington knew it at the time. The Americans in charge of national security began to think about the unthinkable, and the advent of nuclear weapons changed the ways they thought. The wisest among them saw that if they were going to have it out with the Russians, the next war would destroy everything we wished to defend, and the living would envy the dead.

When the two sides failed to make peace between them, and set out to struggle for dominance over the nations of the world, they had to find a way to fight one another through the clandestine projection of power—spying and subversion, subterfuge and sabotage, stolen elections and subtle coups, disinformation and deception, repression and assassination. The Americans knew next to nothing of this way of war. The Russians had been at it for four centuries.

Ivan the Terrible, the sixteenth-century czar, had established a primitive secret police. Peter the Great and Catherine the Great had expanded Russian espionage, spying on foreign adversaries as well as on their own people. By the time Napoleon invaded in 1812, Czar Alexander I had strengthened Russia's foreign intelligence and linked it with his military. The Okhrana, formed after the assassination of Alexander II in 1881, spied on enemies within and without Russia in the decades when anarchists were killing kings and queens, princes and archdukes, and, in 1901, the president of the United States. But the Kremlin's spies were crushed by the Bolshevik revolutionaries who seized Russia in 1917. In their stead, in that cold and pitiless December, Vladimir Lenin created his own secret police: the All-Russian Extraordinary Commission for Combating Counter-Revolution and Sabotage—the VChK, known to all as the Cheka. "We stand for organized terror," the first leader of the Cheka, Felix Dzerzhinsky, said in 1918. Stalin gave them unchecked power. In 1934, they instituted the Great Terror: one million people were murdered. By that year, Stalin's spies were at work in the United States. By World War II, they had burrowed into the government—the State Department, the Justice Department, the Manhattan Project. In 1954, after Stalin's death, the spy service was rechristened the Committee for State Security: the KGB. Charged with conducting espionage, subverting enemies with disinformation and political sabotage, securing the state, protecting its rulers, and crushing dissent, the KGB was a ministry of fear, combining the missions of J. Edgar Hoover's FBI, the cold-war CIA, and the Nazi Gestapo. It was the biggest intelligence service in the history of the world. If you, like Vladimir Putin, were born into poverty and hunger in the postwar rubble of mid-century Russia, and you aspired to power, the KGB was the place to be.

An immense statue of Dzerzhinsky stood in front of the Lubyanka, the KGB headquarters in Moscow, from 1958 until 1991, when it was toppled by protesters aiming to take down the crumbling architecture of the Soviet Union. The statue wasn't recast and remounted, but Putin rehabilitated Dzerzhinsky as he revived the Soviet intelligence state. Chekist Day is now celebrated every December 20 in the Kremlin. And Putin is a Chekist to the marrow of his bones. What that means is what it always has meant: the preservation of the leader's power, at all costs; the imprisonment and assassination of his domestic opponents; and the conduct of political warfare to mystify, mislead, and surprise his enemies, to trick them into acting against their own best interests, and to weaken their position in the world.

The United States never had a peacetime spy service until Congress created the Central Intelligence Agency in 1947. Though we Americans have learned a great deal about the craft of intelligence in the ensuing years, often through embittering experience, at the outset we were amateurs in almost every aspect, particularly at political warfare, and especially in the dark arts of deception and disinformation. In its first days the CIA was only two hundred officers strong. Its mission was to fight the cold war and prevent the next Pearl Harbor. Its forces grew a hundredfold in five years, controlling covert armies around the world, running paramilitary missions from Russia to China, mounting coups, seeking to crack the Iron Curtain.

The White House and the Kremlin ordered their spies and diplomats to manipulate at least 117 national elections all over the world during the twentieth century. They fought to control nations across Africa and Asia and Latin America and the Middle East, buying allegiances with guns and money but never coming directly to blows. Each side shored up strongmen and despots, and subverted the other's favorite regimes, covertly backing guerrilla armies and underground movements and pliant political leaders. The United States fought the war on communism in the jungles of Vietnam, and the Russians smuggled arms and ammunition to America's enemies in Southeast Asia. The Russians seized Afghanistan, and the CIA shipped billions of dollars in weapons to the Islamic holy warriors who fought them. Americans beamed news and propaganda over the Iron Curtain via Radio Free Europe. The Russians fought back with torrents of disinformation disseminated by the KGB.

And in the end, after trillions of dollars spent on armaments in Washington and Moscow, and millions of lives lost in the nations where the great powers had contended, the Soviet Union collapsed under the dead weight of its self-deceptions. The Kremlin could not sustain its founding falsehood, the big lie that Soviet communism was more noble an experiment than American democracy. "Imagine a country that flies into space, launches Sputniks, creates such a defense system, and it can't resolve the problem of women's pantyhose," Mikhail Gorbachev, the last leader of the Soviet Union, lamented after the hammer and sickle was furled for the last time. "There's no toothpaste, no soap powder, not the basic necessities of life. It was incredible and humiliating to work in such a government."

The dream of the Americans who fought the cold war had been realized: the map of the world had been remade by the collapse of the Soviet Union. The tide of liberal democracy had risen, and the nations of Eastern Europe had been freed from the suffocating grip in which Stalin and his successors had held them. And another war had been fought and won, when the United States crushed the Iraqi army in 1991. The Gulf War was a shockwave in which the Pentagon wielded new weapons of strategic deception, perception management, and information warfare. They proved as devastating as smart bombs and cruise missiles.

The United States bestrode the earth like a colossus in those days, as it had after World War II, and the prevailing wisdom in the high councils of Washington was that the world was going our way. "There weren't any foreign policy problems" when George H. W. Bush left office in January 1993, said his secretary of state, James A. Baker III. "Everybody wanted to be friends with the United States. . . . Everybody wanted to embrace free markets. Everybody wanted to embrace democracy, with the sole exceptions of North Korea, Cuba, Iran, Iraq, and Libya. Everybody was ours." Everybody loved America— including the Russians. Or so we wanted to believe.

Wiser minds, though not many, were wary about the spirit of strutting triumphalism ruling the day. The warrior-statesman Colin L. Powell, by turns chairman of the Joint Chiefs of Staff and secretary of state, quoted the Prussian military strategist Carl von Clausewitz: "Beware the vividness of transient impressions." Few looked beyond the fleeting events; fewer still envisioned how the conflicts of the cold war could be rekindled in the twenty-first century. "What we did not realize was that the seeds of future struggle were already sprouting. There were early stirrings of future great power rivalry," wrote Bob Gates, then a former director of Central Intelligence and a future secretary of defense, who served presidents from Lyndon Johnson to Barack Obama. "In Russia, resentment and bitterness were taking root as a result of the economic chaos and corruption that followed the dissolution of the Soviet Union"—along with the American push to expand the NATO military alliance eastward to Russia's border—and "no Russian was more angered by this turn of events than Vladimir Putin." The Russian leader had been a KGB lieutenant colonel watching from his post in East Germany as his nation's empire crumbled. He knew something about the practice of political warfare.

When he rose to power at the turn of the twenty-first century, he took the shattered components of the old KGB and reconstructed a new version of the Soviet state in which he controlled not only soldiers and spies but manipulated television and the internet to invent perceptions of reality. After he won his third term as president in 2012, Putin focused the full spectrum of his powers, readied his forces, and took aim at America. In the words of Mike Morell, a former acting director of the CIA, he "turned significantly back towards what was essentially Russian behavior during the cold war, which is to challenge the United States everywhere you can in the world, and do whatever you can to undermine what they're trying to accomplish. Do whatever you can to weaken them."

Americans tend to see war and peace as night and day. Russians see a never-ending battle. They may be right, for while the circumstances of combat change, the nature of war is immutable. For twenty years, Putin has used the power of his military and intelligence services to create new strategies and tactics for political warfare against the United States. Their counterattack slowly came into force, a blitzkrieg unseen until after it had struck at the heart of the American body politic.

Not long ago, on a winter's night in Moscow, a senior adviser to Vladimir Putin named Andrey Krutskikh, an expert in political warfare who now serves as an ambassador at large of the Russian Federation, delivered a stark threat at a public forum. "You think we are living in 2016," he said. "No, we are living in 1948. And do you know why? Because in 1949, the Soviet Union had its first atomic bomb test. And if, until that moment, the Soviet Union was trying to reach agreement with Truman to ban nuclear weapons, and the Americans were not taking us seriously, in 1949 everything changed and they started talking to us on an equal footing.

"I'm warning you," he continued. "We are at the verge of having 'something' in the information arena, which will allow us to talk to the Americans as equals."

Now we know what that weapon was. We have to understand its origins and its history, and we have to understand that it threatens permanent damage to American democracy, and the potential for its downfall. We are reliving a moment that began a lifetime ago, when the great powers began to clash by night, and the fate of the world was at stake. One great difference stands between then and now. America is bereft of a strategic vision to replace what it had in the cold war. And where there is no vision, as the Book of Proverbs says, the people perish.

But in 1948, America had a strategy to fight fire with fire. It was the work of a single solitary figure who made his voice heard around the world. It guided ten presidents, it governed the decisions and the stratagems of diplomats and spies, and it spurred the destruction of the Soviet Union.

CHAPTER 2

THE PERPETUAL
RHYTHM

The strategy that shaped the cold war was the brainchild of George F. Kennan, second in command at the American embassy in Moscow during and after World War II. He had spent most of his adult life studying the calculations and the cruelties of Generalissimo Joseph Stalin, the absolute ruler of the Soviet Union since 1924; the penetrating gaze of Kennan's brilliantly blue eyes had been fixed on the enormity of the Soviet empire for nearly twenty years. He saw Stalin as "a man of incredible criminality, of a criminality effectively without limits; a man apparently foreign to the very experience of love, without pity or mercy . . . most dangerous of all to those who were his closest collaborators in crime, because he liked to be the sole custodian of his own secrets, and disliked to share his memories with others who, being still alive, had tongues and consciences."

Stalin, like his true heir, Vladimir Putin, aimed not only to penetrate the American government with espionage and to get inside the minds of its leaders, but to seize control of nations within his reach, to defeat leaders he detested, to pick suppliants or useful idiots he could manipulate, and to make Russia a great global power, feared by allies and enemies alike, and to achieve all this in the wake of a devastating struggle. Alone among Americans in the months after the war ended, Kennan grasped all this, and he tried with increasing force to make American leaders understand it too. He had deep insight into what went on inside the Kremlin; he had nearly seven years' experience inside Stalin's Russia, and he knew it better than he knew America. "He was terribly absorbed—personally involved, somehow—in the terrible nature of the regime," wrote the Russian-born Oxford don Isaiah Berlin, then serving at the British embassy in Moscow. The Russians were a nation of stage managers, Kennan wrote at the end of the war, and their deepest conviction was that things are not what they are, but only what they seemed to be.

Kennan saw that the sun would soon set on Russia's wartime alliance with America and that the shadow of Soviet power would lengthen westward, falling on one hundred million souls in Europe and beyond. "No one in Moscow believes that the western world, once confronted with the life-size wolf of Soviet displeasure standing at the door and threatening to blow the house in, would be able to stand firm. And it is on this disbelief that Soviet global policy is based," Kennan had written in a May 1945 cable from Moscow to Washington, a warning unread at the White House, newly occupied by President Harry Truman. But he believed that America could contain the hungry wolf. If it stood steadfast against the ambitions of the Kremlin and confronted them with confidence, "Moscow would have played its last real card." Though no one heeded his words at the time, they would become the core principle of American foreign policy for the rest of the twentieth century.

Harry Truman thought he could find a way to get along with the man he called Uncle Joe. They were set to meet for the first time at Potsdam, on the outskirts of Berlin, on the afternoon of July 16, 1945. But Stalin stood him up.

Truman was a pure product of America, born into the Missouri of the outlaw Jesse James to parents who traded in mules and horses

and farmed the fertile earth. He was straightforward and plainspo-
ken. He never went to college. A veteran of World War I, a failed
haberdasher, a county judge by the grace of the Kansas City political
machine, somewhat miraculously elected to the United States Senate
in 1934, and ten years after that, a startling last-minute choice as President Franklin D. Roosevelt's third vice president, Truman served
for eighty-two days under FDR. The president was a ghostly figure
to him, rarely seen, wraithlike in the flesh. When Roosevelt died on
April 12, 1945, Truman said, "I felt like the moon, the stars, and all
the planets had fallen on me."

Stalin was the dictator of 180 million people; his rule reached
five thousand miles from Berlin to the Pacific Ocean, and from the
cold Baltic Sea south to the balmy shores of the Adriatic. Born to an
alcoholic shoemaker and a laundress, his face scarred by childhood
smallpox, he had been expelled from a seminary and set out to be a
revolutionary. He had edited the Bolshevik newspaper *Pravda*, run
extortion rackets to raise money for the party, survived four years
of exile to Siberia during World War I, and risen to power through
ruthless cunning.

He was a master of conspiracy and a mass murderer. Truman
was an innocent. He had no notion of foreign policy or statecraft.
He was unprepared for power, and he knew it. For eight years, these
two men would hold the fate of the earth in their hands.

When Stalin failed to show up at Potsdam that afternoon, Truman took a motorcade through what remained of Berlin, once the
world's fourth-biggest city, now a hellscape of death and destruction,
stinking of rotting flesh. The rubble of the Reich was piled ten yards
high along the boulevards. "I thought of Carthage, Baalbek, Jerusa-
lem, Rome, Atlantis," Truman wrote in his diary that night. "I hope
for some sort of peace—but I fear that machines are ahead of morals
by some centuries and when morals catch up perhaps there'll be no
reason for any of it." As Truman toured the ruined city, it was dawn
in the high desert of New Mexico. At 5:29 a.m., the scientists and

soldiers of the Manhattan Project witnessed a blinding light brighter than the sun and watched the rising mushroom cloud of the world's first nuclear explosion. Truman got the news that night.

The Potsdam conference, intended to settle some of the most pressing problems of postwar Europe, foundered from the start. Prime Minister Winston Churchill, who would be voted out of office the next week, was an exhausted volcano, his words great gusts of wind. Stalin was war-weary but wily, cautious but calculating. Churchill talked without coming to a point, Truman wrote; Stalin just grunted, but you knew what he meant. The one moment of great consequence came on July 24. The day's talks at the Cecilienhof Palace, a mock Tudor mansion built during World War I, had been fruitless. After conferring with Churchill and their respective military chiefs, Truman decided to share his secret with Stalin that afternoon. He walked around the table as the late afternoon light slanted into the dark-beamed room and spoke quietly to the generalissimo and his interpreter. He said in a casual tone that he possessed a new weapon of great force with which to end the war against Japan. He came away thinking that Stalin didn't understand what he saying. Stalin knew exactly what he meant.

Truman came home believing he could do business with Uncle Joe. Months passed before he knew he'd been naive. Through the summer and into the fall, the glow of victory began to fade and the chill of a darkening twilight descended on Washington. No one knew where to steer the American ship of state. Truman had no firm policy toward the Soviet Union and little basis on which to build one. What did Stalin want? How far west would he project his power? What should the United States do? In late January 1946, an urgent appeal for enlightenment on these questions arrived at Kennan's desk at the American embassy in Moscow, in the depths of the Russian winter. His title was minister-counselor, but he was running the show. Ambassador Averell Harriman had left Moscow, and three months would pass before the arrival of his replacement, General Walter Bedell Smith, who had

been chief of staff to the supreme allied commander, General Dwight
D. Eisenhower, and who went on to lead the CIA during the Korean
War. Bedell Smith was desperate to understand Stalin's thinking. So
were the president and the secretary of state and the secretary of war.
The State Department had turned to Kennan for wisdom after ignoring his cables for months. He was sick in bed, as he often was, suffering from the flu and a throbbing headache; his mood by turns highly
strung and deeply melancholy. But he was roused by Washington's
plea for an understanding of the Kremlin. "They have asked for it," he
thought to himself. "Now, by God, they will have it." He unleashed
an eight-thousand-word dispatch, the "Long Telegram," the longest in
the history of American diplomacy and by far the most widely read. It
circulated all over Washington and through American embassies and
military outposts around the world. Every member of the newly emerging national-security establishment absorbed it, and Stalin, thanks to
his spies, read it, too.

Kennan set out to address questions "so strange to our form of
thought" that they required intricate answers. He wanted his superiors to understand that the truth in Russia was whatever Stalin said
it was: "The very disrespect of Russians for objective truth—indeed,
their disbelief in its existence—leads them to view all stated facts
as instruments for furtherance of one ulterior purpose or another."
The Russians conducted their affairs on two levels: the official realm
of public policy and diplomacy, in which lip service would be paid
to international relations with its allies, and the subterranean one,
carried out by secret intelligence and security agencies, through espionage and subversion.

"There is good reason to suspect that this Government is actually
a conspiracy within a conspiracy," Kennan wrote. Stalin had dissolved
the Communist International, or Comintern, in its aboveground
role as a world congress in 1943, as a gesture to his wartime allies,
the United States and Great Britain. But the international network
under his direction and control was "a concealed Comintern . . . an

underground operating directorate of world communism." Although J. Edgar Hoover didn't know it yet, Soviet spies in America had stolen the secrets of the atomic bomb, burrowing into the Manhattan Project from the first. They had a long start on the FBI and the CIA. They had more than two hundred agents and sources inside the United States government, the military-industrial complex, and the media. Soviet intelligence was "an apparatus of amazing flexibility and versatility," Kennan wrote, "managed by people whose experience and skill in underground methods are presumably without parallel in history."

The Kremlin was "a political force committed fanatically to the belief . . . that it is desirable and necessary that the internal harmony of our society be disrupted," Kennan wrote, in a passage foreshadowing the political warfare waged by Putin against American democracy. The Kremlin would seek through covert means "to disrupt national self-confidence, to hamstring measures of national defense, to increase social and industrial unrest, to stimulate all forms of disunity. . . . Poor will be set against rich, black against white, young against old, newcomers against established residents"—all of which presaged the Russian attack that lay seventy years ahead.

Fighting back against this new enemy would constitute the greatest task that American diplomacy had ever faced, he warned. He proposed that the United States had to harness its strengths in a way that had little to do with armies and air forces but everything to do with the projection of political power. Stalin and the Soviet Union might be "impervious to the logic of reason," Kennan concluded, but they were "highly sensitive to the logic of force"—not tanks and troops, but American political resistance designed to thwart the Kremlin's dreams of glory. He was writing himself into history by imagining that America could fight Russia without weapons.

Three months later, Kennan went back to the United States, a nation he hardly knew, lecturing at universities and public forums and, starting in September 1946, teaching at the newly established National War College at Fort McNair in Washington. The college had been created to help weave together the disparate strands of thinking about the postwar world, bringing together officers and civilians from the Departments of War, Navy, and State. No other mechanism existed. The war and navy brass handled military strategy. State handled foreign policy. Nobody had a handle on intelligence. Only one man in America—the president of the United States—had the job of harnessing military power to political and diplomatic purposes. And that task was beyond the mind of Harry Truman.

At his first War College lecture, Kennan struck a theme that resonated throughout the government. The Soviets, like the Nazis, would pursue their goals without moral inhibitions and through all manner of skullduggery—intimidation, deceit, corruption, subversion, psychological and economic pressure, blackmail, and murder. The United States had to defend itself and counter the Kremlin by building alliances abroad and showing the Soviets that America possessed "a preponderance of strength." Kennan was working out the rudiments of a strategy, sketching a new theory of American warfare. His adherents now included navy secretary James Forrestal, a volatile Wall Street magnate soon to be the first secretary of defense, and the newly appointed secretary of state, General George C. Marshall, who as army chief of staff under FDR had organized the biggest military expansion in history.

The cold war was coming into the forefront of the American mind by the start of 1947. Kennan was expanding on his work, polishing an article to be published in a forthcoming issue of the quarterly journal *Foreign Affairs*. The title was "The Sources of Soviet Conduct," and the byline was "X," but his intended audience would know the words were Kennan's. It made him America's Kremlinologist, the man who understood how to confront the Soviets. He argued in it that "the main element of any United States policy toward the Soviet Union must be that of a long-term, patient but firm and vigilant containment" of Russia's imperial ambitions. And

there it was, the word that would define a world. Containment
became the compass of the cold war.

"Soviet pressure against the free institutions of the Western world
is something that can be contained by the adroit and vigilant application of counterforce," he wrote. "The Russians look forward to a duel
of infinite duration, and they see that already they have scored great
successes." Stalin had seized nearly half of Europe, and he had his sights
on Italy and Turkey and Greece and Iran. But the United States would
win the duel in time—if it could "confront the Russians with unalter-
able counterforce at every point where they show signs of encroaching
upon the interest of a peaceful and stable world." American generals
thought counterforce meant the deployment of an overwhelming military power. Kennan explained that the point was to prevent another
all-out war. He wrote that the nation should not simply apply the logic
of force but the force of logic: The United States had to show the Soviets and the world that it was "a country which knows what it wants,
which is coping successfully with the problems of its internal life and
with the responsibilities of a world power." That might prove to be the
most valuable force of all.

Kennan's concepts meant different things to different people,
including Kennan. He was writing political poetry; he didn't set
his terms in concrete, and he would come to despair at how politicians and generals twisted his ideas. Some saw containment as stopping Stalin from spreading Soviet ideology deeper into the Western
world. Some wanted to push him out of Europe, back to Russia's
borders. Some wanted to deter him or, if it came to that, destroy
him by building an arsenal of nuclear weapons that could reduce
Russia to a smoking, radiating ruin. The argument over the best
means by which to achieve the end was ceaseless and schismatic.
But the concept of containment at its core was the fundament of
American foreign policy until the hammer and sickle went down
over the Kremlin for the last time, the principle around which millions of soldiers and sailors and trillions of dollars in weaponry were

organized, and the only strategic concept in the battle against the Kremlin that retained its value when the cold war was over.

Kennan did not say how an American counterforce could be created, or who would be in charge. But those ideas were coming to fruition in Washington in the spring of 1947. And many took shape at Sunday night suppers in the elegant Georgetown home of Frank and Polly Wisner, where Kennan and his wife, Annelise, had a seat at the table among the wealthy, powerful, influential men who created the American national security state and a political culture that lasted for twenty years until Vietnam tore it apart. Henry Kissinger is said to have once remarked that the hand that mixes the Georgetown martini guides the destiny of the Western world. This seemed almost true at the time, at least while Frank Wisner, who became commander of covert operations at the CIA, was stirring the drinks. Wisner was Mississippi gentry, a white-shoe New York lawyer in the 1930s, scalded by wartime experience inflicted by Stalin's shock troops against the partisans he had worked with as an intelligence officer in Romania. He was genteel, witty, given to grandiloquence after the second or third drink. His favored guests included Charles Bohlen, who would in time replace Kennan as ambassador to Moscow, and Dean Acheson, who served as General Marshall's second-in-command and would succeed him as the secretary of state. They gathered for cocktails in the garden under the tulip trees, conversed at the dinner table, and reconvened in the parlor for brandy and cigars thereafter, pondering the problems Kennan had defined and the strategies that might guide the United States through uncharted seas. In April, Acheson recruited Kennan to run the new policy planning staff at the State Department. The office was next to General Marshall's, and the door was always open to Kennan. "The General," Acheson wrote, wanted Kennan "to look ahead, not into the distant future, but beyond the vision of the operating officers caught in the smoke and crises of current battle; far enough ahead to see the emerging form of things to come and outline what should be done to meet or anticipate them."

That spring and summer, a strategy for the cold war started taking shape in the crucible of Kennan's mind. One brainchild grew into the Marshall Plan, which would deliver billions of dollars to rebuild the shattered cities of Western Europe and feed millions of people who faced hunger and starvation. Another gave rise to Radio Free Europe, which soon started beaming powerful signals in many languages and on many frequencies across the Iron Curtain to bolster American influence and subvert Soviet ideology. A third became the covert-operations directorate of the new and inchoate Central Intelligence Agency. On September 27, 1947, two months after the CIA was established under law as an intelligence-gathering organization, Kennan sent Secretary of Defense Forrestal a proposal that flowed from the conversations at Wisner's table. The United States had to create a "guerrilla warfare corps" to counter the Soviets abroad—a force with which "to fight fire with fire."

A few days later, one of Kennan's first major policy planning papers went to the newly established National Security Council, where he served as Marshall's representative, and it landed on President Truman's desk in October. Surveying Soviet aims around the world, it drew particular attention to a growing political crisis in Italy, which had been the subject of the very first meeting of the NSC only two weeks earlier. Half a million Italians had died fighting fascism in World War II, a toll far greater than all American combat deaths. American forces stationed in Italy since the war were set to withdraw. National elections would take place in April 1948. The Kremlin would order Italian communists "to resort to virtual civil war" in order to seize power, Kennan predicted, and the Russians would try to keep their hand hidden by using spies rather than soldiers. "Our best answer to this is to strengthen in every way local forces of resistance," he argued. "We should be free to call the play." The call led to the first major covert operation in the history of the CIA.

On December 17, the NSC issued a sweeping directive in which

Kennan had a firm hand. It ordered the CIA to conceive and execute "covert psychological operations" against Moscow. The intended end was clear, but the means to achieve it were not. The last major psychological operations the United States had run were the strategic deceptions that supported General Eisenhower's D-Day invasion in 1944. This was a different field of battle. Nothing in the NSC's command defined what these operations should look like. Nothing in the CIA's charter empowered it to run them. No law authorized them. No legislation financed them. A mad scramble for money and manpower ensued at the CIA's ramshackle Washington headquarters, at Forrestal's Pentagon, and in Italy, where the communist Popular Front, whose members included battle-hardened veterans who had fought Mussolini's Fascists, contested the conservative Vatican-backed Christian Democrats for political control of the nation. The Italian operation was carried out in an atmosphere of apocalyptic urgency. The CIA's analysts painted it as a contest between Stalin and the Pope—a battle for Western civilization. President Truman ordered Forrestal to secretly ship arms and ammunition to Italian government security forces. High-ranking army intelligence officers made contingency plans to back a military coup if the communists won. At the palatial American embassy in Rome, the army attaché met with the ambassador and the CIA station chief, James Angleton, and reported that all agreed a communist victory could "start World War III."

On March 8, 1948, the NSC weighed the likelihood that the Communists could win power by legal means and then transform Italy into a totalitarian state in thrall to Moscow. All of the first three major NSC reports dealt with Italy, and this one, the third, endorsed financial support for the Christian Democrats and other anti-communist parties and a "full-scale, vigorous and openly anti-Communist campaign" of political propaganda. It was in fact a formal approval of operations already underway. The Christian Democrats and their political allies received at least $10 million in support through the

CIA; a 1948 dollar is a ten-dollar bill today. Every penny was off the books: the agency had to mount a major money-laundering scheme to finance the operation. This legerdemain was in great part the work of Forrestal and his good friend Allen Dulles, the future CIA director. In one part of the effort, they tapped a Treasury Department cache of funds earmarked for the reconstruction of postwar Europe. Great sums flowed from the Treasury to wealthy Americans, who signed personal checks to CIA-created fronts, then used a prearranged code to write the money off as a charitable deduction. More money came from wealthy friends of Forrestal and Dulles through Swiss banks. CIA officers in Rome handed over suitcases filled with cash to political candidates and politically savvy Catholic priests in four-star hotels. The money financed every essential element of the Christian Democrats' campaign, including radio broadcasts, newsreels, posters, pamphlets, and propaganda to sway public opinion. It brought them the votes to win control of the Italian parliament on April 18, with a 48.48 percent plurality; the CIA kept backing the party for a quarter of a century.

The clandestine operation didn't win the election on its own. But it was proof to America's new national security chiefs at the CIA, the NSC, the State Department, and the Pentagon that covert action could change the course of human events.

On May 4, sixteen days after the Italian election, Kennan delivered a manifesto titled "The inauguration of organized political warfare." Strikingly, crucial paragraphs of this document remain classified top secret today. It was deemed too explosive to serve as an official policy planning paper; only a handful of copies were printed. Kennan was shooting a flaming arrow into the air, and it struck home. He began by citing Clausewitz's doctrine that war was a political instrument. Then he made a leap: if wars were politics, politics could be warfare. "Political warfare is the logical application of Clausewitz's doctrine in time of peace," he wrote. "Political warfare is the employment of all the means at a nation's command, short of war, to achieve its national objectives."

Thus the Marshall Plan was political warfare. The creation of NATO as an American-led political and military alliance in Western Europe, precisely eleven months away, was political warfare. Espionage, sabotage, propaganda, and the "encouragement of underground resistance in hostile states" all were essential elements of political warfare. American leaders needed to understand that the British Empire had been built and maintained in part by four centuries of political warfare and that "the Kremlin's conduct of political warfare has become the most refined and effective of any in history."

Americans now had to join that battle. Their view of the world had been blinkered by their belief in "a basic difference between peace and war, by a tendency to view war as a sort of sporting contest outside of all political context, by a national tendency to seek for a political cure-all, and by a reluctance to recognize the realities of international relations—the perpetual rhythm of struggle, in and out of war." That rhythm was the cadence of the cold war.

The United States had to confront "the full might of the Kremlin's political warfare," as Stalin worked his will on nations like Czechoslovakia, Hungary, and Poland, and threatened to push westward if unchallenged. "We cannot afford to leave unmobilized our resources for covert political warfare," Kennan argued. "We cannot afford in the future, in perhaps more serious political crises, to scramble into impromptu covert operations"—like the Italian adventure. He proposed four new ways to fight.

First came "Liberation Committees"—overseen by Americans but filled with political refugees from the Soviet Union and its satellites, who would "provide an inspiration for continuing popular resistance" in Eastern Europe. The refugees would create "organized public support of resistance to tyranny." And if the cold war turned hot, they could form "all-out liberation movements." For now, their

American sponsors would select leaders "to keep alive as public figures with access to printing presses and microphones." From this seed grew the National Committee for a Free Europe, a CIA front organization led by Allen Dulles, ardently backed by General Eisenhower, and supported behind the scenes by Kennan. And from the committee came Radio Free Europe, which began beaming broadcasts behind the Iron Curtain in July 1950 and served as the most powerful American weapon of information warfare in the twentieth century.

Kennan called for carrying out covert operations in countries where Soviet political warfare threatened American national security, and wanted it done as "a matter of urgency," because the communists were seeking to disrupt the delivery of Marshall Plan aid. And herein lay a crucial link. Congress still had given the CIA no money and no authority for covert operations. It had given the Marshall Plan billions to rebuild Europe. The Marshall Plan's top administrators were, in Paris, Averell Harriman, Kennan's old boss, and in Washington, Richard Bissell, very much a member of Kennan's circle, and later the CIA baron responsible for the U-2 spy plane and the Bay of Pigs invasion. Kennan sent them a trusted emissary—Frank Wisner—who asked them to finance covert operations in Europe, and they readily agreed. Money was no object; they had far more at hand than they could spend. CIA officers in Europe and Asia thus had access to $685 million from the Marshall Plan's coffers over the course of the next five years. This off-the-books financing was crucial to the development of the CIA as a clandestine service with missions around the world.

The first such operations were personally authorized by Kennan. The most immediate threat was that communist labor leaders, through strikes and intimidation, sought to block the distribution of Marshall Plan aid and military materiel being offloaded by American ships in Marseilles and Naples. The operation was mounted in a matter of weeks, delivering money to labor groups in France and

Italy, and to the gangsters who served as their enforcers, via a trusted associate in the labor movement named Irving Brown, a conduit for the CIA's political warfare in Europe for the next four decades. The military and economic aid got through.

Kennan now turned to paramilitary operations "to prevent vital installations, other material, or personnel from being sabotaged or liquidated or captured intact" by the Soviets. He was addressing ever-mounting demands from Forrestal and the Joint Chiefs, who were preparing for the prospect of World War III. They wanted foreign refugees to be recruited and trained to fight the Red Army; they needed plans to sabotage the oil wells and refineries of Saudi Arabia, Iran, and Iraq, in order to keep them from Russian hands in wartime; they sought ways to evacuate foreign leaders and allies who might be threatened in a political crisis. These demands would grow more urgent as the cold war deepened.

All of this was a preamble for Kennan's boldest idea. "The time is now fully ripe for the creation of a covert political warfare operations directorate within the Government," he wrote. "They must be under unified direction. One man must be boss." And the man he chose was Frank Wisner, then the deputy assistant secretary of state overseeing operations in American-occupied Berlin. He created the job Wisner would hold for a decade—the chief of America's covert operations.

Stalin's soldiers and spies by now had seized Poland, Czechoslovakia, Hungary, Romania, and the Baltics; they had threatened Iran, Greece, and Turkey; they were seeking to subvert the politics and diplomacy of Western Europe in Paris, Rome, and London; they had blockaded Berlin. The United States should strive to "reduce the power and influence of Moscow to limits where they will no longer constitute a threat to the peace and stability of the world family of nations," Kennan wrote on August 20. This concept went beyond containment to coercion, and it was the cornerstone of a secret order, titled NSC 20/4, which President Truman signed after narrowly winning reelection in November and then circulated to his cabinet on December 3.

The United States, it said, would seek to take back the spoils of war from Stalin, to roll back the Soviet tide that had swept to the edge of Western Europe, to push back until it achieved "the gradual retraction of undue Russian power and influence . . . and the emergence of the satellite countries as entities independent of the USSR." The goal was to liberate Eastern Europe through political warfare.

"As the international situation develops," Kennan told Wisner on January 6, 1949, "every day makes more evident the importance of the role which will have to be played by covert operations if our national interests are to be adequately protected." Wisner went forth and built an entirely new and utterly secret branch of American government, with the backing of the Pentagon, the Joint Chiefs of Staff, and the State Department: the clandestine service of the CIA. He proudly noted that "the original architects of the whole deal" included Marshall, Harriman, Forrestal, and Kennan.

By the end of Truman's presidency four years later, Wisner had launched hundreds of major covert operations and spent close to $2 billion; and he and his superior had drawn up a budget for the coming year in excess of $700 million, or roughly 1 percent of the nation's gross domestic product. In the decade that Wisner ran America's boldest political warfare operations, he gave his men the sense that they were America's Knights Templar. They could make or break presidents and kings, prime ministers, and political parties around the world; they could buy or rent the loyalties of generals, dictators, spy chiefs, internal-security ministers, union bosses, and newspaper publishers; they were enmeshed in the political fortunes of France, Germany, Greece, Pakistan, Egypt, Syria, Jordan, Thailand, the Philippines, South Korea, and South Vietnam, among many other nations. And for five years, from the summer of 1949 onward, they were training and deploying exiles and émigrés and refugees and other foreign agents to serve as liberation armies behind enemy lines in Eastern Europe. Nearly every one of these paramilitary operations ended in death and disaster.

They were launched under the auspices of an overarching strategy put forth by Kennan on August 25, 1949, and approved by Truman in the form of a secret presidential directive shortly thereafter. It was the first concrete plan to drive the Soviets out of Poland, Czechoslovakia, Hungary, Albania, and the rest of Eastern Europe—to free the captive nations through an all-encompassing campaign of political warfare. "Since V-E Day," Kennan wrote, "we have checked the westward advance of Soviet power, at least for the time being," and "made substantial strides in developing Western Europe as a counter-force to Communism. These are defensive accomplishments. The time is now ripe for us to place greater emphasis on the offensive" and to seek "the elimination or at least a reduction of predominant Soviet influence in the satellite states of Eastern Europe." As an "essential prerequisite," the United States had to push for "the withdrawal of Soviet troops from satellite countries," he continued. A combination of intensive diplomatic pressure, economic power, and political attack would be required. So was the projection of power by American forces through the newly created realm of the NATO military alliance, and the dissemination of propaganda designed to promote heresies against Stalin. The most secret codicil to this strategy was covert action.

The CIA recruited exiles and émigrés made stateless by the war, trained them at American military bases in occupied Germany, and dropped wave after wave of the unfortunate foreign agents into desperately poor and isolated Albania, a Soviet satellite bordered by Greece, Yugoslavia, and the Adriatic Sea. Year after year, whether the guerrilla teams arrived by air, land, or sea, almost all of them were doomed. A second front was opened on September 5, 1949, when a charter member of the CIA, Steve Tanner, sent Ukrainian partisans—émigrés recruited in Munich—behind the Iron Curtain to a rendezvous near Lviv, a major city seized from Poland by the Red Army a decade earlier and incorporated into Ukraine. The CIA believed that the operation would spark a major underground resistance movement in Ukraine,

the breadbasket of the Soviet Union and its largest republic outside
Russia. Wisner approved air drops of several dozen more armed members of the Supreme Council for the Liberation of Ukraine over the
next four years. All were captured or killed; Soviet intelligence officers compelled those who survived to radio back encouragement to
their CIA case officers, who organized and dispatched another set
of partisans, and another. None survived. But the idea that the Iron
Curtain could be pierced by American intelligence was electrifying.
The CIA began to launch paramilitary operations into Russia, Poland,
Romania, and the Baltic States. They were suicide missions, for the
exile and émigré groups recruited for these exploits were shot through
with Soviet informants, and their plans were relayed to Moscow by
the British intelligence liaison in Washington, who worked hand in
glove with the CIA. He was Kim Philby, Moscow's foremost recruited
foreign agent of the cold war.

Soviet espionage had made Stalin Truman's equal on the world
stage. The very day that Tanner's team parachuted into the forests of
Ukraine, the United States detected the atmospheric fallout from
Moscow's first atomic-bomb test. Stalin's spies in America had sped
the success of his scientists by at least three or four years. Truman
responded to the Soviet test by authorizing the development of the
hydrogen bomb. Stalin soon followed suit, but even he saw the bomb
as a poisoned chalice; he rued the fact that "atomic weapons can
hardly be used without spelling the end of the world." Both men
knew, at the same time, in the same way, that the most destructive weapons in history could not be used in war, lest they destroy
humanity. "No one wants to use it," Truman said. "But . . . we have
got to have it, if only for bargaining purposes with the Russians."

The American H-bomb test came on November 1, 1952—three
days before Dwight Eisenhower won the presidency. The Soviet
test came the following year, five months after Stalin's death. Each
blast was hundreds of times more powerful than the bombs that had
destroyed Hiroshima and Nagasaki. These were not armaments for

a war that had a strategy, but instruments of genocide or suicide, or both. They were political weapons. Their existence ensured, by virtue of their terrible force, that the cold war would be fought by political warfare. The Soviets would tighten their grip by force. The Americans would keep seeking, against all odds, to loosen it.

CHAPTER 3

TRUTH IS NOT ENOUGH

General Dwight D. Eisenhower had gone to Moscow to meet with Stalin in August 1945, two days after Truman unleashed the bomb and forced Japan into unconditional surrender. On the thousand-mile flight from Berlin, accompanied by his Red Army counterpart, Marshal Georgy Zhukov, he had looked down from the window of his low-flying four-engine turboprop, and he could not see a building still standing on Russian soil. The bones of millions of civilians and soldiers lay in that blood-soaked land. At a great feast in the Kremlin, Ike and Uncle Joe drank champagne toasts to each other. Eisenhower found Stalin, flush with victory, a strangely fatherly figure. Stalin, in turn, judged the American commander a humane and kindhearted man. Eisenhower later told reporters at a news conference in Moscow: "I see nothing in the future that would prevent Russia and the United States from being the closest possible friends." That vision proved to be an illusion.

By the time President Truman recalled Eisenhower to duty at the end of 1950 to serve as the first military chief of NATO, it looked as if World War III might be at hand; one bolt from the blue might

start the final conflagration. The North Atlantic Treaty Organization had been founded in April 1949 to prevent that disaster, but
it existed almost entirely on paper at the time Ike took command.
NATO united America and eleven European nations in a military
alliance of mutual defense. The United States gave explicit nuclear
and conventional military guarantees to every member through the
NATO treaty, and in return American military power was cemented
on European soil. The linchpin was an agreement that an attack on
one NATO nation was an attack on all.

Eisenhower dismissed as propaganda the Russians' threats
against America arming NATO. Though the fear of an attack on
Western Europe was immense, and American forces spent the
next four decades arming and training and war-gaming for it, Ike
doubted that the Russians would launch it at the time or thereafter.
"I personally think those guys in the Kremlin like their jobs. They
can't see their way through to winning a war now and I don't think
they'll start one," he told the president and his cabinet at a White
House meeting on January 31, 1951, after whirlwind meetings with
the military and political leaders of the NATO nations. "They know
they'll lose their jobs, and their necks, if they start something they
can't win." The most pressing political problem in Europe, he said,
was not communism. It was poverty. It was fear. The only solution
he saw was a united front put forth by America, its wartime allies,
and West Germany. And why so great a fear of Russia? Ike asked.
Why be afraid of "190 million backward people?" The answer was
simple: "There is unity on behalf of the Russians and disunity on
behalf of the West. Russian unity is forced unity, it is unity at the
point of a bayonet, but it is still unity." His mission, he said, was
to bring a sense of common purpose to the West. In the course of
a year, through force of will, he transformed NATO from a concept into a force, with half a million men in uniform—thirty-five
divisions, six of which were American—and a fleet of almost three
thousand aircraft. But NATO needed more than warplanes, tanks,

and troops, Ike told the president. "The most pressing thing," he wrote to Truman, "is the will to fight—confidence." And he was confident. As the supreme commander of all Allied and American forces in Europe, Eisenhower provided that essential element. "In a very real sense," his most capable biographer wrote, "Ike was NATO and NATO was Ike."

Truman offered Eisenhower the presidency on the Democratic ticket at Christmas 1951, and not for the first time, but for the fourth. "If I do what I want to do, I'll go back to Missouri," Truman confided in a handwritten letter to Eisenhower. "If you decide to finish the European job (and I don't know who else can) I must keep the isolationists out of the White House. I wish you would let me know what you intend to do. It will be between us and no one else." He had assumed, without knowing, that the general would accept the Democratic nomination. No one knew for sure what party Ike liked. The only political factions that might undermine him were within the conservative wing of the Republican Party—the isolationists, the America Firsters, the McCarthyites. The Republicans were set to nominate Ohio senator Robert Taft, a president's son who had spent two decades fighting progress. He had fought the New Deal. He was foursquare against America's entering World War II. He condemned the Nuremberg trials of Nazi war criminals. He bitterly opposed the creation of NATO. And he seemed to have three-quarters of the party's convention delegates locked up.

Ike played a hidden hand. In February 1952, skirting the military code against active-duty officers seeking political office, Eisenhower secretly sent word that he was available through a close friend, the retired general Lucius Clay, who had succeeded him as the high commissioner of occupied Germany and broken the Soviet blockade of Berlin. Eisenhower allowed his name to appear on the New Hampshire Republican primary ballot. He won it, and after a bitter fight with Taft, he won the nomination, and in November he won the presidency in a landslide against the Democratic candidate Adlai

Stevenson, a senator too liberal for a majority of Americans deep in the grip of the cold war's fears. The decisive moment came two weeks before Election Day, when Eisenhower pledged to end the Korean War, which had become a bloody stalemate in which more than twenty-five thousand Americans had died.

Inaugurated on January 20, 1953, he spent the next eight years trying to wage peace. After he settled Korea, not a single American soldier died in combat on his watch. He believed that the only way to win a third world war was to avoid it.

But the ambitions of Ike's cold warriors were infinite, and the ideas they brought to the table for the president's approval were breathtaking. Overthrow governments around the world in the name of anti-communism. Inspire the Red Army to revolt against the Politburo. Liberate Eastern Europe, whether by force of arms or sabotage and subversion. Drop the bomb on North Vietnam, which was fighting half a million French soldiers. And before it was too late, launch a nuclear sneak attack on Moscow. Eisenhower needed an architecture to impose some discipline and order on these soaring aspirations. An elemental framework came from Charles Bohlen, whom Eisenhower appointed to succeed George Kennan as the American ambassador to Moscow; the Soviets had expelled Kennan for openly attacking the Kremlin's repression after keeping him under suffocating surveillance for a year.

On March 7, 1953, two days after the death of Stalin, Bohlen posed the problem in black and white: "Hanging over all our plans and actions," he wrote, "is the question of whether this nation has now or will find itself shortly committed to the overthrow of the Kremlin." Or would it instead seek some kind of peaceful coexistence in public, while still striving in secret to undermine the Soviets? The question hung fire for nearly three years. And in those thousand days, Eisenhower's Christian soldiers marched onward to an unknown destination.

From the outset, Eisenhower reshaped the presidency in the service of the struggle against the Soviets. He used the National Security Council to orchestrate the instruments of his power. The council met weekly at the great round mahogany table in the Cabinet Room at the White House, and he presided, doodling caricatures and coffee cups on a legal pad as he weighed the fate of the world. The NSC was the crucible in which the strategies to attack the power of the Kremlin were shaped. After the president, it was dominated by Secretary of State John Foster Dulles and his brother Allen, the director of Central Intelligence. Foster Dulles had campaigned for Eisenhower by hammering the theme of liberating the captive nations of Eastern Europe. Allen had been the CIA's deputy director since August 1951; he had served under Walter Bedell Smith, now the undersecretary of state, and a powerful presence at the NSC. They were joined by, among others, the secretary of defense, the chairman of the Joint Chiefs of Staff, and the top military commanders. The secretary of the treasury was there as well, in part to enforce Eisenhower's emphatic desire that the military would not bankrupt the nation as it built an arsenal for war. Allen Dulles usually began the meetings with a twenty-minute tour of the world, with special attention to places ripe for the CIA's covert operations. With his militant brother by his side, unlimited funds at his command, and most importantly, the president's ear, he made the CIA as important a weapon in Ike's quiver as the rapidly expanding American nuclear arsenal.

Ike would rely on nuclear weapons and covert action as a double-barreled force to project American power. Though costly, they were far cheaper than the immense buildup of conventional military forces that his generals, admirals, and war planners deeply desired. He spent up to $110 billion a year in today's dollars building more than twenty-two thousand nuclear warheads, along with the intercontinental ballistic missiles and the strategic bombers to deliver them. (The United States would spend more than a trillion dollars on nuclear weaponry between the start of the Korean War in 1950 and the introduction of combat troops in Vietnam in 1965.) He did this while fighting back ceaseless pleas from the military brass for massive increases in the conventional army; military spending fell dramatically as a percentage of the booming American economy under Eisenhower. That was his plan all along: a lean military and a muscular body politic.

"Every gun that is made, every warship launched, every rocket fired signifies, in the final sense, a theft from those who hunger and are not fed, those who are cold and are not clothed," he said in his first major foreign policy address on April 16—a speech titled "The Chance for Peace," aimed not only at Americans but at the Russians, whose new troika of leaders printed it in full in *Pravda* while rejecting his proposals to limit armies and arsenals. In the next breath, Eisenhower presented what he deemed, in public, to be a universal principle. "Any nation's right to a form of government and an economic system of its own choosing is inalienable," he said. "Any nation's attempt to dictate to other nations their form of government is indefensible."

This noble ideal meant little or nothing when it came to American efforts to control, manipulate, undermine, overthrow, or on occasion assassinate foreign leaders.

The CIA's covert operations were the pointed end of the spear of American foreign policy, and they were conducted with the broadest authority from the president. The first coup successfully engineered by the CIA overthrew the freely elected prime minister of Iran, Mohammed Mossadegh, who had audaciously wrested control of Iran's oil back from the fading British Empire. (Detailed CIA and State Department records describing the origins, outcome, and aftermath of the coup finally were declassified in 2018.) Allen Dulles, Bedell Smith, Frank Wisner, and Kim Roosevelt, President Theodore Roosevelt's grandson and the CIA's chief of operations in the Near East and Africa, had been working on plans to oust Mossadegh in conjunction with British intelligence since the fall of 1952.

Days after Eisenhower's election, Truman's NSC had declared in a top secret statement: "It is of critical importance to the United States that Iran remain an independent and sovereign nation, not dominated by the USSR. Because of its key strategic position, its petroleum resources, its vulnerability to intervention or armed attack by the USSR, and its vulnerability to political subversion, Iran must be regarded as a continuing objective of Soviet expansion." Truman had authorized "special political operations in Iran and adjacent Middle Eastern areas, including the procurement of such equipment as may be required." By the time Ike was drafting "The Chance for Peace," the CIA had stockpiled guns and ammunition in Iran, sufficient to supply a ten-thousand-man guerrilla force for six months, along with plenty of money to build "a network with numerous press, political, and clerical contacts" in Iran, and a potential coup leader, General Fazlullah Zahedi, whom CIA files described in detail: "Associated with the Nazi efforts in Iran during World War II, he has long been firmly anti-Soviet." Together they had the aim of restoring the pliantly pro-American Shah Reza Pahlavi to the Peacock Throne, where he would ensure the flow of Iranian oil to the West.

Dulles had painted an apocalyptic picture for Eisenhower and the NSC as Stalin lay dying. "The Communists might easily take over" in Iran, and this would transform the world: "Not only would the free world be deprived of the enormous assets represented by Iranian oil production and reserves, but the Russians would secure these assets," Dulles warned. "If Iran succumbed to the Communists there was little doubt that in short order the other areas of the Middle East, with some 60 percent of the world's oil reserves, would fall into Communist control." This shocked Eisenhower, who fully understood the stakes at hand, but it did not lead him to contemplate overthrowing Mossadegh. On the contrary, he thought the United States should support him at almost any cost. The NSC's note taker recorded: "The President said that if a real Soviet move against Iran actually comes, we shall have to face at this council table the question of going to full mobilization"—a shooting war against the Russians—for "if we did not move at that time and in that eventuality, he feared that the United States would descend to the status of a second-rate power. 'If,' said the President, 'I had $500,000,000 of money to spend in secret, I would get $100,000,000 of it to Iran right now'" to shore up the government against the Soviets. That was not at all what Dulles had in mind. One month later the director approved a more modest budget: $1,000,000 in untraceable CIA funds to overthrow Mossadegh, a down payment on an operation that eventually would cost $5,330,000. It took some arm-twisting, but the Dulles brothers and the new American ambassador in Tehran, Loy Henderson, finally convinced the president that the oil question could not be resolved in America's favor so long as Mossadegh remained in power.

Eisenhower gave the green light for a coup on July 11. "It was cleared directly with the President," Dulles told his brother. The operation collapsed into chaos five weeks later. "Mossadegh, learning of the plan through a leak in our military covert apparatus, took immediate counteraction to neutralize the plan," the CIA subsequently reported. The shah fled the country, and the coup plotters went into hiding.

And then—miraculously, in Roosevelt's eyes—a spontaneous combustion flared up in the streets of Tehran three days later. In a euphoric cable to CIA headquarters, he called it a "genuine peoples [sic] uprising led by nobody until leaders were provided." The street protest was inflamed by the glowing embers of the CIA's political propaganda, in particular a fabricated interview with Zahedi dictated by Roosevelt that flooded the newspapers and airwaves in Tehran, part of a fake news campaign that had gone on for months. "This demonstration began in small way in bazaar area but initial small flame found amazingly large amount combustible material and was soon roaring blaze which during course of day swept through entire city," Ambassador Henderson reported. "Prime Minister's house overrun and gutted. . . . Almost simultaneously General Zahedi occupied desk in Prime Minister's office." Roosevelt had fished

Zahedi out of a CIA safe house where he was cowering, clad in a
dirty undershirt and khakis, pulled him up, stiffened his spine, and
frog-marched him into power. "The time has come now," he told the
disheveled general. "You are going to have to get out on the streets
and take command of the situation, and we have Radio Tehran."

When Roosevelt recounted the tale for Eisenhower, leaving out
the more unsavory parts, the president said it sounded like a dime-
store novel. Ike wrote in his diary a few weeks later that the CIA
had brought about "the restoration of the Shah to power in Iran and
the elimination of Mossadegh. The things we did were 'covert.' If
knowledge of them became public, we would not only be embarrassed in that region, but our chances to do anything of like nature
in the future would almost totally disappear."

The CIA and Iran fell into a passionate embrace once the shah
was in power. "The Shah and the Prime Minister, cognizant of the
need for assistance in their effort to capitalize on the present situation, have become willing collaborators with CIA," the agency's
political warfare planners reported, and with that, Dulles and Wisner set out to buy the allegiances of Iran's military, political, religious,
and intellectual leaders, along with its press corps, in a major effort "to
support a political action/psychological warfare program in Iran." The
CIA underscored the continuing need for that program in a detailed
report at the end of 1954, which noted that the American hand had
not gone unseen in Iran. "The principal new features of the present
power situation," agency analysts reported, were "the extensive use
of authoritarian means—martial law, censorship, and prosecution or
repression of opponents—to curtail opposition to the regime and to
the government," and "the emergence of the U.S., which many Iranians hold responsible for effecting Mossadegh's downfall and which
has since been the chief financial backer of the government, as an
acknowledged major influence in the situation." These concerns
were brushed aside by a spirit of celebration that did not fade in the
passing years. "The Shah is now our boy," Roosevelt told his superiors

after he returned to CIA headquarters. And so the shah remained for a quarter of a century, buying billions of dollars of American weaponry and providing a bulwark of anti-communist power in the Middle East. America's overthrow of a freely chosen foreign leader stayed an official secret for a generation, though not to the generation of Iranians who were oppressed by the shah and took their revenge twenty-five years later. The world still lives with the consequences of their countercoup, an Islamic revolution that shook the world.

The CIA had proved to Ike's satisfaction that covert action was a powerful instrument of political warfare. Eisenhower enthusiastically gave it a free hand to overthrow governments from Guatemala to Indonesia, to create governments, shore up juntas, swing elections, and sway popular opinions with cash and propaganda all over the world. And propaganda was perhaps the most promisingly potent weapon of all, the NSC advised Eisenhower. (The word *propaganda* comes from the work of Catholic missionaries and their propagation of the faith among the unbelievers.) American cold warriors worked tirelessly to fine-tune messages for foreigners that could convert them from communism, spark anti-Stalinist heresies among them, and convince them that their self-interests were at one with the United States.

Stratagems for propaganda in the service of political warfare to undermine the Kremlin were already under way on the fourth day of Eisenhower's presidency. He ordered a close confidant, William H. Jackson—a key intelligence aide for the deceptions that secured the D-Day invasion, Dulles's predecessor as deputy director of central intelligence, and a senior civilian consultant to the CIA—to develop a battle plan. Political warfare that sought to capture hearts and minds had been scattershot under Truman, and the president told Jackson he wanted a "unified and dynamic effort" in the field, deeming it "essential to the security of the United States and of the other peoples in the community of free nations." Ike had an expansive concept of political warfare: he said it could encompass "anything from the singing of a beautiful hymn up to the most extraordinary kind of physical sabotage."

Jackson worked in tandem with Robert Cutler, the president's national security adviser. Their key staff members included two CIA cold warriors, Frank Lindsay, who had been Wisner's chief covert-operations aide, and Henry Loomis, later a director of the Voice of America under Eisenhower. Jackson and Cutler harnessed the best minds they could find inside and outside the government, interviewing more than 250 people—including two young Harvard academics, the future national security advisers McGeorge Bundy and Henry Kissinger—and they had reported to the president on June 30, 1953, outlining a "Program for World Order" in which political warfare and information operations were paramount. Know your enemy, they counseled, get inside his head, and rearrange his way of seeing the world.

"The best way of affecting Soviet behavior is to confront the Kremlin with difficult choices on matters of great importance," the report asserted. "Political warfare should be designed to bring pressure on the regime to choose a course favorable to United States interests." The key principles underlying American propaganda—"demonstrating to others their self-interest in decisions which the United States wishes them to make"—were essential elements of political warfare. If American leaders could keep that in mind and make clear-eyed plans and actions free from starry-eyed hopes, "we believe that political warfare holds great promise of success in forcing a reduction and retraction of Soviet power and a change in the nature of the Soviet system.

"The objectives of CIA covert propaganda in the free world are to combat communist subversion, counter neutralism, and generally promote United States and Western concepts and interests," the report to the president said. "The dissemination of truth is not enough."

The "Program for World Order" called the work of the National

Committee for a Free Europe—conceived by Kennan, founded by Allen Dulles, and financed by the CIA—the most powerful force the United States had harnessed to achieve that goal. It had joined the battle on the airwaves, pouring vast sums into Radio Free Europe, which reached millions behind the Iron Curtain, primarily in Poland, Hungary, and Czechoslovakia; and its sister network, Radio Liberation (later Radio Liberty), aimed exclusively at the Soviet Union and Soviet troops in Eastern Europe. The Voice of America played one tune, straight news and pointed political commentary on behalf of the American government, and the CIA's radios played another, propaganda purporting to be the voice of liberation forces from within the countries they targeted. The agency also floated an armada of balloons carrying propaganda pamphlets behind the Iron Curtain, more than three hundred million leaflets in the mid-1950s. All were keys in what Wisner called "the mighty Wurlitzer"—the instrument of propaganda that provided a soundtrack for the daily drama of the cold war. The CIA would write the lyrics, compose the score, and conduct the orchestra for political warfare.

But the report ended with a cautionary note of common sense. "The cold war cannot be won by words alone," it concluded. "What we do will continue to be vastly more important than what we say."

As the report went to the printer, the people of East Germany were trying to strike off their chains. The rebellion was the first of its kind in the cold war—and the first to let American national security officers imagine that their dreams of liberation could come true. What began in Berlin on June 17 as a labor protest against production quotas imposed by Stalinist bureaucrats spread over the following days to more than four hundred cities, towns, and villages throughout East Germany. The uprising was violent and volatile, and it shocked and frightened the political commissars. "Death to Communism!" demonstrators chanted. "Long live Eisenhower!" The Kremlin, still without a chosen leader to replace Stalin, revved up its tanks and readied shoot-to-kill orders for its soldiers.

On June 25, President Eisenhower, Vice President Richard M. Nixon, and the Dulles brothers met at the National Security Council, and Ike approved a secret presidential directive, NSC 158. (It wasn't fully declassified until 2017.) It said that the United States should "covertly stimulate acts and attitudes of resistance short of mass rebellion" in East Germany. It ordered the CIA to "encourage elimination of key puppet officials" through foreign agents, and "train and equip underground organizations capable of launching large-scale raids or sustained warfare when directed" throughout the Soviet satellite states of Eastern Europe. The goal was to "nourish resistance to communist oppression" and to "convince the free world, particularly Western Europe, that love of liberty and hatred of alien oppression are stronger behind the Iron Curtain than it has been dared to believe and that resistance to totalitarianism is less hopeless than has been imagined."

Strong words, but they were only words. The American response to the struggle in East Germany and a smaller but similar protest in Poland that summer was far weaker than the rhetoric. The CIA's Richard Helms, a future director of central intelligence, wrote to Wisner, his immediate superior in the clandestine service, that there was a great deal of "fuzzy thinking" in high circles of the government about what could be done in Eastern Europe. The wishful bluster about freeing the captive nations, emanating from leaders like Richard Nixon and Foster Dulles, sprang from their desire "to make good on certain campaign pledges," and it came at "the expense of hard-headed appraisals of . . . the basic facts of life. There seemed an inclination to raise hob in the satellites . . . since this would be popular on the domestic political scene, but there is no compensating intention to devote the necessary overt forces and support to insure a favorable outcome to such aggressive cold war approaches." The CIA's chief for Eastern Europe, John Bross, told

Allen Dulles that the prospect of a victorious revolution in East Germany was approximately zero. The Red Army had twenty-two divisions stationed there, about 350,000 soldiers in arms. Unless the United States smuggled vast quantities of weapons into the country, and "undoubtedly unless U.S. military forces were overtly committed to support an East German revolt, we believe that the resistance elements would be liquidated in a very short time." He estimated that the chances for a successful uprising in Poland, Hungary, or Czechoslovakia were "nil."

Eisenhower wasn't ready to run the risk of war with the Soviets. He feared that a thermonuclear war could be triggered by the next harebrained paramilitary mission behind the Iron Curtain. The Soviets had tested a hydrogen bomb on August 12, 1953, and both nations would conduct intermittent and increasingly powerful aboveground H-bomb blasts for ten years. Moscow eventually detonated a weapon with a yield of at least fifty megatons, roughly equal to four thousand Hiroshimas; the fireball rose five miles high, and the shock wave was felt nearly six hundred miles away. That bomb, if dropped on New York City, would kill more than ten million people in an instant. The threat of annihilation under a mushroom cloud occluded a clear vision of a way forward for Eisenhower.

The Red Scare was in full flower in the fall of 1953, with the charlatan Senator Joe McCarthy at the height of his powers, and the FBI at war against both Soviet spies and the American left. Tension and fear ran deep and wide in Washington. At the NSC meeting on September 26, the note taker recorded Ike thinking out loud: "It looked to him . . . as though the hour of decision were at hand, and that we would presently have to really face the question of whether or not we would have to throw everything at once against the enemy. . . . The United States was confronted with a very terrible threat, and the truth of the matter was that we have devised no way of meeting this threat without imposing ever-greater controls on our economy and on the freedom of our people."

We were engaged, continued the President . . . in the defense of a way
of life, and the great danger was that in defending this way of life
we would find ourselves resorting to methods that endangered this
way of life. The real problem, as the President saw it, was to devise
methods of meeting the Soviet threat and of adopting controls, if
necessary, that would not result in our transformation into a garrison
state. The whole thing, said the President, was a paradox . . . of trying
to meet the threat to our values and institutions by methods which
themselves endangered these institutions.

Here was an existential dilemma of the cold war: using undem-
ocratic methods to defend American democracy. But Eisenhower
believed that the ends would justify the means when the issue was
national survival.

Early in 1954, he set a team of high-powered investigators on
the CIA, headed by General Jimmy Doolittle, who had led the fire-
bombing of Tokyo in World War II. They issued a scorching report
on September 30. They noted the failure of dozens of paramilitary
missions into Russia, China, North Korea, Poland, Albania, and
beyond. They found that the information obtained from these operations was useless or nonexistent and that the cost in dollars and
lives was appalling. And in the same breath they urged the president
onward. The United States had to "subvert, sabotage and destroy
our enemies by more clever, more sophisticated and more effective
methods than those used against us," they told Ike. "We are facing
an implacable enemy whose avowed objective is world domination
by whatever means and at whatever cost. There are no rules in such
a game. Hitherto acceptable norms of human conduct do not apply.
If the United States is to survive, long-standing American concepts
of 'fair play' must be reconsidered."

Mounting political warfare against a closed and totalitarian
nation was far harder than attacking an open democracy. The CIA
had not placed a spy of any note inside the Soviet Union, nor would

it for years to come; it gathered next to no firsthand intelligence from nations such as Poland, Hungary, and Czechoslovakia. By contrast, communist spies had penetrated the ramparts of American national security, sped the Soviets' development of nuclear weapons, paralyzed American code-breakers, sabotaged crucial covert operations, and subtly subverted the CIA's political front groups and propaganda organizations. To date, it had been an almost complete rout. For five years, the goal of American cold warriors had been pushing the Russians out of Eastern Europe and rolling them back to the point where the Soviets would no longer threaten the United States or its NATO allies. That ideal had proved impossible to achieve.

After a debate that had raged from the start of his presidency, Eisenhower resolved that militant covert action could not overthrow the Kremlin. Ike was going to talk to the Russians, to see what could be accomplished in the name of peaceful coexistence, in the hope of avoiding a nuclear holocaust.

In July 1955, Eisenhower went to a peace conference in Geneva, and a measure of goodwill flowed. He addressed his new adversary, the Soviet leader Nikita Khrushchev, and his old ally, Marshal Zhukov, now the Soviet defense minister, who together had just created the Warsaw Pact, a military alliance among the Red Army and the seven Soviet satellites, as a counterweight to NATO. In the soaring chambers of the Palais des Nations, Ike offered the Russians a surprising and stunningly innovative proposal. He called it "Open Skies," and it was a beautiful vision. Washington and Moscow could fly over the other side's military bases, looking down with reconnaissance planes, to reduce the dangers of surprise attack, and thus to increase the chance for peace. As he concluded his speech, a great clap of thunder erupted, a blinding flash of lightning split the sky, and all the lights went out. The American delegation presumed divine providence was applauding Eisenhower.

The idea went nowhere with the Soviets, who feared the Americans would see their weakness in full. But Ike had the U-2 spy plane up his sleeve. The first test flight took place the following week.

A new NSC directive on political warfare went forth at the end
of 1955. Abandoning the goal of rolling back the Soviets, it nonetheless resolved to oppose the Russians and the Red Chinese at every
turn in Eastern Europe and in Asia. "Create and exploit trouble-
some problems for International Communism," the president commanded. More ambitiously: "Reduce International Communist
control . . . and increase the capacity and will of such peoples and
nations" to resist it. The new orders were to be carried out by the old
methods: propaganda, sabotage, subversion, deception, and support
for liberation armies around the world.

The CIA met the first of these requirements—and scored an epic
victory—by slipping a story to the *New York Times* that scooped the
world: the text of a "secret speech" by Khrushchev. Stalin had been
dead for almost three years when the Twentieth Congress of the
Soviet Communist Party convened; after it had come to a formal
end, Khrushchev summoned the Russian delegates back to the Great
Hall of the Kremlin at midnight on February 25, 1956—pointedly
barring the press and party members from outside the Soviet Union
from his four-hour address. A Reuters correspondent in Moscow,
John Rettie, was packing his bags when his phone rang. A Russian
friend wanted to meet him immediately. And his message was urgent.
"Khrushchev, it was said, had made a shattering report," Rettie wrote
fifty years later, "openly denouncing Stalin by name as a murderer
and torturer of party members. This was so traumatic that it is now
said some delegates had heart attacks during the speech, and others
committed suicide afterwards." Rettie left for Stockholm and, after
careful consideration, filed a cautious dispatch.

In Washington, Allen Dulles read the news with joy. He told
Eisenhower that while there was always "the possibility that Khrushchev had been drunk," the speech, if authenticated, gave the United
States "a great opportunity, both covertly and overtly, to exploit the
situation to its advantage. Stalin had been the chief theoretician of
the Soviet Union. He had been its great war hero in addition to his

more familiar role as dictator of the Soviet Union for twenty-five years. What would the Soviets now do?" How could communism thrive without a doctrine? The CIA director instructed his top aides to do anything in their power to put their hands on the speech. My kingdom for a copy! Weeks went by without a word. Then, on Friday, April 13, a courier pouch from the Israeli embassy in Warsaw arrived at the office of Amos Manor, the head of the Shin Bet, Israel's internal security service. There it was: seventy pages, in Polish. Manor took the speech to Israel's prime minister, David Ben-Gurion, a Pole by birth. He read it and exclaimed: "If it's authentic, it's an historic document, and 30 years from now there will be a liberal regime in Moscow."

Manor had it translated and flew an English-language text to the Israeli embassy in Washington, with instructions to hand it over to James Angleton, the CIA's chief of counterintelligence and its liaison to Israel's spies. With the speech in hand, Allen Dulles sought to validate its authenticity. He sent a copy to a man whose identity was known only to him, and to all others in the government as "the expert." This was George Kennan, banished from the State Department by Foster Dulles in a fit of high dudgeon for a perceived lack of political loyalty. (A foolish move: Foster's political platform of liberating Eastern Europe had been built in large part with Kennan's planks.) In exile from the government, in his sinecure at Princeton University, Kennan remained a highly valued CIA consultant in good graces with the director. He thought the transcript of the speech was the genuine article. Allen Dulles was delighted, and thus assured by his spy chief, the president authorized its disclosure. Dulles chose to give it to Harrison Salisbury, who had been the Moscow bureau chief for the *New York Times*, and who had shared his expertise with the CIA's director over private luncheons when on home leave.

"KHRUSHCHEV TALK ON STALIN BARES DETAILS OF RULE BASED ON TERROR; CHARGES PLOT FOR KREMLIN PURGES; U.S. ISSUES A TEXT; Dead Dictator Painted as

Savage, Half-Mad and Power-Crazed," read the headline atop page
1 on June 5. "Stalin, as he is pictured by Mr. Khrushchev, turned the
world about him into a miasma of treachery, treason, and nightmar-
ish plots," Salisbury wrote. "The picture was one that beggared the
wildest surmise of political opponents of communism." The paper
printed the full text—twenty-six thousand words—and the political
axis of the world shifted. The truth, in this case, was enough.

The reverberations in the United States were immense, if largely
invisible. The American Communist Party was shattered by the publication of the secret speech. Its membership plummeted from about
fifty thousand to about five thousand in a matter of months. The
networks of Soviet espionage in the United States, once supported
by an American communist underground, withered along with it.

The CIA beamed highlights of the speech eastward over the
Iron Curtain on Radio Free Europe, which also broadcast heartfelt
pledges from President Eisenhower that the emancipation of Eastern Europe was still a centerpiece of American foreign policy. These
bulletins ignited a great hope against the grinding fear. In October,
student demonstrators in the Hungarian capital of Budapest rose
up against Big Brother; they were joined by tens of thousands of
workers as they fought against the Kremlin's control. Soviet troops
entered the city two days later, and the battle was joined. Radio Free
Europe crackled with messages of liberation, and the people took it
to heart. Surely America would come to the rescue! "Virtually every
Hungarian of scores spoken to in past 24 hours have demanded 'Give
us arms,' 'Give us diplomatic assistance,' 'What is America going to
do for us in this hour?'" the American embassy reported on October
24. No answer came.

Allen Dulles told Eisenhower two days later that "the revolt
in Hungary constituted the most serious threat yet to be posed
to continued Soviet control of the satellites." The president
responded: "If they could have some kind of existence, choose their
own government and what they want, then we are satisfied and

this would really solve one of the greatest problems in the world that is standing in the way of world peace." Foster Dulles gave a stirring speech in Dallas, with Ike's approval: "The heroic people of Hungary challenge the murderous fire of Red Army tanks. These patriots value liberty more than life itself. And all who peacefully enjoy liberty have a solemn duty to seek, by all truly helpful means, that those who now die for freedom will not have died in vain."

But as they started dying, and no help came, the American ambassador across the border in Vienna sent a warning to Washington on October 28. Hundreds of Radio Free Europe broadcasts and thousands of propaganda leaflets airlifted in balloons had "incited the Hungarians to action," and fingers were being pointed at "our failure to do anything effective for them now that they have risen against their Communist oppressors." That same day, the CIA's covert-ops chief Frank Wisner told Radio Free Europe's senior policy adviser to amplify the call to arms. This led to an urgent message from RFE's director in New York to his Hungarian staff in Munich: "All restraints have gone off. No holds barred. Repeat: No holds barred." That evening, Radio Free Europe urged the people of Hungary to sabotage the railroads, hurl Molotov cocktails into the ventilators of Soviet tanks, and fight to the finish: "Freedom or death!"

For a moment, it looked like they had won. On October 30, Prime Minister Imre Nagy announced the abolition of one-party rule. Hungarian soldiers joined with the protesters. *Pravda*, the daily paper of the Soviet Communist Party, published a statement from the Politburo regretting the bloodshed. In Moscow, Marshal Zhukov told Ambassador Bohlen that Soviet troops were pulling out of Hungary. The next day, the American embassy in Budapest cabled: "In dramatic overnight change, it became virtually certain in Budapest this morning that this Hungarian revolution now fact of history." The president, on the verge of an overwhelming reelection victory, went on television to address the American people that evening: "A new Hungary is rising from this struggle, a Hungary which we hope from our hearts will know full and free nationhood," Ike said. "If the Soviet Union indeed faithfully acts upon its announced intention, the world will witness the greatest forward stride toward justice, trust, and understanding among nations in our generation."

At the National Security Council meeting the following morning, Allen Dulles spoke to Eisenhower in a state of ecstasy at the fact of history in Hungary. "What had occurred there was a miracle," he said. "Events had belied all our past views that a popular revolt in the face of modern weapons was an utter impossibility. Nevertheless, the impossible had happened, and because of the power of public opinion, armed force could not effectively be used. . . . Soviet troops themselves had had no stomach for shooting down Hungarians, except in Budapest." Foster Dulles told Nixon that it was the beginning of the collapse of the Soviet empire.

But the CIA had no one to gather intelligence in Hungary, and the State Department had no way to see that two hundred thousand Red Army troops were ready to conquer the country. Nor was the KGB chief, Ivan Serov, possessed of wisdom or foresight. Serov had gone to Budapest after the start of the uprising; once there, he had reported to the Politburo on October 28 that the United Nations, backed by the United States, was weighing a massive military intervention to back the Hungarian revolutionaries. That report was utterly false, and fatally so, for it sent the tanks and armored personnel carriers rolling toward Budapest.

On November 1, Imre Nagy and his cabinet urgently summoned Moscow's ambassador in Budapest, Yuri Andropov, the future chairman of the KGB and Soviet general secretary. They asked Andropov about the reports of troop movements. His explanation was evidently unconvincing. The Hungarian government immediately renounced the Warsaw Pact and declared Hungary's neutrality. The Soviets began to encircle the city the next day. When the leaders of Hungary attempted to negotiate their way out of the crisis on the evening of November 3, KGB officers burst into the meeting and arrested them. The Soviet attack on Budapest began at four o'clock the next morning. The fiercest fighting in Europe since World War II erupted, and as the Hungarians threw themselves against Soviet tanks, twenty thousand of them died; hundreds of thousands fled across the border to Austria. Imre Nagy was arrested and executed. Wisner flew to Vienna, drove to the Hungarian border, watched the river of desperate refugees fleeing the horror in the dark of night, and suffered a devastating nervous breakdown, the first of three that in time would drive him to suicide, a living emblem of the short-circuiting network of covert action and clandestine plans against the Kremlin.

Eisenhower and the Dulles brothers were devastated that they could do nothing to support the uprising. It was the end of a decade's dreams of glory, erasing all the bold statements about subverting the Soviets and supporting democracy in Eastern Europe. Newly reelected, Ike convened the National Security Council on November 8. "The President said that this was indeed a bitter pill for us to swallow," the minutes read. "What can we do that is really constructive? Should we break off diplomatic relations with the USSR? What would be gained by this action? The Soviets don't care. The whole business was shocking to the point of being unbelievable." The most essential part of political warfare was the image of the United States as a force for freedom in the eyes of the world, and now that ideal was damaged in Eastern Europe and beyond. The American vision of dissolving the Kremlin's power, freeing the captive nations, and drawing them into the embrace of the West vanished for a generation. Twenty-five years would pass before the United States found a way to challenge the Soviets' control over half of Europe.

But even before he was sworn in for a second term in January 1957, Eisenhower began preparing to confront the Soviets in the Third World—the newly coined name for the developing nations of Latin America, Africa, Asia, and the Middle East, many unaligned with America or Russia. He had long ago laid out the most famous cold war doctrine of all: if you took a row of dominoes and knocked over the first one, the last one would fall quickly. And Eisenhower now saw dominoes wobbling around the world. He gave particular attention to shoring up pro-American governments in nations from Lebanon to Japan. And he tried to overthrow leaders suspected of communist sympathies from Indonesia to Iraq to the islands of the Caribbean.

He immediately set forth an "Eisenhower Doctrine" regarding the Arabs and their oil. "Russia's rulers have long sought to dominate the Middle East. That was true of the Czars and it is true of the Bolsheviks," he said in a message to Congress. "We have just seen the subjugation of Hungary by naked armed force. In the aftermath . . . international communism needs and seeks a recognizable success." He sought and was granted $200 million to protect and defend nations of the Middle East in good graces with America. He vowed that American troops would guard them against aggression, and he sent the army and the marines into Lebanon the following year. But in private, the president despaired that anything resembling democracy would take root in the Middle East. "If you go and live with these Arabs, you will find that they simply cannot understand our ideas of freedom or human dignity," he later told the National Security Council. "They have lived so long under dictatorships of one form or another, how can we expect them to run successfully a free government?"

He unleashed his fury at President Sukarno of Indonesia, a Muslim who ruled eighty million people and sat on perhaps twenty billion barrels of untapped oil. Sukarno had sinned, in Ike's eyes, by convening twenty-nine Asian, Arab, and African heads of state and proposing that they create an alliance of the unaligned—a third path for the Third World, apart from both NATO and the Warsaw Pact. This was too much for the White House: either you were for the United States or you were against it. The CIA considered assassinating Sukarno, dropped that idea when its agent couldn't get a clean shot, and instead began financing his political opponents. In July 1957, Ike received a report from a trusted NSC aide he'd dispatched to confer with the CIA's Near East chief in the Indonesian capital of Jakarta. The gist of it was grim: almost all of America's allies in the region then called Indochina—South Vietnam, South Korea, Taiwan, Laos—were led by unpopular and corrupt dictators. But Sukarno posed a different problem: he was highly popular and was taking Indonesia leftward through elections—subversion by the ballot box. Allen Dulles was not about to let that happen. He played his ominous theme music for the NSC: Sukarno was going communist, he was at the point of no return, and if Indonesia fell, all Indochina was in peril. On September 25, Eisenhower authorized the CIA to mount a coup.

Three days later, the Bombay *Blitz*, an English-language weekly whose editors were highly susceptible to suggestions from the KGB, ran a banner headline: AMERICAN PLOT TO OVERTHROW SUKARNO. What followed was the most incoherent operation in the CIA's cold war history, culminating in the bombing and strafing of the innocent citizens of a neutral nation and its staunchly anti-communist armed forces, whose elite commanders had been trained in the United States and called themselves "Sons of Eisenhower." The CIA's air force, crewed by Polish recruits who had been working for the agency since the late 1940s, mistakenly dropped five tons of arms and ammunition along with bundles of cash into the hands of Sukarno's troops. The CIA's pilots intentionally killed hundreds of civilians and sank a British freighter. The chaotic covert action was no secret to the Indonesians, though it was all but unknown to the American people, and it went on for six months until it collapsed in June 1958. Dulles tried to conceal the depths of the disaster from the president, and succeeded in part, but the operation was Frank Wisner's last hurrah. He returned from a tour of the Far East and went mad. The diagnosis was psychotic mania, and the treatment was six months of electroshocks. He emerged a broken man, and though Dulles gave him a sinecure as chief of station in London, his decade as the field marshal for American political warfare was done.

His replacement was Richard Bissell, the Marshall Plan admin-
istrator who had siphoned its funds into the coffers of the CIA in
the late 1940s and early 1950s. He had brought the U-2 spy plane
from the drawing board to the runway in two years' time in 1956;
a crucial mission for the U-2 in its flights over Soviet terrain was to
prove that the "missile gap"—the incendiary assertion that Russia
was outpacing America in nuclear weaponry—was a falsehood. Bissell, the bespectacled scion of an immensely wealthy insurance company magnate, and an exemplar of the American establishment, was
a brilliant manager of money and machines, but he had a murderous
tinge to his blue blood. He took over as the commander of political
warfare on January 1, 1959, the same day that Fidel Castro took power
in Cuba. The CIA looked on in fascination, then fear, then fury, as
it slowly realized that the *comandante* was a communist. Before the
year was out, Dick Bissell proposed to kill him.

Khrushchev and the KGB took close note of Eisenhower's pivot
to the Third World. They saw America's increasingly muscular overt
and covert operations gathering strength in Indochina, where American special forces and the CIA fought shadow wars in Vietnam and
Laos. In the Middle East, American diplomats and spies worked to
counter the communist threat among the Arabs. In Africa, centuries
of European conquest and control were coming to an agonizing end,
and the colonial powers would leave the continent up for grabs. That
struggle could become "the decisive factor in the conflict between
the forces of freedom and international Communism," Vice President
Nixon had told Eisenhower upon his return from a three-week tour
in 1957, and he strongly recommended that the American policy of
containing communism in Europe should apply forcefully in Africa.
All told, three dozen newly independent nations had emerged in
Asia and Africa in the decade since the late 1940s. The Kremlin and
the White House were preparing to contest for power in almost
every one of them. Both sides paid special heed to national liberation movements trying to throw off the yoke of empires. In a perfect

world, Eisenhower could have tried to harness any one of them to the ideals of the Declaration of Independence; even Mao Tse-tung knew something about of the spirit of the American Revolution. But Mao was implacably militant, pushing Khrushchev back toward the relentlessness and ruthlessness of Stalin. It was Mao who had helped convince him to change course and crush Hungary, Mao who pushed him to support Ho Chi Minh in Vietnam, and Mao who urged him to arm Africans, Asians, and Latin Americans in the name of anti-imperialism. In time, Mao proved too much of a tyrant for even the Kremlin; their two nations would come close to war at the close of the 1960s.

The KGB adjusted its strategies against America after Ike's reelection, as its leaders determined that Americans were amateurs at political warfare and particularly unpracticed at the art of deception. The Soviet spy known as Colonel Rudolf Abel, arrested in New York in June 1957 after working under deep cover for nine years, had told his FBI interrogators that American intelligence walked in "baby shoes." That opinion was shared by two successive KGB chiefs: Ivan Serov, who ran the spy service from 1954 to 1958, and Alexander Shelepin, who took over when Serov moved to command the Soviet military intelligence agency, the GRU. They worked together to transform the intelligence powers of the Kremlin. Soviet espionage in America was at a low ebb in the late 1950s, as its support system within the shrunken Communist Party of the United States evaporated and its underground networks faced intense pressure from J. Edgar Hoover's counterintelligence gumshoes. The KGB took the great game to its next level by creating a new directorate to undermine America: Department D.

D as in *dezinformatsiya*, a Russian word defined in the 1952 *Great Soviet Encyclopedia* as the "dissemination (in the press, on the radio, etc.) of false reports intended to mislead public opinion." The Department of Disinformation was the world's first industrial factory of fake news. It set to work creating a myriad of forgeries of official-looking U.S. government documents and planting them in overseas print and broadcast outlets. The CIA eventually caught wind of thirty-two of these fictions, a fraction of what the department created between 1957 and 1961. "Some of these were sniper shots," as a CIA analyst noted, and others were prolonged assaults, but all depicted the United States as an imperialist aggressor and a threat to world peace. Like the best propaganda, a few of the stories were wound around a core of hard facts—like the charge that the United States sought to overthrow Indonesia. The goal was to defame the United States and corrode the ties among America and its allies. In a 1965 study, the CIA saw Department D's aims as threefold. First, destroy the confidence of Congress and the American people in their government's cold war agencies—in particular the CIA and the FBI. Second, damage American prestige in Europe, "thereby contributing directly to the breakup of the NATO alliance." And third, sow distrust against the United States in the Third World. Department D's dedicated work over the next thirty years provided a strong and lasting template for the global network of political warfare launched by Vladimir Putin in the twenty-first century.

The doctrine of deception wasn't yet perfected in Moscow. The future Soviet leader Yuri Andropov would try to see to that task when he rose to the top of the KGB hierarchy a decade later. But the Kremlin's spies, like the CIA's, already controlled news outlets all over the world. The Bombay *Blitz* was a favorite; its KGB-conceived articles were often picked up and disseminated by international wire services, especially the ones run by the Soviets and their allies. The *Blitz* produced any number of bogus scoops in 1958 and 1959. One described a secret pact between Foster Dulles and the Japanese premier Nobusuke Kishi—who was, in reality, a CIA agent of influence—to permit the use of Japanese troops anywhere in Asia. Another falsely purported to reveal American plans to build nuclear weapons bases on the Indonesian island of Sumatra. The biggest scoop produced by the fake news fabricators was a phony letter to President Eisenhower from Nelson

Rockefeller, who had served as a White House special assistant for psychological warfare under Eisenhower and went on to become the vice president of the United States. In this widely disseminated diatribe, the mega-millionaire Rockefeller, the personification of capitalism, pushed a plan for world domination using economic assistance as a Trojan horse to secure American military and political control overseas. There would be many more such skillful forgeries in the years to come. The KGB could take a grain of truth and upon it build a crooked tower of lies.

The CIA's own news and propaganda operations grew mightily in the 1950s, gilding the image of the United States at home and abroad. Its domestic branches were a social network relying more on the manipulation of information than the manufacture of disinformation; its goal was subtly shaping public opinion rather than bludgeoning minds through the power of mass media. Many corporate media chiefs and more than a few reporters collaborated. Allen Dulles had influential and readily influenced friends who ran CBS News, *Time* and *Life* magazines, and the *New York Times*, whose publisher, Arthur Hays Sulzberger, signed an agreement shielding their professional relationship and readily did personal favors for Dulles, like pulling a *Times* reporter out of Guatemala to protect the secrecy of the CIA's 1954 coup against that nation's duly elected president. Those powerful news organizations, along with ABC News, the *Wall Street Journal*, *Newsweek* magazine, the Associated Press, and a dozen others each had on their rosters at least one journalist working or moonlighting for the CIA, and their editors often were unaware that their reporters served two masters. Scores if not hundreds of credentialed stringers and freelancers working overseas were CIA officers under cover or recruited foreign agents.

Journalism was the perfect cover for espionage; spies could serve as reporters and reporters as spies. Joseph Alsop, the most widely read foreign affairs columnist of the era, whose work appeared in the *New York Herald Tribune*, *Newsweek*, and the *Saturday Evening Post*, undertook assignments in the Philippines and Laos at the behest of the CIA in the 1950s, reporting to the agency as well as to his readers, and his work consistently reflected the agency's thinking; in 1957 the agency helped to protect Alsop, a closeted homosexual, when he was entrapped by a handsome KGB officer in a Moscow hotel room and photographed in flagrante delicto. Twenty years later, he said he was proud to have served the founding fathers of the CIA; they were bosom buddies, drinking from the same pitcher of Georgetown martinis. "Dick Bissell was my oldest friend from childhood," he told the reporter Carl Bernstein. "It was a social thing, my dear fellow. I never received a dollar. I never signed a secrecy agreement. I didn't have to. . . . I've done things for them when I thought they were the right thing to do. I call it doing my duty as a citizen."

The CIA's international propaganda arm owned or underwrote roughly fifty newspapers, radio stations, magazines, and news services around the world, publishing its version of events in almost every international capital of consequence. Forum World Features, a London-based news syndicate created at the agency's behest by the multimillionaire John Hay Whitney, Eisenhower's ambassador to the United Kingdom, packaged reliably hawkish articles for both American and international audiences. Prominent American publishing houses printed about two dozen English-language books financed or produced by the CIA in the 1950s and early 1960s. The leading example was Doubleday & Company's *The Penkovsky Papers*, the purported diary of a Soviet spy working in secret for the CIA. The best-selling book was fabricated from CIA records by a worldly-wise reporter, Frank Gibney, who counted Allen Dulles as a confidant, and Peter Deriabin, a KGB defector working for the agency. The protagonist of the story was real—the Soviets had captured and executed him— though the idea that a spy would keep a diary was preposterous if you thought about it. Few did at the time. The top editors and publishers at the most powerful media corporations, and a handful of their journalists, believed that working with the CIA was no crime. Sig Mickelson, president of CBS News and the CIA's point of contact there from 1954 to 1961, later the director of Radio Free Europe, thought it was "a normal relationship at the time. This was at the height of the Cold War and I assumed the communications media were cooperating." In Eisenhower's America, my country right or wrong was the prevailing point of view in newsrooms and boardrooms, and that consensus stayed strong until the war in Vietnam shattered it.

As his presidency neared its end, Eisenhower continued to do what he could to promote the ideal of peaceful coexistence with the Soviets. He invited Khrushchev to the United States in September 1959; the two men talked for three days at Camp David and watched Westerns in the evening. In public, they exchanged pleasantries; in private, they butted heads and groped for common ground. The president said plaintively that he was "afraid of nuclear war and that to his mind everyone should be. During the last war, he said, he may have had moments of exhilaration in commanding huge armies, but now war has become nothing more than a struggle for survival." Those days of shining glory had devolved into a dark era defined by human folly.

Khrushchev tried to end on a high note. While he couldn't say "where the barometer pointed—to clear, changing, or stormy" in his relationship with the United States, he said, he wanted to invite Eisenhower to return to Russia in May, "when the weather was good and everything was in full bloom. The beautiful scenery and the wonderful scent of blooming trees might help the President and himself in their talks." Eisenhower accepted with pleasure.

But all hope for a thaw in the cold war vanished on May Day 1960, when the Soviets shot down a U-2 over Russian soil and captured its pilot alive. Eisenhower had wanted to end the flights—he had feared for years that they could trigger World War III—but Dick Bissell was the air traffic controller and he had insisted on one last mission. Allen Dulles had convinced the president for years that such a disaster was impossible. The U-2's final mission aimed to put an end to the false issue of the missile gap, which the Democratic Party candidate for president, Senator John F. Kennedy, had been using to hammer the Eisenhower administration and his Republican opponent, Vice President Nixon. NASA put out a cover story that the plane was gathering meteorological data. That fell apart when Khrushchev produced the pilot, the wreckage of the plane, and the film it had shot of Soviet air bases and fighter planes—proving, as he said, that Allen Dulles was no weatherman. The State Department put out another falsehood, saying the president had not authorized the flight. This was ultimately too much for Eisenhower. He walked into the Oval Office on May 9 and told his secretary that he wanted to resign. In retirement, Ike would reflect: "I didn't realize how high a price we were going to have to pay for that lie."

The shootdown embarrassed America in the eyes of the world, shattered the idea that a bodyguard of lies could plausibly protect American political warfare, and for the first time proved to the public that presidents deceived the American people. Khrushchev called Eisenhower a liar and wrecked their plans to talk of peace. Ike's chief scientific adviser listened as the president said, with great sorrow, that "the stupid U-2 mess had ruined all his efforts" to end the cold war, and "he had nothing worthwhile left for him to do now until the end of his presidency." His sadness soon turned into a smoldering rage.

He was bitter and exhausted, taking a double dose of sleeping pills before bed but suffering nightmares instead of finding respite, and by midsummer he was in a murderous mood. He set out to clean up some of the messes that the next president might otherwise inherit. In August he set the CIA to work on plans for a paramilitary invasion of Cuba and approved a $13 million budget for the operation. He gave at least tacit approval to the elimination of Castro and, as a political counterweight in the Caribbean, to the disposal of the right-wing dictator Rafael Trujillo in the Dominican Republic. *Elimination* and *disposal* were the euphemisms Dwight Eisenhower and Allen Dulles used when they were talking about political assassinations. The president was more straightforward at the National Security Council meeting on August 18 when he issued an order to do away with Patrice Lumumba, the new prime minister of the Congo.

American political warfare soon would come to a crescendo. But at the last, Eisenhower said in despair that he was leaving a world of trouble to his successor.

CHAPTER 4

THE LAST HOPE
FOR THE WEST

Dwight David Eisenhower and John Fitzgerald Kennedy met alone in the Oval Office on the morning of January 19, 1961, the day before the torch of power was passed. The president wasn't confident of JFK, who had won the November election over Vice President Nixon by 118,550 votes out of nearly 69 million cast, a margin owing much to Kennedy's rhetoric that the Russians were winning the cold war. Ike was a five-star general handing over the secret protocols for launching nuclear war and the stratagems of covert operations to a young man who had been a navy lieutenant, junior grade, in World War II.

They walked out together and met with the old and the new secretaries of state, defense, and treasury in the Cabinet Room. Kennedy raised the question of the CIA's plans to invade Cuba. Nine days before, a headline on the front page of the *New York Times* had blazoned: "U.S. Helps Train an Anti-Castro Force at Secret Guatemalan Air-Ground Base; Clash with Cuba Feared." Ike said it had to be done: the United States could not live with Castro in power, and for good measure it should dispose with the Dominican dictator Trujillo at the same time. At that moment, a diplomatic pouch of small arms dispatched by the CIA was en route to the Dominican Republic. And at the same hour, the deposed prime minister of the Congo, Patrice Lumumba, the target of a CIA-sponsored coup spurred by Ike's wrath, had just been sent to his death in a squalid prison.

Kennedy had inherited the most powerful political warfare machine in the world. But he was forty-three years old, the youngest president ever elected, and his inexperience showed in the shakiness of his command soon after he was inaugurated. His supreme self-confidence was shattered by the Bay of Pigs invasion. The doomed mission exposed America's incapacity to coordinate its military, intelligence, and diplomatic powers. On April 27, a week after 118 of the CIA's Cubans were killed and 1,202 captured as their commando assault collapsed, Kennedy sought with a measure of desperation to draw a distinction between how the United States conducted itself in such affairs of state and how the Soviets did it.

"We are opposed around the world by a monolithic and ruthless conspiracy that relies primarily on covert means for expanding its sphere of influence—on infiltration instead of invasion, on subversion instead of elections, on intimidation instead of free choice, on guerrillas by night instead of armies by day," he said in a speech before the American Newspaper Publishers Association. "It is a system which has conscripted vast human and material resources into the building of a tightly knit, highly efficient machine that combines military, diplomatic, intelligence, economic, scientific and political operations." The president was projecting his own thoughts and fears. He now knew that the American machine was less than well-knit and in need of an urgent overhaul.

The Kremlin had sized up JFK as a weakling. He took a shellacking when he held a summit meeting with Khrushchev in Vienna in June; the Soviet leader was warlike and bellicose, brusquely challenging the president. Kennedy said Khrushchev beat him up because of the Bay of Pigs, because he thought any president so young and inexperienced as to get in that mess could be taken easily, and that anyone who got into it and didn't see it through had no guts. This was an accurate assessment. Khrushchev immediately went forward with plans to erect the Berlin Wall—millions already had fled communist East Germany for the West—and within a year he was shipping nuclear weapons to Cuba, to protect it as a launching pad for revolution in the Western Hemisphere.

Far from abandoning covert action, JFK handed control over the CIA's paramilitary operations to his thirty-five-year-old brother, Attorney General Robert F. Kennedy, and in less than three years they launched 163 of them, on average one a week, almost as many as Eisenhower had undertaken in eight years. The Kennedys put Castro in their crosshairs, following up on the assassination plots first mounted by the Eisenhower White House. They embraced the most muscular clandestine operations as essential weapons for political warfare, as a catapult for projecting and protecting American power and influence in the eyes of the world, and as magic bullets for the escalating battles America faced in Southeast Asia, Central America, and Africa.

The Soviets did the same: the doctrine emerging at the KGB was that the war between the United States and the Soviet Union would be fought and won on the battlefields of the Third World. Shortly after the Vienna summit, KGB chief Alexander Shelepin sent Khrushchev a breathtakingly ambitious plan to "create circumstances in different areas of the world which would assist in diverting the attention and forces of the United States and its allies." A key part of the plan was to use the national liberation movements rising in Africa, Asia, and Latin America as part of the larger struggle against Washington, and to spark "armed uprisings against pro-Western reactionary governments." Nowhere was riper for revolution and counterrevolution than Africa. In the past year alone, seventeen African nations had freed themselves from the chains of their white masters. America saw chaos afoot as colonialism crumbled; chaos incubated communism; the next Castro could arise unseen at any time. The threat that any nation could go communist was absolute anathema at the White House.

No country was a bigger prize than the Congo. It was "the heart of the Cold War struggle" in the 1960s, said Frank Carlucci, in those days a political officer at the newest American embassy in Africa, later deputy director of the CIA and the secretary of defense. And it was the target of a political warfare operation that went on under eight presidents and lasted for more than thirty years. The secret history of American influence in the Congo, limned in documents declassified in 2014, reveals what could happen when the United States sought to harmonize its military, diplomatic, intelligence, and economic instruments during the cold war. It could control the fate of a huge and strategically crucial country, the cornerstone of a continent, with a hidden hand.

The Congo was the largest and potentially most powerful of the emerging black African nations: nearly one million square miles, one-third the size of the United States. It held great riches: two-thirds of the world's diamonds, half its cobalt, a tenth of its copper, the uranium at the core of America's nuclear weapons, gold and oil and rubber and rare earths. Its people had suffered seventy-five years of oppression under Belgium, the most vicious colonial regime of the twentieth century. The cruel and avaricious King Leopold took everything he could steal in "the vilest scramble for loot that ever disfigured the history of human consciousness," wrote Joseph Conrad, whose *Heart of Darkness* captured the rape of the Congo as it happened. Leopold became one of the richest men on earth, and his minions murdered millions as they pillaged. The nation's ruling class was engorged with the wealth it had mined from the Congo until World War II shattered five centuries of European colonial power, and the sun started setting on the last of the great empires.

The Belgians had dreamed that they could stave off independence for decades to come. They were deluding themselves. A year before Kennedy was inaugurated, in January 1960, they had reluctantly convened the thin ranks of Congolese leaders at a conference in Brussels, gambling on finding a prime minister to serve as their pliant puppet. They had made few other provisions for the peaceful transfer of power. To the horror of the colonizers, the delegates elected Patrice Lumumba, who had just been released from prison, where he had been locked up for preaching liberation. The United States knew very little about Lumumba. The files of the CIA and the State Department held the barest biographical sketch of his life. He was thirty-four, a postal clerk turned political firebrand, and "the first voice really to shout for independence," said Owen Roberts, an American consul in the Congo; "he was a charismatic, loud leader" who had gotten his ideas from reading Voltaire and Rousseau, not Marx and Engels. Roberts testified to Congress that Lumumba was an African nationalist, not the communist he was caricatured to be: "Yes, he was radical, but he could hardly be a communist because there weren't any communist materials in the Belgian Congo. Or any communists." The Soviets concurred in this judgment. Lumumba had met with B. A. Savinov, a mid-level Soviet diplomat in Brussels, to ask for material aid from Moscow for his political movement. Savinov conveyed the request to the Ministry of Foreign Affairs with a cautionary note: Lumumba did not qualify as a communist; his ideology was inchoate.

The United States feared him nevertheless. Everyone held their breath as Independence Day drew near. Robinson McIlvaine was sent to open the American embassy as chargé d'affaires in the capital of Léopoldville, a city of white buildings and deep green tropical foliage on the banks of the swirling, churning Congo River. He had no firm instructions from his superiors. "There was almost nobody who had any idea what was going to happen," he said. "I don't think anybody in the U.S. Government had much idea about this part of the world." This was not entirely the case. Robert D. Murphy represented the United States at the independence ceremonies. He had been Truman's ambassador in Brussels, and he had admired the strength of Belgian rule in the Congo firsthand. He had been Ike's chief political adviser during World War II, one of his key cold war advisers at the White House, and most recently in charge of political affairs at the State

Department. He would go on to serve as an intelligence and foreign affairs consultant to Presidents Kennedy, Johnson, Nixon, Ford, and Carter. On the day of the Congo's independence, he was a director of Morgan Guaranty Trust, deeply invested with Société Générale and American companies holding immense stakes at risk in the nation's minerals and mines. Eisenhower's secretary of defense, his undersecretary of state, and his ambassador in Belgium all were business magnates whose corporate portfolios had millions at risk, and they had an intense interest in what was going to happen in the Congo.

Things happened fast. "Independence was June thirtieth. I arrived the week before," McIlvaine remembered. "We got through the Fourth of July. It was the sixth when the whole place fell apart." The Congolese army, the *Force Publique*, had twenty-four thousand black soldiers in its ranks, led by one thousand Belgian officers, and on the fifth of July, their commander, General Émile Janssens, had written an edict on a blackboard: "Before independence equals after independence." But the soldiers wanted promotions and pay raises now that their white officers were leaving, and when Lumumba didn't immediately increase their ranks and salaries, they ran riot. The Belgians flew in paratroopers to seize the national airport and the mines. Fighting to turn back time, they orchestrated the secession of Katanga, the immense southern province where the great mineral riches lay, creating a military base and a shadow government in its capital, Elisabethville. The Belgians proclaimed the Republic of Katanga, anointed their favorite political figure in the Congo, Moise Tshombe, as its president, and gave it a constitution, a flag, and a national anthem.

The UN Secretary-General Dag Hammarskjöld moved with great speed in the second half of July to win approval for a peacekeeping mission, the biggest and most complex mobilization of its kind the UN ever had undertaken. The goal was enforcing a ceasefire and compelling Belgium to withdraw its troops. Lumumba flew to New York, appealed to the United Nations for more forceful support, and then on July 27 made a quick trip to Washington, where he asked the leaders of the State Department for financial and technical help. The minutes of the meeting read: "The Prime Minister said that he did not wish the Congo to emerge from a colonial status only to fall under the domination of some other form of dictatorship or ideological influence. We are, he said, Africans and wish to remain so." The patrician undersecretary of state C. Douglas Dillon found him appalling. "Just not a rational being," he sniffed.

The White House, the leaders of the CIA, and the members of the NSC looked upon Lumumba with great dismay. They saw him as another Castro and the Congo as a ripe target for a Soviet coup. Allen Dulles told Eisenhower, without evidence, that it was safe to go on the assumption that Lumumba had been bought out by the Belgian Communist Party on orders from Moscow. The CIA officer whom Dulles had assigned to take care of the Congo, Lawrence R. Devlin, had told the director that if the Soviets got their hooks into Lumumba, they would soon control the country's diamonds, oil, and uranium; use the Congo as a base to extend their influence throughout Africa; and vastly increase their power, influence, and prestige throughout the Third World. On July 29, the Joint Chiefs of Staff reported to Eisenhower:

> The United States must be prepared at any time to take appropriate military action as necessary to prevent or defeat Soviet military intervention in the Congo. Multilateral action would be preferable but unilateral action may be necessary. In the present Soviet belligerent mood, the USSR could estimate that the United States would not oppose them. We must be prepared to oppose and defeat them. In order to prevent their making such a rash move, they must be made to understand that we will not tolerate a Soviet military takeover of the Congo.

A note-taker recorded that Ike told his national security team on August 1: "In the last twelve months, the world has developed a kind of ferment greater than he could remember in recent times. The Communists are trying to take control of this and have succeeded to the extent that [college students] are now saying the Communists are thinking of the common man, while the United States is dedicated to supporting outmoded regimes." America could not afford to lose *that* battle.

A few days thereafter, more than eleven thousand troops had arrived in the Congo under the UN banner, a majority from African countries, with orders to shoot only in self-defense in their mission to ease out the Belgians. Lumumba's faith in the mission wavered when he saw that the West would not use force to help him secure his power against his colonial oppressors and that any aid that the United States deigned to send him would be channeled through the UN. Sometime during the next two weeks or so, he secretly determined to ask the Soviets for military support: weapons, transport planes, trucks, and communications gear.

The country was up for grabs. Into the maelstrom flew Larry Devlin, the new CIA chief of station. He soon became the proconsul of the Congo. Devlin cut a sharp figure, *très sportif:* slicked-back black hair, dark lightweight suit, open-necked white shirt, Ray-Bans shielding his eyes. He had just turned thirty-eight, and he had long been a man of the world. He'd fought in North Africa and Europe under Eisenhower in World War II, and in 1949, while he was studying for a master's degree in international relations at Harvard, he'd been recruited for the CIA by a visiting lecturer named McGeorge Bundy. (At that time, Bundy was the youngest member of a secret group perfecting the Marshall Plan's mechanisms to finance the CIA's covert operations; the Council on Foreign Relations conclave included Dwight Eisenhower, Allen Dulles, Dick Bissell, and George Kennan. In January 1961, Bundy left his post as dean of Harvard's Faculty of Arts and Sciences to become President Kennedy's national security adviser.) In his first years as a spy, Devlin had traveled the globe in the guise of a writer of travel guides, excellent cover for the craft of espionage. His last posting had been in Brussels, where he'd posed as a diplomat, and with his onward assignment to the Congo in hand, he'd observed the tumultuous conference that made Lumumba prime minister.

Devlin was whip-smart, courageous, tireless, devoted to skullduggery, and every bit as devious as his profession demanded him to be. He was convinced that he was witnessing a Soviet effort to take over the Congo and to use it as the foundation for building a communist Africa. "We had a very clear mission to conduct political warfare," he said almost half a century later, and "we were working for the president of the United States." The spirit of the mission was gung ho: money was no object, no holds barred, no questions asked. In the days after he arrived in the Congo, he began to help shape American foreign policy. And that policy was the overthrow of Patrice Lumumba.

"Lumumba moving left and Commie influence increasing," Devlin wrote to CIA headquarters in the chopped syntax of cablese on August 11, 1960. "Unless he stopped near future, believe he will become strongman, eliminating moderate opposition and establishing regime under influence if not fully controlled by Commies. Thus believe fall Lumumba would assist Western objectives . . . all Station efforts concentrated this campaign on crash basis." On August 18, he wrote: "Whether or not Lumumba actually Commie or just playing Commie game to assist his solidifying power, anti-West forces rapidly increasing power Congo and there may be little time left in which take action to avoid another Cuba." This got the president's full attention. On that same day an extraordinary meeting of the National Security Council took place in the elegant seaside setting of Newport, Rhode Island, where Eisenhower was vacationing. The note taker, an NSC staffer named Robert Johnson, later testified under oath that he heard Eisenhower turn to Allen Dulles and say that Lumumba should be assassinated. A stunned silence ensued.

That same week, perhaps that same day, Soviet pilots flew fifteen transport planes into Stanleyville, Lumumba's home base and the locus of his political support, which lay sixteen hundred rough miles of road from the capital. Their objective, never fulfilled, was to support Lumumba in a military assault on the Belgian forces in Katanga, to be carried out by Congolese army troops. Over the summer, as Devlin later determined, hundreds of Soviets and Czechs had streamed into Léopoldville, ostensibly to deliver food and offer economic aid and to help Lumumba run his ministries, but in reality with the hope of planting the hammer and sickle in the heart of Africa. The new Soviet ambassador arrived the same week Devlin did, as did a three-man KGB contingent. After presenting his credentials, the envoy handed Lumumba a note from Khrushchev expressing solidarity and comparing the situation in the Congo to the early days of the Soviet Union, which had been invaded by foreign soldiers, including Americans, after the triumph of the Russian revolution.

On August 27, Dulles wrote to Devlin: The White House had decided that if Lumumba continued in power, "the inevitable result will at best be chaos and at worst pave the way to Communist takeover of the Congo with disastrous consequences. . . . Consequently we conclude that his removal must be an urgent and prime objective and that under existing conditions this should be a high priority of our covert action." He authorized Devlin to spend up to $100,000 on any single aspect of that covert action without asking headquarters—an extraordinary grant of power. The station chief already was drawing up what he called "a three-page plan, step-by-step-by-step, as to what should be done and when, right from the time of buying the first senator." These steps were not limited to buying or renting the allegiances of politicians, trying to fix votes for a parliamentary motion of censure against Lumumba, and paying demonstrators to shout him down when he spoke at a meeting of African foreign ministers in Léopoldville. Devlin had to find the new leader of the Congo.

The station chief left the embassy for the presidential palace on the night of September 13 looking for Lumumba. He encountered instead a slender young soldier in full military dress named Joseph-Désiré Mobutu, who was twenty-nine, had served as a sergeant major under the Belgians, the highest rank attainable, and had been their paid informer in the Congo since 1956. The two men had met before, in Brussels, during the run-up to the election, and they had sized one another up in full: a good spy's fingertips start tingling when he spots talent, and Mobutu recognized power when he saw it. They quickly got down to business. Colonel Mobutu told Devlin that the army was prepared to overthrow Lumumba—if the United States would recognize the new junta. On the spot, Devlin agreed on behalf of his country to back a coup. Mobutu boldly asked for $5,000 in cash, and without hesitation, Devlin said he'd have it in the morning. The station chief returned to the embassy and then, at 2 a.m., went to the residence of the new American ambassador, Clare Timberlake, waking him to tell him what he'd done.

Like his compatriots in Washington, Timberlake, a thirty-year veteran of the Foreign Service, thought that chaos in the Congo would give the Soviets a golden opportunity to create a surging communist front in Africa. Unlike most of them, he also saw that if the Belgians resurrected their colonial powers at gunpoint in the name of conquering chaos, black Africa could collectively recoil from the West. The chances of success of the unarmed and unprecedented United Nations mission in the Congo were unknowable. Here was a way for the United States to impose its own order on its own terms. The ambassador gave the station chief the go-ahead. Devlin immediately cabled Dulles to report that he had recruited Mobutu, who had the promise of long-term "political action potential, provided he does not destroy himself in plot." The director was overjoyed. He dropped a hint with a wink and a smile at the next National Security Council meeting: it wasn't easy to run a coup in the Congo, he said, but he had the wheels in motion.

The Congo had been front-page news all summer, and many of the world's leading foreign correspondents had converged at the Regina Hotel in Léopoldville. After midnight on September 15, Mobutu called a press conference at the hotel. He leaped upon a table and announced a bloodless coup. He proclaimed himself the commander of the army, and said he had decided to neutralize the chief of state, the government, and the legislature. Lumumba, he said, was under house arrest. This was not a coup d'état, he insisted, but a peaceful revolution. To make his allegiances clear, he was shuttering the Soviet embassy and expelling its diplomats and spies; 480 Russian and Czech personnel were declared personae non gratae and ordered to leave on the next plane.

Devlin sent a flash message, the highest priority, to CIA headquarters. In his excitement, he forgot the code word for *coup* and instead used the word for *war*. That got the president of the United States out of bed. The station chief quickly followed up with a plan for a "crash operation" to bolster Colonel Mobutu. "A: Mobutu needs financial assistance to pay certain troops and officers, provide gas for troop movements. B. Mobutu needs French-speaking economic, political and security advisers. C. Mobutu desires security team to work against Lumumba and Communists." The National Security Council approved all of this and more: a steady flow of arms and ammunition. A briefing paper for the White House by American intelligence analysts concluded that the fractious Congo now had one true center of power: "The Mobutu military dictatorship." General Mobutu and the CIA were running the country now.

But as Dulles told the president: "Lumumba was not yet disposed of and remained a grave danger." CIA deputy director Richard Bissell, who had more than one murder plot already on his hands, let Devlin know that he wanted Lumumba dead before Eisenhower left office on January 20. Bissell sent the CIA's top scientist, a clubfooted biochemist named Sidney Gottlieb, out to Léopoldville. Gottlieb ran the CIA's search for methods of mind control; he had dosed legions of unsuspecting human guinea pigs with LSD, and he himself had taken the drug a hundred times or more. One of his sidelines was chemical warfare: specifically, the use of poison to assassinate political leaders. He arrived carrying a satchel filled with syringes and toxins.

Plan A was to inject poison into Lumumba's toothpaste. He said it was now Devlin's job to find an agent in Mobutu's camp and order him to kill Patrice Lumumba.

"Jesus H. Christ!" Devlin said. "Who authorized this?"

"President Eisenhower," the doctor replied.

Devlin locked the murder weapons in his office safe and agonized. He had killed the enemy in war, but this was different. He couldn't bring himself to do it, but he couldn't tell that to his superiors. In November, Bissell dispatched two more men to finish the job: a CIA officer named Justin O'Donnell and a hit man known to history only by his cryptonym of QJ/WIN, a foreign citizen with a criminal background recruited by the CIA somewhere in Europe. A third man sent to assist Devlin was WI/ROGUE, a stateless soldier of fortune whose resume included forgery and bank robbery. The poison-toothpaste operation never came off, and in time Devlin buried the contents of the satchel on the banks of the Congo River. He proposed to Mobutu that the job should be done the old-fashioned way—with a bullet—when the time was ripe. But the CIA's assassins never got near their target, and neither did Mobutu's allies. Lumumba was under house arrest, guarded by 150 troops from the army and the United Nations— the Congolese to prevent him from escaping into UN custody and the UN to prevent him from being killed by the Congolese. And then, as a violent thunderstorm struck on the night of November 27, Lumumba slipped past his guards and set out for Stanleyville.

Devlin told headquarters that he was working with Mobutu to get the roads blocked and his troops alerted. Lumumba was captured four days later, flown back to the capital, jailed, and beaten. Mobutu came by to spit in his face. On January 17, 1961, by a twist of fate, Frank Carlucci and a visiting United States senator were the last two Americans to see him alive. "We were having a drink about mid-afternoon at a sidewalk café and a truck went by," Carlucci recalled. "Lumumba had his hands tied behind his back and was in the rear part of the truck. The truck was on the way to the airport." A DC-4 flew the prisoner to Elisabethville in Katanga province, the southern-most city of the Congo, and into the hands of his enemies. The CIA base chief in Katanga cabled Devlin that Lumumba had debarked in chains, badly beaten, his teeth knocked from his head, and taken to a prison where he was guarded by white soldiers.

On the evening of January 19, the last full day of the Eisenhower administration, the base chief reported that a Belgian officer had executed Lumumba with a burst of submachine gunfire. He was not deeply mourned in Moscow. Khrushchev told the American ambassador in Moscow, Llewellyn Thompson, that his imprisonment and death had served the Soviets' interests. The ambassador reported: "With respect to Congo K said what had happened there and particularly murder of Lumumba had helped communism. Lumumba was not Communist and he doubted if he would have become one." In the Kremlin's eyes, the chances of a Communist takeover at independence had been nil.

The White House and the CIA started to cement their plans for political control of the Congo as soon as Kennedy was sworn in. CIA headquarters sent Mobutu $250,000 along with a fresh injection of weapons and direct instructions from on high: he should take the role of the power behind the throne. Devlin was to assure him that he'd get all the money he wanted for himself, to be the paymaster for his troops in Léopoldville, and to expand his power in the capital and in the provinces. From the start, the CIA would send Mobutu a list of candidates for president, prime minister, and cabinet officials for his approval. He would then meet with these handpicked political leaders and tell them they could not obtain office nor run the government without him. Mobutu accepted the plan.

Devlin told his superiors: "Agree political realities require some form constitutionality for new govt. However if we to be realistic, must be satisfied with democratic façade."

On March 3, 1961, President Kennedy and his National Security Council—CIA director Allen Dulles, Secretary of State Dean Rusk,

Secretary of Defense Robert McNamara, and National Security Adviser McGeorge Bundy—discussed political warfare plans for the Congo at a two-hour meeting in the White House. JFK said he wanted the CIA to expedite and expand its "silver bullets" program in the Congo. A bandolier of silver bullets was at hand. Dulles immediately notified Devlin, using the CIA's own code word for itself, *KUBARK.* "At high level policy meeting three March KUBARK received reaffirmation of authority to expend funds both to bribe [deleted] forces and supplement pay of selected Mobutu forces where needed to assure loyalty," the director wrote to Devlin. "Urge you canvass all means for using funds securely and effectively for these purposes."

President Kennedy was well aware of these payments and their purposes in their minutest details. "As you requested last week, we are arranging a meeting at which all of our clandestine activities in support of political leaders and parties will be discussed with you. In particular, at that meeting, there will be presented a proposal for action in the Congo which has the support of the ambassador and our Department of State," Bundy wrote to the president on June 10, 1961. "Meanwhile, one small aspect of this Congo proposal has been presented with an urgency which has led me to approve it in your absence, on the basis of clear State Department concurrence. This is an expenditure of $23,000 in support of particular activities designed to strengthen the moderate camp in the Congo. Very much larger sums have been spent in the past in the same direction, through the same channels and without embarrassment." Bundy trusted Devlin's judgment, and why wouldn't he? He himself had recruited the man from the hallowed halls of Harvard into the labyrinth of the CIA.

Over the course of six years, the CIA poured at least $11.7 million into the political warfare campaign to put Mobutu in power and keep him there, more than $100 million in today's dollars, insofar as can be documented. The declassified annals of the cold war do not thus far reveal another military strongman who received that level of personal financial assistance from the United States. Devlin

delivered more than $1 million of that money to Mobutu in the first
months of the Kennedy administration. It paid for weapons, communications gear, trucks, and jeeps. It went to bribe the Congo's
principal military and civilian leaders. It underwrote a political coalition to control the parliament when it reconvened. It created propaganda, print and broadcast. And it met Mobutu's endlessly mounting
demands for himself. Devlin consolidated his political control by
putting Mobutu's two closest allies, Justin Bamboko, the minister of
foreign affairs, and Victor Nendaka, the chief of the secret police, on
the CIA's payroll. These three were the core of the Binza group, so
named after the neighborhood where they convened. The group was
the true government. Devlin was its leader. They set out to run the
country and to select its next prime minister.

This wasn't enough for Devlin. In increasingly urgent and
occasionally angry dispatches to CIA headquarters, he called for a
rethinking of American foreign policy in all of Africa. "Independence in the Congo has resulted in chaos, great difficulties for the
West and an opportunity for the Soviet Bloc to exploit the situation to its own ends," he wrote on October 12. "The time for ad hoc
KUBARK action to meet the emergency must now give way to a
detailed and organized plan of action which looks beyond today to
the eventual form that [the United States] wishes to see the future
take in the Congo and, for that matter, in Central Africa. KUBARK
can take major credit for the fall of the Lumumba govt [and] the
success of the Mobutu coup," he wrote. But "instead of becoming a
strong force for the preservation of law and order, the army . . . has
taken the law into its own hands, arbitrarily arresting Congolese
and foreigners, robbing banks and looting." They were "little more
than an armed mob." And now the Soviets were creeping back in
the picture, covertly supporting a breakaway political group led by
Lumumba's deputy up the Congo River in Stanleyville, reopening
their embassy, and offering military aid to Mobutu's many enemies.
A KGB beachhead in Stanleyville had been established that summer

in cohort with the Czech intelligence service, the StB. It set up an arms pipeline that trickled and sputtered while the Czechs set up safe houses for Lumumba's supporters in the capital.

Devlin said the United States wasn't doing enough to stop communism and its ally, chaos, in the Congo. What was needed, he argued, was a more massive political warfare operation, including military support and training for the army, planes and helicopters for an air force, foreign aid and food programs, building roads and bridges, ginning up more muscular diplomacy and propaganda and public information operations—all the available means at America's control. Mobutu had made an impassioned plea for direct support from the United States, and Devlin agreed with him. He reiterated that Mobutu was the key to success for American foreign policy in all of Africa and a cornerstone for the global struggle against the Soviets.

The president and the Special Group, the White House covert-action panel led by Bobby Kennedy, strongly agreed with Devlin. They expanded the CIA's financial support for Mobutu, the Binza group, and their handpicked front man, Prime Minister Cyrille Adoula, in November. JFK also authorized an injection of money and propaganda to "enhance the political image of Prime Minister Adoula domestically and internationally and to furnish him and his closest collaborators with a base of domestic power." Devlin reported that it would be necessary to "grease many palms" to build that base. But, working through the State Department, he helped secure an invitation for Adoula to meet President Kennedy at the White House. He prepped the prime minister as best he could. The meeting on February 5, 1962, was desultory; Adoula complained at length that the army was twice the size it should be but said he had no idea what to do with the thousands of otherwise unemployable soldiers who should be stripped from its ranks.

Over the next year, Devlin held Mobutu as closely as he could, drinking and dining with him several times a week, meeting his every demand for money. He reported continually to Washington that Mobutu remained the only man with the political and military qualifications needed to keep the country from chaos. He assured Mobutu that he, too, would one day get to the White House. And after some wrangling, he secured that invitation, though it was highly unusual for a military commander, much less a coup leader, to meet one-on-one with the president of the United States. Plans were set for a two-week trip: a full-dress reception by the chairman of the Joint Chiefs of Staff, a tour of the United States Military Academy at West Point, lunch at the CIA's new headquarters in the wooded hills above the Potomac, and an hour in the Oval Office. The royal treatment reflected the power vested in Mobutu.

Devlin sent more than two hundred reports to headquarters in 1962, the gist of which he and his superiors summarized for the State Department and the White House in March 1963. "A multitude of nearly insoluble problems" had plagued the Congo since independence. Yet the station chief and his recruited agents had created "a government which was as pro-American as any that could be expected in Africa," and the CIA had held that government together: "On numerous occasions, financial support as well as political guidance to Adoula and his principal supporters have enabled them to survive immediate, short-term crises, failure in which might have resulted in the downfall of the government." The CIA was financing and feeding information to "a new newspaper which is generally recognized to be a government outlet." It was bankrolling a major labor union. It had created a paramilitary force for counterinsurgency. And, as ever, it was enriching General Mobutu and his allies. President Kennedy personally approved all of this.

In May, Devlin won a promotion to the CIA's equivalent of a one-star general and a new assignment as chief of the East Africa division at headquarters. He planned to leave as soon as Mobutu returned from his visit to Washington. As he was on his way out, a new chief political officer, the State Department's Lewis Hoffacker, arrived at the American embassy. Like Devlin, he'd been in the

Congo for nearly three years, most of it at the Elisabethville consulate in Katanga. His reporting was so riveting that the president had called him back to Washington for a personal briefing. Hoffacker was mightily impressed by the empire that the station chief had built. "CIA was very big and conspicuous," he observed. "They were everywhere: in the government, in the military, and in the embassy. Everybody knew who they were; they were the backbone of the central government." He was less impressed after a long meeting with Mobutu: "He was a lazy lout," and his army was "a rabble. Rape and pillage was their first priority. They did not provide any security for the Congolese. They were just corrupt, ineffective and he was likewise, from the very beginning, just taking care of himself."

On May 23, 1963, Mobutu lunched with the CIA's chieftains in Langley, Virginia. That day, Devlin cabled what he thought would be his final report from the Congo: Mobutu was America's best friend in Africa, and although he had his failings, the United States should continue to bet on him. There was no alternative to his power. Eight days later, President Kennedy sat down with the general in the White House. He asked what more the United States could do for the Congo. Deliver us direct military aid, Mobutu said—American training, trucks, communications, and other war materiel for his troops. "If you give me equipment," he told JFK, "I'll be ready." But he'd need three years to straighten out his country. Mobutu also wanted a few things for himself: four weeks of parachute training at Fort Benning, two weeks at the Special Warfare School at Fort Bragg, and a command aircraft, an African Air Force One. The president said he'd be delighted to provide all that and more. The floodgates were open: in the 1960s, Congo received about $800 million in economic aid, more than any other country in black Africa. The president told Mobutu that there was nobody in the world who had done more to maintain freedom in Africa. "General," he said, "if it hadn't been for you, the whole thing would have collapsed and the Communists would have taken over." Mobutu replied, "I do what I am able to do." The president told him he'd done an outstanding job. In September Mobutu and his allies dissolved the parliament and declared martial law. The political parties who opposed them were banned, and they went underground.

The Soviets had sent a new diplomatic delegation to the Congo, along with a new KGB station chief, Boris Voronin, whose orders were to work with the banished opposition. He was fingered by the CIA, and Mobutu decided to crush him. On November 19, 1963, Voronin was arrested, beaten within an inch of his life, and the next evening transported to the Ndola prison, a circle of hell inside a military base. Mobutu came in the middle of the night. His men dragged their captive into the prison yard, and he told the Russian spy that it was his last chance to confess. The soldiers raised their rifles. And then Mobutu called off the show in his theater of cruelty. In the morning, he cut off the electricity and telephone lines to the Soviet embassy and ordered it shuttered and its personnel expelled for the second time in two years. On the morning of November 21, an American—very likely Ben Cushing, the new CIA chief of station—braced a bruised and barefoot Boris Voronin and suggested without success that he might prefer a new life in the West to the prospect of "Siberian exile." Spy-versus-spy confrontations like this, the CIA face-to-face with the KGB, were rare moments in the war inside the cold war.

President Kennedy was assassinated the next day in Dallas by a United States Marine veteran who had defected to Moscow and returned to America. By all reliable accounts, Khrushchev and Castro were horrified, and the KGB's hands were clean, but the killing still haunts the imagination, and for millions, the murder remains the black hole of American history. In the immediate aftermath of the assassination, CIA director John McCone had to swear to his fellow Catholic Bobby Kennedy, with an invocation of the sacramental blood and body of Christ, that his officers were innocent in the death of the president.

Among JFK's many legacies to President Lyndon B. Johnson was a growing confrontation with communism throughout the Third World, from Saigon to Stanleyville. At the highest levels of the government, men like McCone and Secretary of State Rusk worried that the United States was losing the contest for hearts and minds in Africa. Rusk suggested a global divide-and-conquer operation. He asked "that CIA do everything possible covertly to stimulate and incite resentment" between black Africans and "the Muslim slave traders" of the Arab world. McCone assured him that "the covert support we were giving had turned the tide of the battle."

But the Kremlin and the KGB were aligning with governments and liberation movements from Algeria to South Africa, where Nelson Mandela of the African National Congress, a secret member of the Communist Party, had been arrested and sentenced to life in prison in 1962. (A CIA officer, Donald Rickard, undercover as the American vice-consul in Durban, gave the South African government the tip-off that led to his capture; he later called Mandela the most dangerous communist in the world outside the Soviet Union.) The year before, the Soviets had created Patrice Lumumba University in Moscow as an international magnet school; the KGB oversaw it, its officers recruiting and training promising young men for future battles in Africa, the Middle East, and Latin America. The Soviets were trying with mixed success to arm Lumumba's followers for a countercoup in the Congo once the United Nations peacekeeping force withdrew in June 1964. Those loyalists, enraged by the rottenness of their government and dreaming of taking power in the name of their slain prime minister, aimed to establish a people's republic based in Stanleyville. Mobutu's undisciplined army was ill-equipped to meet that threat. Voicing widely held fears, the Pentagon's special-operations commander, General Paul Adams, wrote to the Joint Chiefs that a victory by the insurgents would lead directly to a communist-dominated black Africa. The stalwart diplomat Averell Harriman, now the undersecretary of state for political affairs, went to the Congo and pledged that American military aircraft would be delivered with great speed. The list included weaponry never before seen in that part of the world: B-26 bombers, helicopters, and light aircraft equipped with .50-caliber machine guns, rockets, and five-hundred-pound bombs for counterinsurgency missions. Devlin would be the commander of this air force.

LBJ had appointed a new ambassador, the veteran diplomat G. McMurtrie "Mac" Godley, who arrived in March. The core of the country team—Godley, CIA station chief Cushing, and the exceptionally erudite deputy chief of station, Charles Cogan, magna cum laude, Harvard, class of '49—all had the benefit of Devlin's guidance from headquarters. They worked with a new figurehead prime minister, Moise Tshombe, darling of the Belgians and their erstwhile emperor of Katanga. ("Tshombe had little external support," Cogan wrote half a century later. "Other African nations, for example, refused to have anything to do with him.") The Americans now had an impressive military force ready to deploy against the Stanleyville rebels. The growing CIA paramilitary team worked with hundreds of white mercenaries, most from the racist regimes of South Africa and Rhodesia, led by a well-known commando named "Mad Mike" Hoare. The CIA's air force in the Congo had the power to inflict shock and awe; the pilots included CIA officers and contractors, as well as Cuban veterans of the Bay of Pigs. In June, Mobutu talked two of the American pilots into assaulting rebel positions for three days. The Joint Chiefs pushed back hard when the State Department expressed queasiness over the fact that Americans were dropping napalm on Africans.

By late July the strongest of the rebel forces, who called themselves the Simba, Swahili for "Lions," had surrounded Stanleyville, and hundreds of American and European missionaries, along with the small United States consulate, were at their mercy. Ambassador Godley ordered the American consul, Mike Hoyt, to hold the fort. This proved a misjudgment. Hoyt, the CIA base chief David Grinwis (undercover as the vice-consul), a CIA communications officer, and two more staffers were captured when the city fell, creating the first American hostage crisis of the cold war. "I knew it was foolhardy to stay," Hoyt remembered; the rebels had made it very plain "that Americans were on their shit list." The Simba leaders told Hoyt to send a cable to Washington, warning that he would be killed unless the CIA's air force was grounded. Devlin immediately returned to the Congo to lead a mission to rescue the hostages.

"Stanleyville is in rebel hands," the NSC staff reported to President Johnson on August 6. "Central Government may collapse in next several weeks. . . . There is real danger Communists will be able to exploit in near future." The White House was already on a knife's edge: LBJ was about to send aircraft carriers and warplanes to attack North Vietnam for the first time. On August 10, Devlin reported to headquarters in a cable from the CIA station in the capital that he could foresee a "Commie field day in the Congo" if the tide didn't turn. "If Commies worked fast enough, they might be able to exploit rebel govt for Commie ends [and launch] subversion ops into many east, central and west African countries."

The president, Secretary of Defense McNamara, Secretary of State Rusk, and CIA director McCone convened at an NSC meeting the next day. LBJ was intensely worried. Time was running out, he said, and the Congo had to be saved. At McCone's direction, Devlin drew up a plan requisitioning seven long-range bombers, two military transports, combat helicopters, pilots, and air crews for an air war in the Congo. The ground war was a bigger problem. "The Congolese Army is totally ineffective," he wrote, and "only with Belgian or other white officers can an effective striking force be put in the field." The United States should "support the immediate development of a 3,000-man force with 200 white mercenaries," and the CIA would pay the commandos.

This looked less like political warfare and more like a resurgence of imperial power to Carl Rowan, the African American director of the United States Information Agency, and the only member of LBJ's inner circle who wasn't a white man. He wrote to the president: "United States planes are hauling in Belgian guns to be used by South African and Southern Rhodesian mercenaries to kill Africans," and he pointed out, "Saving the present situation in the Congo . . . could lose us the longer-range struggle for all of Africa." Devlin and the CIA pressed on through that moral quagmire. They sought, and the White House approved, a large injection of hard currency for the white mercenaries and $750,000 for Mobutu. The general then requisitioned an additional $35 million for his spies and security forces, whose ranks would be beefed up by Belgians. Ambassador Godley was taken aback by all this. On August 19, he cabled Washington with a warning that "we may well soon find ourselves in all-out support, alone or with Belgians, of minority regime being propped up by . . . US financed secret police" and firmly aligned with apartheid regimes "against most, if not all of this vast continent." This fact was not soon forgotten among the African nations caught in the cross fire between Moscow and Washington. As the civil rights movement in the United States reached a crescendo, America had wrapped itself in a colonial flag in Africa, in alliance with the covert armies of apartheid.

On November 24, twelve American C-130 transports flew 545 Belgian paratroopers to Stanleyville. After the CIA's bombers dropped air strikes on rebel positions, the Belgian commandos and a CIA strike force of eighteen Cubans seized the town by force and mowed the Simbas down by the hundreds. Twenty-one hostages, including two Americans, were killed; the consular and CIA officers were freed. Two days later Hoyt and Grinwis were drinking champagne on an Air France flight to New York. The president got the word at his Texas ranch, where he'd been basking in the aftermath of a landslide election victory. LBJ had had grave doubts about the mission. He didn't want to turn the country and perhaps the continent into another Vietnam. But in the end, he felt he had no choice, for the CIA reported that the international forces of communism in Africa—soon to be led in a disastrous mission commanded by Castro's field marshal Che Guevara—would never stop trying to seize the Congo.

Richard Helms, soon to become the CIA's director, wanted no country where his officers had a measure of control over the course of human events to go communist on his watch. He called Devlin into his office at headquarters in the spring of 1965. Helms possessed all the social graces and an iron fist to complement them. He allowed that it would be an excellent idea if Devlin returned to the Congo. Devlin thought not: he wanted to fight the CIA's battles in the Vietnam War. Helms was compelled to order him back to Africa. The command was auspicious. On July 19, Devlin, newly reinstalled, dined and drank once again with Mobutu. The general asked: How did Devlin like the climate? He meant the political climate. The puppet president and prime minister were two scorpions in a bottle corked by Mobutu, each seeking to depose the other.

The tensions in the capital were boiling over by the time the rainy season started in late October. The CIA officer and his prized asset had a come-to-Jesus meeting on the night of November 19. "Mobutu turned to Devlin and stated he wished seek latter's personal advice. He emphasized he speaking to Devlin as friend," the station chief reported in a cable. Mobutu proposed to resolve the conflict once and for all. "Mobutu stressed he does not repeat not wish to stage another coup d'état. However said he believes it to be his duty to try find compromise solution to current political impasse. Thus, he asked Devlin if he could suggest a solution." He was looking for a green light. Devlin reported: "Since Station knows of no satisfactory alternative to Mobutu as commander of army, and in view of Mobutu's long-time cooperation . . . Station believes it is incumbent upon USG to try help Mobutu." They met again, two days later, on November 21. Mobutu wanted $100,000 immediately. Devlin reported that this request represented America's last opportunity to influence the fate of the nation.

"*Crisis in Congo*," the NSC aide Robert "Blowtorch Bob" Komer wrote to Bundy at roughly the same hour. "Mobutu is the key; perhaps he can force a compromise. You'll probably have a new plea at 303 for baksheesh to this end." The 303 Committee—formerly the Special Group—was Bundy and the number two men at CIA, State, and Defense; it was the clearinghouse for major covert actions. The four conferred by telephone. Bundy had in hand a detailed memo from his staff that concluded: "We can back Mobutu. We could either back him in a coup or let him put together the best formula he can. . . . He is already our man. He controls the army (with our help). He has shown himself the most sensible leader in the current mess. At the moment, he knows the ins and outs of the situation better than we do." Mobutu was a master manipulator of the men who thought they could manipulate him.

At five o'clock in the morning on November 25, Mobutu announced that he had taken over the Congo and deposed the president and prime minister. Devlin went to see him at eleven-thirty. Mobutu struck the pose of a statesman, saying that he understood that the United States might not immediately recognize his regime, but stressing that he was counting on America's support for his survival. For his part, Devlin cabled the CIA: "Mobutu said he would appreciate receiving all advisors that KUBARK can provide. He specifically cited need for advisor to guide information ministry [and] a political advisor to provide him with guidance. . . . He stressed he looking to KUBARK for advice and guidance now and in future. . . . He wants to maintain close working relationship with Station." Headquarters wrote back commending Devlin for a job well done and instructing him to continue to support Mobutu to the utmost. The station chief followed up on December 13. He wrote that Mobutu was "the last hope for the West in the Congo."

So began the slow death of a nation.

One of the first things Mobutu did upon taking power was to hang four former cabinet ministers before a crowd of fifty thousand.

The CIA kept him on the payroll for at least two years thereafter. Soon he did not need its money. He revived the mines that produced the Congo's wealth—diamonds, silver, gold, copper, cobalt, tin, uranium, zinc, and more—and then he seized control of their riches. By 1970, they were his and his alone. The diamonds were "flown off to Belgium for Mobutu's account," said Michael Newlin, the deputy chief of mission at the American embassy from 1972 to 1975. The gold went to Switzerland. And he took not only the diamonds and the gold, but everything from which wealth could be extracted, and the lion's share of the revenues from foreign exchange and state marketing operations. "There was no investment in the country by Mobutu and his rich relatives and cronies. They were skimming off everything," Newlin said. "Through, I guess, intercepts, we found out that the central bank was about to ship the silver deposit, the entire silver deposit in the national bank, to a storefront in Jersey City." By 1973, Mobutu had seized full or partial control of every major foreign-owned company in the country—factories, farms, wholesale firms—and made them his private property. He now pocketed half of the nation's revenues or more. By the end of the decade, he was one of the wealthiest men in the world; his ever-expanding fortune eventually was estimated at $5 billion. He jailed his real and imagined enemies at will. A man could be Mobutu's minister one day and his prisoner at the point of death the next. He had become the new King Leopold.

Larry Devlin had a ringside seat to this carnival of corruption. He returned to the nation he had saved from chaos and communism after he retired from the CIA as chief of the Africa division in 1974. He was for many years thereafter the chief business agent in Africa for Maurice Tempelsman, a fabulously wealthy Belgian American diamond merchant and mining kingpin, Mobutu's silent business partner, the longtime companion of Jacqueline Kennedy Onassis, and later in life a major financial contributor and confidant to President Bill Clinton. Shortly before Devlin's death in 2008, he spoke proudly about his service with the CIA: "In those years, we kept the

Soviets from taking over Africa, or a very large part of Africa. We were in the business of political warfare. And we didn't win 'em all. But we won that one."

Mobutu remained in the good graces of the United States for the rest of the cold war, continuing to receive significant American military and economic aid despite his corruption and his human rights abuses, in great part due to his relationship with the CIA. When the agency wanted to supply weapons to would-be African leaders it supported, such as the Angolan rebel Jonas Savimbi, Mobutu would provide airfields for transshipment. He sent troops to back CIA-supported governments and insurgencies in Africa, and he served as a vital switchboard for American intelligence. Even Jimmy Carter, the president who made human rights the lodestar of his foreign policy, welcomed him to the White House with an honor guard and ruffles and flourishes. (On the occasion of that visit, two senior State Department officials made a friendly wager. Frank G. Wisner, the son of the CIA's covert-operations czar, bet William C. Harrop, an experienced Africa hand, a dollar that Mobutu had worn out his welcome in the Oval Office. Harrop kept that dollar framed above his desk for the next forty years as proof that human rights would seldom prevail in American foreign policy.)

"Mobutu had a tremendous amount of charisma, human magnetism, charm. He was also a brilliant schemer and plotter," said Robert Oakley, the American ambassador from 1979 to 1982. "Not once do I remember Mobutu making any comments or showing any interest in the benefits that our assistance was providing his country. He was neither grateful or interested; he just wanted more." Mobutu stole his nation's wealth, Oakley said, with the help of the Société Générale in Brussels, which served by turns as a holding company for Belgium's colonial wealth, the privy purse of the king, a laundromat for Mobutu's money, and the repository for much of his loot. "He did share some of these illegal profits with his Belgian buddies, so that everyone except the people benefitted," Oakley said. As he and his

cronies enjoyed the spoils of his power, his nation's most basic infra-
structures rotted in the heat, the jungle began to reclaim the towns
and cities beyond the capital, and his soldiers brutally oppressed his
citizens. A formal CIA assessment of Mobutu, prepared in advance
of his meeting with President Reagan in December 1986, presented
the rationale for the unwavering support he had received from the
United States. "President Mobutu is arguably unique in Africa in his
support for US national security objectives," it began, "and his political demise would have serious implications for the United States and
cost Washington its closest friend in Africa." The feeling was mutual:
"Mobutu perceives that the United States has repeatedly responded
to his needs when he has been faced with major threats to his government, and he sees this as a special relationship." The CIA recommended that when Mobutu came to the White House, he should be
"recognized as an African statesman."

Reagan so recognized him. Three years later, President George
H. W. Bush, a former CIA director, was especially effusive in his welcome. He called Mobutu one of America's oldest and most valued
allies. But as Mobutu's wealth grew, so did his cruelty, said Brandon
Grove, the American ambassador under Reagan: "There was great
fear of Mobutu, and of his army in particular, by people in villages
and the countryside who suffered constantly from pillaging, brutality
and rape by his underpaid or unpaid soldiers, who exacted their 'pay'
from villagers by stealing food." Mobutu had his enormous yacht,
Kamaniola, where he received Reagan's CIA director, William E.
Casey, and Bush's secretary of state, James A. Baker III, on the River
Congo. He had his palaces in Switzerland and France and Spain and
Italy, his extraordinary apartment on the Avenue Foch in Paris, and
his immense fortune, and it still was not enough. He built a Versailles
in the rain forest, a huge palace of Italian marble and green mala-
chite at Gbadolite, his ancestral village in the northwest corner of
the Congo, with a discotheque, a nuclear fallout shelter, Louis XIV
furniture, and an airport outfitted for the Concorde. He began to

spend more and more time in the Oz world of Gbadolite, while doing "almost nothing to provide schools and functioning hospitals, roads, water, sanitation, electricity, housing, or anything else," Grove said. "Democratic institutions and respect for human rights had no place in his schemes. Mobutu felt himself accountable to no one." Every American president from Kennedy onward had seen him as an instrument of American political warfare in Africa, and their unwavering support had protected him and burnished his image, against all evidence, in the eyes of the world.

"I think that, looking back, historians are going to say, 'How could the United States have been wedded to such a dictator for so long? Because there was a confrontation with the Soviet Union, a consideration which, in the end, proved specious?' But that was the situation," said Bill Harrop, the American ambassador under Reagan and Bush. In 1993, two years after Harrop left that post, and as the country fell into abject ruin, he reflected that Mobutu was "a genius at manipulating the ethnic, military, and regional politics of his country. He was also a genius at manipulating the United States of America ... the National Security Council, the Department of State, the Central Intelligence Agency, and the Department of Defense." He continued:

> If we needed African support or help on issues before the UN, General Mobutu was always there. Our relationship was by no means just a one-way street. For instance, if there were a vote in the Security Council about the exclusion of Israel from some body, or if we needed support in the Security Council to do with Korea, Puerto Rico, or whatever the classic issues of the day were, we could always count on President Mobutu.
>
> So there were a lot of reasons why the United States embraced this extraordinary, authoritarian, selfish dictator. But these were the facts and that was the way we operated. Part of his genius was utilizing the United States, explaining that one reason that he was in power was that he was America's man.

That rationale was destroyed by the end of the cold war. But by then the Congo was destroyed as well. In 1997, thirty-seven years after his rapprochement with America, Mobutu fled in the face of an armed rebellion, and he soon died in exile. The Congo erupted into an epochal conflagration, an African world war in which nine nations fought and five million people were killed or injured. Our man had stockpiled the arsenal and lit the fuse.

CHAPTER 5

THE VOICE OF AMERICA

Americans who came of age after the cold war might look back and wonder: Who were these people we supported? What did we win in the end? Where is democracy triumphant today? In this harsh light, the long struggle might seem like folly.

It didn't look that way at the time to a great many people who waged political warfare on behalf of the United States. Americans had allied with Stalin against Hitler, and if now they struck a devil's bargain with the likes of the shah and Mobutu against the Kremlin, it was all for the greater glory of God and country. They believed that they were engaged in a battle between good and evil, pure and simple. If their faith ever faltered, they could find consolation in an old Balkan proverb often quoted by FDR: "My children, it is permitted in time of grave danger to walk with the devil until you have crossed the bridge." And they believed that one day they would cross over into a new world.

But they learned to their sorrow that their enemies could not be defeated by military might alone. Vietnam was the most bitter lesson: it was a political war, and it could not be won by force of arms. American leaders, at least some of them, would come to understand that victory or defeat in political warfare depended less on American power and statecraft than on the spirit of the people in the lands where they were waged. The longest and most glorious of these struggles took place over more than forty years in a country that had seen more war in its thousand years than any place on earth, and whose national anthem begins: "Poland has not yet perished."

Once, in the seventeenth century, Poland had been the largest country in Europe. Attacked on all fronts by the Swedes, the Turks, and the Russians, then carved up by Russia, Prussia, and the Austrian monarchy, it was wiped off the map for 140 years, until the end of World War I. Hitler and Stalin invaded it together in 1939. Then the Nazis stormed eastward through Poland on their way to Stalingrad, and the Red Army stormed back on the way to Berlin. Polish divisions fought under the command of General Eisenhower from 1943 to 1945, but they could not save their nation from near-total destruction. At the end of the war, hardly a stone stood upon a stone in Warsaw, and every stone was stained by Polish blood. Cities, towns, and villages vanished. Six million Poles died in the war, a fifth of the population. Three million of the dead were Jews annihilated by the Nazis; Poland was the epicenter of the Holocaust. One and a half million Poles suffered and died in the gulags of Siberia. Yet the Poles were never conquered, even after the Soviets seized them. "Communism does not fit the Poles," Stalin said in 1944. "They are too individualistic."

The Poles saw their history through the prism of Christ's martyrdom and resurrection. They were beautiful losers, romantic visionaries, the Irish of Eastern Europe. Their link to America was immutable: five million Polish immigrants lived in the United States at the end of World War II, ten million more in the years thereafter. Polish exiles in Europe were desperate to serve as a resistance army for the fledgling CIA—and the CIA was determined to use them. If the United States were to achieve its dream of rolling back communism, Poland looked like as good a place as any to start.

The CIA had believed from its beginnings in 1947 that it could mobilize an underground army known as the Freedom and Independence Movement—the initials in Polish were WiN—through a council of exiles in London. The covert-operations czar Frank Wisner envisioned arming and equipping 20,000 paramilitary fighters and 100,000 sympathizers who could rise up in rebellion against communist oppression. A Pole had turned up in London with photos of Soviets tanks that WiN had destroyed; he gave them to a former Polish general who asked the CIA for help. The London exiles and the CIA received a constant stream of messages from inside Poland depicting a growing rebellion in the making. From 1950 onward, the CIA responded by parachuting at least three dozen Polish patriots— along with weapons, clandestine radios, spy gear, and about $5 million in cash and gold—over the Iron Curtain to support WiN. And then, on December 28, 1952, in the last days of the Truman administration, Polish state radio went on the air with a devastating bulletin.

WiN was a sting—a creation of the Soviet and Polish intelligence services. They had controlled and managed the deception all along. It constituted one of the biggest American intelligence catastrophes of the early cold war—"a monumental disaster," John McMahon, then a young CIA officer in Germany, said fifty years later, after he had retired as deputy director of central intelligence. WiN was the first mission for a freshman CIA officer named Ted Shackley, and the sight of his colleagues wrestling with the realization that five years of plotting and millions of dollars had been lost to a double cross was seared into his memory. Soon he would have a chance to strike back.

When the American embassy in Warsaw relayed the gloating Polish state radio reports detailing the deception to Washington, the news enraged Robert Joyce, who had succeeded George Kennan at the State Department's policy planning department. He had worked closely with Kennan and the CIA from the outset as they had inaugurated political warfare—and this was what they had wrought. "I need not point out that this affair represents an appalling setback," he wrote on New Year's Eve 1952. He pointed out that, in Poland and elsewhere in the Soviet orbit, the "perfection of totalitarian police state techniques is approaching '1984' efficiency to a degree where 'resistance' can probably exist only *in the minds* of the enslaved peoples."

The battle for the minds of the people was on in full. Six months later, in Munich, a newly minted Harvard PhD named Zbigniew Brzezinski met another Harvard man named Paul Henze at the headquarters of Radio Free Europe, where Henze served as the deputy political adviser. The two men began a lifelong friendship, an alliance that would continue a quarter-century later at the National Security Council, where they formed their own resistance cell. Brzezinski, born in Warsaw in 1928, was the son of a Polish diplomat who had been posted in Germany as Hitler and the Nazis seized power. His doctoral thesis dealt with the evolution of Stalin's empire, and the suffering of Poland shaped his perception of the world. Henze, born in 1924 in the minuscule Minnesota hamlet of Redwood Falls, had served in Eisenhower's army and earned a master's in Soviet studies under the GI Bill at Harvard; the program served as a CIA incubator, and he entered duty June 21, 1950, four days before the Korean War erupted. Brzezinski and Henze were ambitious and adventurous men in their twenties, thrilled to be at the heart of a huge political warfare operation. Brzezinski thought the world of his colleague: "I was struck from the very beginning by his devotion to the cause of freedom for the East Europeans then under Stalin's rule, and by his realization—novel at the time—that truthful radio broadcasts could eventually negate the communist monopoly of power."

George Kennan conceived Radio Free Europe, Frank Wisner midwifed it, and Allen Dulles raised it. Kennan wanted to harness the energies and intellects of exiles and émigrés who had fled Eastern Europe. Wisner and Dulles helped to gather them in American-occupied West

Germany, put them on the air, and beam their voices back beyond the Iron Curtain. In 1949, Dulles, then a private citizen, a powerfully influential White House consultant, and in effect the shadow CIA director in the absence of a strong leader at the agency, had created the National Committee for a Free Europe as a public entity in New York with a giant covert component overseas. The committee received many millions from the CIA to finance Radio Free Europe; the agency paid the salaries of hundreds and then thousands of employees, built the Munich headquarters at the edge of the city's elegant English Garden, and developed the themes that went out over the airwaves. The first programs had gone out on July 4, 1950, and by 1951 they had reached Poland and four other nations under Stalin's bootheels. Over the years, the broadcasts, at their best, became a brilliant blend of news and entertainment, political satire and propaganda. At their worst they could be venomous—a poison factory, as one top RFE official put it. Free Europe committee directors in the fifties spoke longingly of creating chaos; they saw the radios first and foremost as weapons of the most militant political warfare, and they wanted the spears sharpened.

"During the first broadcasts, they really didn't know what they were doing," said RFE's Richard H. Cummings, later director of security at the Munich headquarters. "It was all hit or miss. They didn't care. They were just putting something out there. I would say it was propaganda. You could call it 'fake news.'"

The Poles nonetheless listened religiously; Radio Free Europe created a cathedral in the air. They were ecstatic to hear the voice of Jan Nowak, a hero of the 1944 Warsaw Uprising against the Nazis and the new director of RFE's Polish-language service. In his first commentary to listeners in May 1952, he captured the spirit of the time: "The struggle is being waged not in the forest, streets, or in the underground, but in Polish souls—within the four walls of a Polish home. It is this struggle that we wish to join here on the airwaves of Radio Free Europe." His American overseers wanted less poetry and more vitriol. "Why don't we advocate sabotage in Poland?" one Free Europe committee director in New York asked bluntly in July 1953. In Munich, Paul Henze railed against the "psy-warriors" in Washington and their "stupid" and "hare-brained" incitements to violence. This battle ebbed and flowed but never ended.

The most startling voice in the history of Radio Free Europe's Polish service went on the air in the fall of 1954. It belonged to Josef Swiatlo, a senior officer of the Polish secret police. As the deputy director of Department Ten of the Ministry of Public Security, charged with rounding up enemies of the state, Swiatlo had earned a fearsome reputation. He had arrested Wladyslaw Gomulka, the former secretary general of the Polish Communist Party, who had fallen out of Stalin's favor, and Poland's Catholic primate, Stefan Cardinal Wyszynski. Then, in December 1953, fearing for his own future after Stalin's death, he defected to the United States in occupied Berlin.

The CIA sent Ted Shackley to meet him. They talked in a safe house near Frankfurt for four months, and the defector described in detail the dirty work he'd done under orders from his Soviet overseers. The litany was long. Shackley wanted to know if Gomulka was alive. Swiatlo said he was comfortably ensconced in a Department Ten villa—and that an anti-Stalinist faction in the Polish Communist Party was alive and well, too. This was sweet music to the CIA. "If there was turmoil in the Polish leadership," Shackley wrote a half century later, "we wanted to keep the pot boiling." So the CIA flew Swiatlo to the United States, and after a far more intense interrogation, it sent him to Radio Free Europe's New York office. It intended to play back his testimony to Poland. The first tape arrived in Jan Nowak's office in Munich on September 17.

"The Inside Story of the Secret Police and the Party" went on the air in October 1954 and ran for seventy-seven weekly installments. In February 1955, the CIA and RFE began printing eight hundred thousand brochures with the text of the programs and sending them into Poland on a flotilla of balloons. Warsaw and Moscow treated this operation as a major threat and formally protested to Washington that it constituted a violation of Poland's sovereignty. The Swiatlo story shook the Polish Communist Party to its core; it led to the abolition of Department Ten, the jailing of secret police commissars, the disgrace and dismissal of the internal-security chief, and a wave of panic in the ministries of fear. A twenty-first-century Radio Free Europe historian wrote that the programs were arguably "the most successful case of influencing an adversarial regime in the history of international broadcasting." Then the CIA struck fire in June 1956 by broadcasting Khrushchev's secret speech and his denunciation of Stalin. It was replayed endlessly, along with pointed commentary, and the effect in Eastern Europe was electrifying. It sparked an uprising in the Polish city of Poznań on June 28.

The Poles knew how to organize an underground resistance; the Warsaw Uprising was only twelve years in the past. And this resistance had an audience: hundreds of foreigners were in town for the annual international trade fair in Poznań, among them Richard E. Johnson, an economics expert at the American embassy in Warsaw. Johnson and an embassy colleague found themselves at a nightclub, drinking at the table of a black marketeer, on the night of June 27. "Further on in the evening, as things warmed up and we had a bit more champagne, he whispered to us, 'You know, this place is going to blow sky high tomorrow.' We said, 'What do you mean?' 'Yep, they're going out on the streets and they're gonna raise hell.'" Early the next morning, workers at the Zispo manufacturing plant proclaimed a general strike and marched into the city center, where legions of workers from other factories joined them.

"As the crowd swelled to a hundred thousand people," Johnson recounted, "some attacked a prison and freed inmates; others destroyed equipment on the roof of a government building used to jam Western radio broadcasts." The demonstrators who sabotaged the jamming antennas chanted, "We want to listen to the outside world!" and "We want freedom!" America showed the flag: in the absence of the ambassador, the chargé d'affaires in Warsaw rode to the embattled city in the embassy's limousine, adorned above each headlight with the fluttering Stars and Stripes. His instructions were to be as ostentatious as possible. He drove back and forth through the streets of Poznań to make the American presence felt. That gesture was the extent of American support.

Late that afternoon, the Soviet general who commanded the Polish army sent two armored divisions and two infantry divisions into the city. Ten thousand soldiers backed by the KGB and the Polish secret police brutally suppressed the uprising; they killed at least fifty-seven demonstrators, wounded six hundred, and arrested many hundreds more before they took back control of the city. Poznań was on the front pages of the world's newspapers and a resounding headline on Radio Free Europe. At the National Security Council, the consensus was that the blood of Polish martyrs was a boon to the United States. Allen Dulles, somewhat in the spirit of Stalin, observed that one couldn't make an omelet without breaking eggs. Nixon said that "it wouldn't be an unmixed evil, from the point of view of U.S. interest, if the Soviet iron fist were to come down again on the Soviet bloc."

The Polish Communist Party, to the great surprise of the White House, the State Department, and the CIA, cracked down on itself and not the people. Fifteen thousand copies of the secret speech had circulated among the Polish ministries and the nation's intelligentsia; many among the elites also listened in secret to Radio Free Europe, if and when they could. Taking the great risk of a military invasion from Moscow, the party sided with the dissidents. "Polish regime thoroughly shaken by unexpected Poznań riots which must have raised urgent questions both here and in Moscow," the American embassy in Warsaw reported to Washington; its leaders had been forced to "redress worker grievances and woo general public." The party itself took a step in an agonizingly long march to freedom in Poland by purging its most devout Stalinists, rehabilitating the old guard's political victims, restoring them to the Polish Politburo, and removing a hated Soviet marshal from his post as the nation's defense minister.

In October, the party elected a new leader—Wladyslaw Gomulka, who had been freed from house arrest a few weeks before, following the broadcasts of Khrushchev's secret speech. Khrushchev himself arrived unannounced in Warsaw, put Soviet forces stationed in Poland on alert, and tried to block Gomulka from gaining power. He failed. On October 20, the new leader described Poznań as the workers' rightful response to "the distortions of the fundamental principles of socialism." He denounced the "clumsy attempt to present the painful Poznań tragedy as the work of imperialist agents." The cause of the upheaval was "to be found in ourselves, in the leadership of the Party, in the Government." He had gone beyond Khrushchev's speech to denounce the evils of the Soviet system itself. And, remarkably, he stopped his government's attempts to jam the broadcasts of Radio Free Europe.

In Washington, the White House, State, and CIA leaped at the chance to encourage Polish independence. On October 23, they agreed to propose a robust program of economic aid. President Eisenhower, addressing a convention of the United Brotherhood of Carpenters and Joiners of America at a campaign rally that evening, said: "A people, like the Poles, who have once known freedom cannot be for always deprived of their national independence. . . . The memory of freedom is not erased by the fear of guns and the love of freedom is more enduring than the power of tyrants." The president told Foster Dulles that the Poles "need have no fear that we might make an effort to incorporate them into NATO or make them part of our alliances. We want to see them have a free choice." Allen and Foster Dulles agreed that the president should back a mini–Marshall Plan for Poland. It would encourage the Poles "to persist in the political attitudes which emerged openly last summer and fall," Allen wrote to his brother, and it would serve as "tangible evidence of American support for Polish efforts gradually to reduce Soviet influence in Polish affairs." The Eisenhower administration quickly approved $55 million in loans and $138 million in agricultural surpluses. This wasn't charity but part of a bigger endeavor: the United States was going to work with Gomulka to weaken the monolith of the Soviet Bloc, using formal diplomacy, intensified information warfare, economic and technological aid, most-favored-nation status for trade, cultural programs, and more.

In the decade since George Kennan had proclaimed the inauguration of political warfare, few countries in the world had experienced its impact more profoundly than Poland. Kennan toured the nation in July 1958 in his capacity as a CIA consultant and recorded his impressions in a letter that Allen Dulles passed on to President Eisenhower. Kennan was impressed by "how much the Poles are getting away with"—including their "complete freedom of speech." He saw that the Polish intelligentsia was unencumbered by any "illusions about the nature of Soviet power." He perceived that the government was now "firmly oriented towards the West." But at the end of the day, he was struck by "how little any of this means that Poland is, or will be in any near future, in a position to shake off communist political control." When Kennan smelled flowers, he looked around for a funeral.

There was one immensely powerful element of American political warfare he had missed, a phenomenon inexplicable to the unhip. And that was jazz.

"The Voice of America had a disc jockey called Willis Conover who played jazz from 10 at night until 1 in the morning," remembered David J. Fischer, then a young officer at the Warsaw embassy, later an American ambassador. "Everyone—and I mean everyone who counted—listened to that program." Conover was a superstar in the communist world and utterly obscure in America.

The Voice of America first went on the air after Pearl Harbor; its first director was John Houseman, a Romanian immigrant who had gained fame as a producer of the staggeringly realistic Orson Welles radio broadcast of "War of the Worlds," and later became an Oscar-winning actor. He put American popular music, predominantly big band jazz, on the air around the world, as far as its signal could reach. The Nazis had banned jazz—they called it *Negermusik*—as a cultural poison produced by African Americans and promoted by Jews. Houseman later reflected: "We found ourselves using music as an instrument of propaganda." In 1953, the VOA became the broadcast arm of the United States Information Agency, newly created by President Eisenhower; other branches included press services, libraries, and documentary films, and Ike wanted it to be the friendly and open face of American political warfare, the smiling soldier who handed out food and sweets to the hungry in the form of information and entertainment.

Conover went on the air in 1955 for a run that lasted forty years until his death, his whiskey- and tobacco-cured baritone becoming instantly familiar to the citizens of Warsaw, Prague, Budapest, and beyond. More than one American who visited these capitals in those days fell into a conversation with a stranger who spoke an unusually idiomatic English, and upon being asked how he learned it, heard the answer: *Villis Conofer.* The television newsman John Chancellor, a future director of the Voice of America, called Conover "the single most effective instrument we had at the Voice." Duke Ellington's "Take the 'A' Train" opened his show, a tune of boundless optimistic energy. He featured the music of—and, importantly, interviews with—the Duke, Billie Holiday, Louis Armstrong, Dizzy Gillespie, and Thelonious Monk, among many other creators of an art form as powerful and as mind-altering as moving pictures. Their music was a force of liberation in an America still trying to segregate and scorn them. Jazz was the sound of freedom; it told the world more about America than most Americans knew.

By early 1959, Conover had received sacks of fan mail from Poland, begging him to come visit. He flew into Warsaw that June. He looked out the window of the plane when he landed, and he saw hundreds of people, some with cameras and tape recorders, girls carrying flowers, and he thought, *I'd better wait until whoever that's for gets off.* Then he saw that he was the last person off the plane. The crowd went wild. That night, and the next, musicians came from all over Poland, at their own expense, to perform for him at the National Philharmonic Hall, to show him what they had learned from listening to his show. If this wasn't winning hearts and minds for America, they could not be won.

Jazz, Conover explained for the unattuned, had the virtues of vitality, strength, social mobility. The musicians agreed on a song, its key, tempo, and harmonies; and "once they've agreed on that, on the range of their performance, they're free to perform whatever they want. And that's parallel to the structure of the U.S.A." Jazz was "a musical reflection of the way things happen in America," he told the *New York Times* upon his return from Poland. "We're not apt to recognize this over here but people in other countries can feel this element of freedom. They love jazz because they love freedom."

A few weeks after Conover came to Warsaw, at the start of August 1959, a very different visitor arrived: Vice President Richard M. Nixon was touring the world in preparation for his presidential campaign. He had a five-hour talk with Gomulka, who gave him an earful. The Polish leader had changed his tune on Radio Free Europe, which had helped him rise to power but now poured vitriol upon him. "RFE is not advocating ideas," he said. "It simply piles abuse on everything and everyone in Poland." But Gomulka was only warming up. His voice rose, his face reddened, and the history of centuries in which no generation of his people had been spared war, or foreign rule, or both, came pouring out. He said he and his nation lived in fear of the rising power of West Germany, implicitly backed by the political and military force of America. "The Poles have seen their relatives and friends shot by Germans, blindfolded before a wall," he said. The war had been over for only fourteen years; he and his people lived with the memory every day. "We do not want to be trampled over," he told Nixon. "I do not believe in war and neither does

Khrushchev. Any war will be suicide. But there are people who want to commit suicide. Eventually there must and will be one world. It is useless to discuss now whether that world will be socialist or capitalist."

Nixon, who thought the Polish leader was cold as steel, tried to warm him up. "Maybe it can be both," Nixon said. "Things change."

Ike's brother and most trusted adviser, Milton, who had accompanied Nixon, drove Gomulka's points home for the president. Radio Free Europe's broadcasts were strengthening the hands of Poland's communist leaders by stirring up anger and fear, he wrote to the president. The Poles wanted to live in peace. Between the Germans, whom they hated, and the Soviets, whom they merely feared, they believed they had no choice but to depend upon Soviet power.

The president read this warning, agreed with it, and forwarded it to Allen Dulles, who did next to nothing to change the radio's tone and tenor. He assured Eisenhower more than once that "Radio Free Europe had to walk a tightrope to avoid, on the one hand, fomenting outbreaks in Poland that would cost Polish lives and, on the other hand, to avoid giving the Poles the impression that the United States had abandoned hope of their ultimate liberation"—and that he would keep walking that rope.

"We have been doing our best to break Poland away from Moscow," Eisenhower told congressional leaders convened at the White House in August 1960. "We do a little here and a little there, as we can." But those efforts soon slowed to a near-halt. The United States kept political warfare in Poland at a very low boil in the 1960s. Warsaw had its annual jazz festivals, Poznań its trade fairs, and American embassy officials drank Scotch and vodka with their Polish counterparts, but little had changed by the time Nixon ran for president again in 1968, and won. By then, Radio Free Europe's ties to the CIA had been exposed by investigative journalists, compromising its credibility. The head of Poland's formidable secret police had started working in lockstep with the new chairman of the KGB,

Yuri Andropov, to run joint operations against the main enemy, the United States, and the "centers of ideological-political sabotage in the West"—especially Radio Free Europe. And the United States had turned away when the people of Poland rose up once again in an early wave of the widespread student rebellions that shook the world in 1968. The president's primary concern as he prepared to return to Warsaw in the spring of 1972 was not the fate of the Polish people but of the Polish vote. A third of the Polish nation now lived in the United States. "Look at what it will mean to us to go into Warsaw and with any kind of a break get a hell of a reception," Nixon told his chief of staff, H. R. Haldeman. "[It] affects Pennsylvania, it affects Ohio, it affects Illinois, and it affects Michigan."

The presidency of Richard Nixon was consumed by the pursuit of détente with the Soviet Union, the disastrous prosecution of the foredoomed war in Vietnam, and at last by the pernicious crimes of Watergate. By the time he fell in August 1974, the cancer on his presidency had metastasized into the institutions of national security and the instruments of political warfare. The Senate investigated those institutions and instruments in 1975, and uncovered the attempted assassinations of Castro and Lumumba, the orchestration of coups against freely elected leaders in Guatemala and Iran, the appalling mind-control experiments with LSD. And they found that the CIA and the FBI had, by turns, spied on Americans, opened their mail, broken into their homes: on orders from every president from Truman to Nixon, they had conducted political warfare against their own people. Beyond the impact that these revelations had on Americans, they were heaven-sent gifts for the KGB. They would provide a decade's worth of fodder for political propaganda and carefully crafted disinformation aimed at destroying America's image in the eyes of the world.

In the face of the Senate's scarifying public reports, the White House all but shut down American political warfare in 1976, and when President Gerald Ford tried to mount a major covert operation of armed support to guerrilla forces in Africa, Congress found out and cut off the funds. On January 13, 1977, the storm-tossed survivors of the Nixon administration—Secretary of State Henry Kissinger, Secretary of Defense Donald Rumsfeld, White House Chief of Staff Dick Cheney, and Director of Central Intelligence George H. W. Bush—gathered with Ford for a final meeting of their National Security Council. They surveyed the battlefield in dismay.

The CIA's capability for covert action was crippled. "We are unable to do it anymore," Kissinger lamented.

"Henry, you are right," Bush said. "We are both ineffective and scared in the covert action area."

"Many things are not even proposed these days because we are afraid to even discuss them, much less implement them," Kissinger mourned. Bush's reply remains classified to this day.

President Jimmy Carter was inaugurated a week later. He had won a narrow victory in the November 1976 election, and one big factor was a blunder Ford made in a presidential debate. Ford had declared that Poland and Eastern Europe were not dominated by the Soviet Union. He had probably meant to say that the Polish people and their neighbors did not consider themselves to be subjugated, that they had retained their strong spirit and their sense of identity in the face of oppression. If so, the nuance was lost on the American people.

Like Truman, and like Eisenhower, Carter sought to undermine the Soviets' control of Poland and Eastern Europe, and to do it in the name of human rights. He was ready and willing to use political warfare to advance that goal. Carter signed almost as many covert-action orders as did Nixon and Ford combined. He looked at political warfare against the Warsaw Pact through the lens of the 1975 Helsinki Agreement, signed by the United States, the Soviet Union, and all the nations of Europe save Albania. It spoke in clear language of the free movement of people and ideas across borders. Stated simply, Carter thought he could use American ideas to crash the Soviet system of subjugation, and to employ the CIA to transmit those ideas, and he meant to do it in ways his predecessors had not conceived. Bob Gates, the future CIA director and secretary of defense, then a CIA analyst serving on the NSC staff, saw him as the first president since Truman to directly challenge the legitimacy of the Soviet government.

The president had the perfect man to pursue that aim: a Polish patriot. Zbigniew Brzezinski was his national security adviser, and Brzezinski hired his old friend Paul Henze, then the CIA station chief in Turkey, to join him at the NSC. They were delighted to find that at least one CIA covert-action program had survived the upheavals of the era: under Ford, in 1976, about $4 million a year had been spent supporting dissidents in the Soviet Union and Eastern Europe, chiefly by smuggling banned books and literature across the Iron Curtain. "The activity of dissidents fighting for greater civil liberties in Poland . . . has greatly increased in the past year," the CIA noted in February 1977. This fired Brzezinski's imagination. He asked the agency's analysts for a full report. They delivered it in April. "The situation in Poland is by far the most volatile in Eastern Europe. A major blow-up could come at any time," they said. "The leadership is acutely aware that . . . a direct confrontation, with the potential creation of martyrs, must be avoided." Brzezinski highlighted that passage and sent the report to the president.

The volatile situation stemmed in no small part from a covert operation overseen by Irving Brown, the longtime Brussels-based European representative of the AFL-CIO, the largest federation of labor unions in the United States. Brown had been the CIA's point man when the United States was shipping wheat and weapons to Western Europe in 1947, hiring muscle-bound dockworkers to protect the operation from being sabotaged by communist union organizers. Brown had been on Kennan's short list of candidates to run the CIA's clandestine service in 1948, losing out to Frank Wisner. For decades since, he had run what might be called the AFL-CIA, working to bolster anti-communist labor unions in coordination with American intelligence officers. "I don't believe I *ever* saw Irving without a nickel in his pocket that didn't belong to CIA," remembered Tom Braden, who ran the agency's international organizations division in the 1950s and kept Irving and his underground support for labor unions around the world well financed.

By early 1977, Brown was handling a conduit of cash and communications gear for KOR—the Komitet Obrony Robotników, or Workers' Defense Committee—a new underground group formed to aid protesting workers who had been jailed or fired by the government. The money and materiel helped KOR run an underground publishing house and the Flying University, a series of lectures organized by students, who discussed ideas about freedom that were dangerous to debate in public. KOR's leaders had a network of contacts with Radio Free Europe's Polish staff in Munich. They kept RFE informed about their work and the government's attempts to suppress it by telephoning Polish exiles in London and Paris. The exiles, in turn, called Munich, and RFE broadcast the information back into Poland, immensely widening the circle of knowledge about the resistance. Lane Kirkland, AFL-CIO's longtime president, saw this as the seed of the movement that became Solidarność—the Solidarity movement. "There was a precursor in Poland to *Solidarność*," he said, "sort of a covert organization called the KOR in Poland, with which we had contacts through Irving in our Paris office." KOR became the intellectual core of Solidarity. And Solidarity became a force that almost no one could have imagined.

Brzezinski reminded President Carter in June 1977 that Poland was ripe for political warfare: "A blow-up there," he wrote hopefully, "cannot be ruled out." He asked what the CIA was doing to stir the pot. It took months for the traumatized agency to comply with a presidential order to step things up, but over the next year, the CIA shipped hundreds of thousands of books and periodicals. "A program such as this contributes as much to our national defense as any of our weaponry—besides which its costs are chicken feed," Paul Henze noted.

On October 18, 1978, Brzezinski was delighted to learn that one of the beneficiaries of the CIA's literary program had sent a thank-you note to his distributor, a postcard expressing gratitude for many mailings of books and magazines in Polish and English. The card came from Cardinal Karol Wojtyla, the archbishop of Kraków. Two days earlier, the cardinal had been elected as the new pope—an electrifying event. Richard Virden, the press attaché at the American embassy, remembered "watching the nightly news broadcast on state television—that's all there was, broadcasting was a state monopoly—when the announcer said, 'And in Rome today Karol Wojtyla of Kraków was selected as the next Roman Catholic pope.' Pregnant stop, then on to something like, 'And now, here's the latest tractor production news. . . .' The announcer didn't have any instructions yet, no one telling him what to make of the news, what it might mean for the party and the country," Virden said. "The Polish people didn't have any doubts though; in Kraków they poured into the streets and squares, and church bells—including one that had rung only once before in a century, at the end of the Second World War—pealed all that night."

Millions greeted the pope when he returned to Poland for a nine-day visit in June 1979. His message was simple and profound: be not afraid. He stood next to the Communist Party leader Edward Gierek and said the role of the church was to make people more confident, more courageous, more conscious of their human rights. He supported the rights of workers in a speech in the industrial city of Nowa Huta, condemning the idea "that man be considered, or that man consider himself, merely as a means of production," a direct attack on communist doctrine. Leaping through that opening, Carter visited Poland at the end of the year and insisted on meeting leaders of the church and the dissidents along with Gierek and his ministers. Doing his part, Brzezinski established covert contacts with the leaders of the growing radical workers' movement in Poland.

The Polish economy slumped from the start of 1980, in part a consequence of a global oil shock following the Iranian revolution that had overthrown the shah and threatened decades of American domination in the Persian Gulf. On July 1, the Polish regime raised food prices nationwide, sparking a series of strikes, stoppages, and slowdowns that swept the country. Radio Free Europe kept listeners in Poland up to date on the demands of ad hoc workers' commit-tees as they bargained with their management and the government, pressing their petitions for more money and more power. RFE now reached almost half the homes in Poland. It also kept the Polish gov-ernment informed. At an August meeting of Poland's Politburo, the defense minister, General Wojciech Jaruzelski, accused the civilian leaders of the government of deceiving themselves, and the people, about the nature of the long-simmering economic crisis. "Two years ago," he contended, "we said that our debt has reached 17 billion, but we knew about it from Free Europe."

A strike at the Lenin shipyard in Gdańsk began on August 14; for the first time, workers demanded that they be allowed to form trade unions independent of government control. They were led by a thirty-six-year-old electrician named Lech Wałęsa, who had worked closely with KOR for four years, work that had gotten him fired, arrested, jailed, and watched over by the secret police. The government tried to keep news of the strike from spreading by instituting a news blackout and cutting off the telephone lines connecting Gdańsk to the rest of the country—a futile gesture. "It was thanks to Free Europe that peo-ple in Gdańsk, in all Poland, and across the world found out that we were on strike," said Bogdan Borusewicz, one of the main organizers, who would one day serve as the marshal of the Polish Senate and, for a few hours, as the acting president of the nation.

Almost overnight, Wałęsa had inspired strikes all across Poland, and the workers and their allies in universities and churches joined forces. "What is going on in Poland could precipitate far-reaching consequences for East-West relations, and even for the future of the Soviet Bloc itself," President Carter wrote to British prime minister Margaret Thatcher on August 27. The best possible outcome, Carter continued, "would involve accommodation between the authorities and the Polish people, without violence. Such an accommodation could well transform the character of the Polish system." Three days later, to the astonishment of the world, the regime accepted most of the rebellious workers' demands. They had not only won the right to form an independent labor union, and the right to strike—revolutionary ideas in a nation under Soviet control—but access to the media, a relaxation of government censorship, and the television and radio broadcasting of mass on Sundays for shut-ins. A formal accord, agreed upon in Gdańsk, was shown on national television. Wałęsa signed with a huge pen. On September 17, three dozen newly independent Polish unions representing some three million workers joined forces under the name of Solidarity.

Brzezinski saw Solidarity as a direct threat to Soviet power. Would the Red Army invade Poland to reestablish Moscow's authority, as it had in Hungary in 1956, Czechoslovakia in 1968, and Afghanistan in 1979? He posed that question at a White House meeting with the secretary of defense, the deputy secretary of state, the acting chairman of the Joint Chiefs of Staff, and the CIA director, Admiral Stansfield Turner, on September 23. He wanted to review the intelligence on Soviet troop movements and American contingency planning for a military intervention. Turner said American spy satellites could detect the readying of Soviet military divisions in time to provide perhaps two weeks of warning—unless cloud cover prevented them from getting a clear picture. The CIA, like Brzezinski, viewed events in Poland as a challenge to the entire communist system. Its analysts said the Kremlin feared "a ripple effect" reverberating throughout Eastern Europe and into the Soviet Union itself.

On Election Day in November 1980, when Ronald Reagan

crushed Jimmy Carter at the polls, the CIA was riveted by a frightening report from its most highly valued source behind the Iron Curtain. The CIA station in Warsaw had received a warning from Colonel Ryszard Kuklinski, who had been working in secret with American spies for nearly a decade. The colonel served as an officer on the Polish General Staff, as an aide to Defense Minister Jaruzelski, and as a liaison with Soviet marshal Viktor Kulikov, the commander of the Warsaw Pact's joint armed forces. He was fifty years old, a chain-smoker, and a tireless reporter. He had delivered copies of more than thirty thousand top secret Soviet and Warsaw Pact military documents—from war plans to weapons data—to the CIA. He treaded very lightly, like a man walking across a frozen lake in a spring thaw. If caught, he would be hanged as a traitor.

He had sent a six-page letter alerting the Americans that he and a small group of fellow officers had been ordered to make plans for the imposition of martial law in Poland. He delivered the letter and photos of draft decrees suspending liberties to a dead drop, a secret hiding place, where a CIA officer in Warsaw found them. In November, CIA analysts pored over spy satellites' photoreconnaissance images of Soviet troop movements—fragments of a mosaic, as impenetrable cloud cover often obscured the terrain—and they tried to read between the lines of the colonel's dispatches. At Thanksgiving, they told the White House without equivocation that it was increasingly likely that the people of Poland would suffer the blows of repression; Bob Gates, newly appointed as the CIA's top analyst on the Soviet Union and Eastern Europe, wrote that Moscow had found the new freedoms won by the Poles intolerable. On December 2, CIA director Turner told the president: "I believe the Soviets are readying their forces for military intervention in Poland."

And then, early on the morning of December 5, a flash message from Kuklinski headlined *Very Urgent!* came to CIA headquarters: he reported that the Soviets had decided to invade Poland with fifteen divisions, two Czechoslovak divisions, and one East German division—

more than a quarter of a million troops—within seventy-two hours. On the afternoon of December 6, a Saturday, Turner told the nation's top national security officials that the Soviets "will go into Poland on Monday or Tuesday." On Sunday, he said that all the preparations for a Soviet invasion of Poland had been completed and that a final "decision to invade" that very night had been made. The president issued a public statement echoing those words.

But none of that was true. The skies over Poland and the western Soviet Union weren't the only cloudy element that weekend. The minds of the president and his national security team were occluded. These were exhausted and humiliated men. American hostages had been held in Iran for 399 days. A rescue mission had ended in disaster. When the Soviets had invaded Afghanistan in December 1979, the CIA had given no warning. Turner and the CIA had been justly criticized for failing to see clear evidence of the impending Soviet military action—and they weren't going to make *that* mistake twice. They made a different mistake instead. For if the Soviets ever did consider an invasion in December 1980, it had already been called off by the time of Turner's call. The Soviets had decided to let the Polish generals handle Solidarity on their own. Significantly, perhaps decisively, KGB chairman Andropov, now a dominant voice in the Politburo, opposed an invasion. The Kremlin did indeed have plans to hold military exercises in Poland, but these maneuvers were always intended as a cover for the imposition of martial law. When the skies briefly cleared two weeks later, American intelligence satellites revealed that only three Soviet motorized rifle divisions in western Russia were at combat readiness.

The military exercises began in Poland on March 23, 1981. The CIA again reported that a Soviet invasion was imminent—another false alarm, and not the last intelligence failure on developments in Poland. The situation in Poland cast a deepening sense of dread in Washington—"a global shadow of tension, the danger of miscalculation, and even possible military conflict between the superpowers,"

Bob Gates wrote. The Reagan administration rushed to complete contingency plans for a buildup of American troops and the deployment of new nuclear weapons in Europe. Kuklinski reported on April 26, in a letter to his longtime CIA case officer, Dave Forden, that the political situation in Poland was gloomy, and the military situation was hopeless. "We Poles realize that we must fight for our own freedom," he wrote. "I remained convinced that the support your country has been giving to all who are fighting for that freedom will bring us closer to our goal."

That support now came from many sources. President Carter had increased financial assistance to $715 million a year, making Poland the largest recipient of American economic aid in the world. Solidarity and KOR had received increasing support from the AFL-CIA. Radio Free Europe gave the Polish people daily reports on the travails of Lech Wałęsa and the nation, and it worked to expose the shortcomings of the regime. American embassy officials maintained close and constant contact with civilians in the upper reaches of the government as well as the leaders of Solidarity and in the Catholic Church. The pope counseled Solidarity on strategy and tactics. And the Communist Party of Poland started shaking up its ranks, elevating liberal and moderate members, and introducing electoral reforms. Such small green shoots, however fragile, made Gates, a devout pessimist, see a ray of light in the shadows that spring. "In my view," he wrote to Casey, "we may be witnessing one of the most significant developments in the post-war period which, if unchecked, may foreshadow a profound change in this decade in the system Stalin created both inside the Soviet Union and in Eastern Europe."

Kuklinski continued to report that the imposition of martial law was imminent: the decrees were ready to go to press and a list of six hundred people who would be jailed had been prepared. And then, on September 15, he sent a fresh alarm to the CIA. The secret police had infiltrated Solidarity and learned that the government's plans, including its code name, Operation Spring, had leaked to the dissidents. The number of people privy to that secret was small, and a search for suspects was under way. On November 2, he was confronted by his superiors. They told him that they had learned from their own sources that the CIA had the plans. He was not arrested on the spot, but he feared he would be soon. He asked the Warsaw station to save him, his wife, and their two sons. Casey sent a message to Ambassador Francis Meehan advising him that an evacuation was imminent. Five days later, the station chief picked up the Kuklinskis in a Volvo, drove them to the embassy, and loaded them into packing crates inside a van with diplomatic plates. The van drove through Poland and East Germany into West Berlin, and then a military aircraft flew them to the United States. By the time they landed, General Jaruzelski knew the colonel was a spy, that the United States had to have his martial law plans in hand, and that the CIA, the State Department, and the White House must therefore know that he was ready to carry them out.

Yet when the crackdown came on December 13, it was a shock to almost everyone in Washington. The CIA—despite Kuklinski's warnings—did not believe the Poles would impose martial law. Astoundingly, the agency seems to have shared his reporting with no one at the State Department and only one man at the White House: the national security adviser, Richard Allen, who had taken a leave of absence after he was enmeshed in a bribery scandal. No one at the CIA ever analyzed the evidence, its ranking Soviet analyst Douglas McEachin found after an exhaustive retrospective review, and in that absence, "the human failings of mindset, bureaucratic turf-guarding, inadequate communication, and simple distraction were free to wreak their damage." These flaws were hardly unique in the annals of intelligence; the 9/11 Commission would cite the same failures as crucial to the success of the attacks. American intelligence had not turned knowledge into foresight, and foresight into action. Had it had that wisdom, it might have forewarned Solidarity, and perhaps forestalled the suppression of democracy in Poland and the human misery that flowed from it. By the end of the winter, more than ten thousand people became political prisoners in Poland, dozens of activists and striking miners had been murdered by the security forces and the secret police, and the Solidarity movement had been driven deep underground, its leaders jailed, its property and funds confiscated, its offices shuttered.

At Christmastime, Reagan sent a letter to Soviet general secretary Leonid Brezhnev that radiated anger: "The recent events in Poland have filled the people of the United States and me with dismay," it began. "Since the imposition of martial law on December 13, the most elementary rights of the Polish people have been violated daily: massive arrests without any legal procedures; incarcerations of trade union leaders and intellectuals in overcrowded jails and freezing detention camps; suspension of all rights of assembly and association; and, last but not least, brutal assaults by security forces on citizens." The Soviet leader's response was as cold as the prison camps.

In fits and starts over the next year, the Reagan administration conceived and began to execute a major covert operation to support Solidarity, building on the foundation laid by Carter and Brzezinski. The full story remains to be written. Key documents—the minutes of National Security Council meetings, the records of the State Department, the files of the CIA's clandestine service—remain classified nearly four decades after the fact. But the essential elements are evident. The United States began pumping tens of millions of dollars into a political warfare campaign to free Poland, using almost all the means at the nation's disposal short of bloodshed.

The turmoil at the top of Reagan's national security team—the swift resignations of two national security advisers, the deputy director of central intelligence, and the secretary of state—was matched by the money and energy it invested in covert action. Bill Casey held cabinet rank, the first CIA director to do so. He was an amoral man, bending rules and laws until they broke. He had been Reagan's campaign manager and held his trust, though he was not a man to be trusted. In the first months of the administration, he won authority to launch aggressive covert operations aimed at Cuba and Nicaragua, all of Central

America, much of Africa, and an audacious plan to sabotage the energy pipelines of the Soviet Union, which led to a malware attack in Siberia that set off an explosion seen from space satellites. But he held off on secret aid for Solidarity at first. In time, the United States would develop what Thomas W. Simons Jr., later the American ambassador to Poland, called "a very robust program of covert assistance to Solidarity . . . very much using the AFL-CIO."

Lane Kirkland, the AFL-CIO's president since November 1979, was the first to leap into action. In coordination with Casey, he reinvigorated the covert apparatus of the AFL-CIA.

"We developed channels and we got some material and some funds into the underground, and we had several alternative ways of doing it, including financing the Brussels office of *Solidarność*," Kirkland recounted. "And we kept them alive during the underground years." The AFL-CIA poured at least $4 million into a pipeline of communications gear flowing to Poland's resistance—video cameras, cassette recorders and tapes, printers, copying machines, carbon paper, newsprint, and printers' ink concealed in bottles of Hershey's chocolate syrup. By the summer of 1982, it was underwriting dozens of newly circulating underground newspapers that constituted a direct challenge to state-run television, where uniformed military officers robotically delivered droning reports. Irving Brown recruited an exiled Solidarity activist, Miroslaw Domińczyk, gave him a code name—Coleslaw—and financed his efforts to smuggle equipment into Poland. Coleslaw in turn paid supporters to travel to London as tourists, take apart a printing press, and spirit it piece by piece back to Warsaw. "The printing presses we got from the West during martial law might be compared to machine guns or tanks during war," said a key member of the underground named Viktor Kulerski.

Martial law in Poland led to a revitalization of Radio Free Europe. RFE had been publicly funded by Congress since 1974, after the White House acknowledged the open secret of the CIA's support. Reagan signed a secret national security directive in June that pumped $21.3 million into RFE and its Russian-language partner Radio Liberty. The money beefed up their programming, boosted the power of their transmitters, and enhanced their ability to defeat jamming by Warsaw and Moscow. It was now a powerful amplifier for liberation, relaying calls for strikes and demonstrations and broadcasting underground bulletins that reached a surging audience. Wałęsa later said that Radio Free Europe served as Solidarity's ministry of culture and its ministry of information. The newly appointed director of RFE's Polish-language service, Zdzislaw Najder, was a Solidarity collaborator. Solid documentary evidence suggests that he smuggled money, laptops, hard drives, and tape recorders into the hands of Solidarity couriers, an operation that bore all the hallmarks of a CIA clandestine program. The regime tried him for treason and sentenced him to death in absentia. His work posed an existential threat to martial law.

Prominent Catholics in the Reagan administration frequently flew to Rome to keep the pope informed on the political, military, and intelligence situation in Poland. These envoys included Casey, who often stopped in at the Vatican while on covert flights to Europe and the Middle East; the roving ambassador, General Vernon Walters, deputy director of central intelligence under Presidents Nixon and Ford, who visited the pope a dozen times and spoke impeccable Italian, the pontiff's working language; the national security adviser, William Clark; his successor, Bud McFarlane; and the chief nuclear arms negotiator, Edward Rowny, a Polish American. They delivered, among other intelligence data, reports on support for Solidarity and spy satellite images of Soviet nuclear arms in Eastern Europe. When the United States beefed up its strategic arsenals and audaciously placed powerful nuclear weapons systems in Western Europe, the pope, who often spoke out against the arms race, did not object.

President Reagan met the pope one-on-one on June 7, 1982. Both men had survived assassination attempts the year before, six weeks apart. Reagan believed that they had a mystical bond, that they had been spared death for a divine purpose. No official transcript exists, but according to Thomas P. Melady, later the American ambassador to the Holy See, they discussed the fates of nations. "The President brought up to the Pope that he had read that the Pope had said that one day Eastern Europe will be free, and Eastern Europe will join with Western Europe. And President Reagan said, 'Your Holiness, when will that be?' And the Pope said, 'In our lifetime.' The President sort of jumped out of his chair and . . . grabbed his hand and said, 'Let's work together.'"

Much has been made of a supposed grand strategy allying the White House, the CIA, the pope, and Solidarity, but in reality, it was at root an intelligence-sharing relationship. Americans gave the pope secrets about Poland and its struggles and the Soviets, and armed with that knowledge, he passed it on to the leaders of Solidarity and their supporters in the church. No less than Radio Free Europe, he was a relay station for political warfare.

In May and in September 1982, Reagan signed secret orders that guided covert action and foreign policy toward the Soviet Union and Eastern Europe. They were forceful reiterations of George Kennan's doctrines dating back to 1948. The first proclaimed that the United States intended to "contain and reverse the expansion of Soviet control and military presence" across the world. The second aimed to support Eastern European nations that "show relative independence from the Soviet Union" by reinforcing "the pro-Western orientation of their peoples," reducing their political dependence on Moscow, and strengthening their ties with the free nations of Western Europe. Poland clearly was the leading candidate for that support. The regime was tightening the screws on the opposition. In October, the government outlawed Solidarity and charged key members of KOR with treason.

On November 4, the president met in the White House Situation Room with the National Security Planning Group, the body that authorized major CIA operations, whose members included Casey,

Bush, Secretary of Defense Caspar Weinberger, and Secretary of State George Shultz. Reagan's diary for that day shows that Poland was on the agenda. The group weighed and approved a secret political warfare program to support Solidarity, in order to help it seek an end to martial law and to win the release of political prisoners. Unlike the CIA's global operation running arms and ammunition into the hands of the Islamic holy warriors in Soviet-occupied Afghanistan, it had to be subtle, and it had to be truly clandestine. These directives inaugurated the CIA operation code-named QR/HELPFUL.

Reagan had the bit between his teeth, said Secretary of State Shultz, and he needed a checkrein: "In the case of *Solidarność* you had to tell him, 'Now be careful, because we are not going to start World War Three. So don't push the edge of the envelope too far, but push.'" Solidarity would be destroyed if it were linked directly to a gung ho CIA covert action. Lech Wałęsa and his allies didn't need guns. They couldn't mount an armed insurrection; they would be crushed. They needed the means to create an alternate world, a counterculture that could challenge authority by printing and broadcasting sharp prose, cutting commentary, pungent satire, democratic ideals, truthful propaganda, and hard facts, along with the occasional hack of the government-controlled media. The weapons of underground political warfare in Poland would be the tools of a free press. Starting in January 1983, the CIA spent no less than $20 million on that arsenal, as best as can be determined. The agency provided Solidarity with the money along with sophisticated printing and broadcasting capabilities, using overland supply routes to Warsaw from major Western European cities—Paris, London, Rome, and West Berlin among them—and establishing an overseas link from Stockholm to Gdańsk.

The first great success was a new wavelength for free speech. The AFL-CIO had provided start-up funds and equipment for an underground Radio Solidarity, which began in 1982 with roving low-wattage broadcasts from moving cars and vans that avoided easy detection by the secret police. The CIA expanded that capability by

providing technology and passing along expertise for more ambitious print and broadcast operations in 1983. The infuriated authorities struck back by stepping up surveillance and raids. The scale of
their searches—and the scope of the resistance—was revealed in
secret police records showing that in those two years, the government seized 1.3 million leaflets, 828,050 books and journals, nine
offset presses, seven Xerox copiers, and close to half a million sheets
of paper. They never did find the transmitters. Suspecting the CIA
was supplying Solidarity, the government started expelling American intelligence officers working under diplomatic cover at the
United States embassy. This proved futile, for the CIA always used
cutouts—third-party intermediaries—when delivering money and
materiel to the underground resistance.

The regime recalibrated its rule in the summer of 1983. The pope
had returned to Poland in June, welcomed by crowds of millions in
Warsaw and Kraków, saluted by Solidarity banners flying amid the seas
of people, and meeting with Lech Wałęsa. As always when he visited,
the repression vanished for a few days. This time his power lingered. A
few weeks after he left, the government lifted martial law, though its ban
on Solidarity and its control of the media and the masses still remained.
Wałęsa won the Nobel Peace Prize in October, and the United States
used the occasion to step up its support for his cause. In November,
Congress created the National Endowment for Democracy, an institution designed to apply "soft power" in support of the principles of democratic rights abroad. Kirkland, who now sat on the governing board
overseeing Radio Free Europe, was a driving force behind the endowment's creation and a confidant to its director. The endowment's initial
funding included $13.8 million for the AFL-CIO's Free Trade Union
Institute, which had supported Solidarity from the start and worked in
close coordination with QR/HELPFUL. The money flowed freely and
continuously. Over time, the endowment pumped roughly $40 million
into the cause of a free Poland.

Solidarity struck a series of subversive blows with CIA technology starting in late 1984 and early 1985. It now had a network of mobile clandestine television transmitters with a one-mile range, guerrilla stations that could break into the government's broadcasts, wave the Solidarity flag on the air, report the real news, and announce the next protests. The *New York Times* Warsaw bureau chief Michael Kaufman was invited into an activist's home one evening as the state-run seven o'clock news began, and he watched in amazement as the words *Solidarity Lives* appeared onscreen, followed by an announcement asking viewers to listen to Radio Solidarity on a certain frequency in thirty minutes. "We could hear the sirens of many police cars and from the windows we could see a blue truck go by with a small disc direction-finder on its cab. 'It's driving the police crazy,' said one of my hosts," Kaufman reported. "'They can't believe we can penetrate their television. They are trying to pinpoint our transmitter, but they won't find it.'"

The CIA smuggled several million dollars' worth of VCRs, video cameras and cassettes, radio scanners and transmitters, computers and floppy discs, photocopiers, and offset duplicators into Poland in the mid-1980s. The deliveries got through despite the best efforts of the Polish, East German, and Soviet spy services. Some four hundred underground periodicals now flourished in Polish cities; the most popular were printed in editions of thirty thousand, and they helped to spread the slow-burning fire of resistance.

The counterculture scored an epic victory in September 1986, when Jaruzelski amnestied most of the jailed underground activists; Solidarity now began to seek ways to work in the open. By the spring of 1987, Radio Solidarity reached audiences across Poland; Solidarity TV broke into the nightly news to urge public demonstrations on the eve of another papal visit. And when the pope held an open-air mass before a great crowd in Gdańsk on the second Sunday of June, he spoke out in a bold new way. "Every day I pray for you," he said. "Every day, I pray for my country, and I pray for men at work, and I pray for this particularly significant Polish symbol, Solidarity."

In Moscow, a new leader was starting to change the political land-scape in the Warsaw Pact nations, in the Soviet Union, and around the world. The terrible dilemma that faced Mikhail Gorbachev was how to change the Soviet system without destroying it. His program of pere-stroika, reforming and restructuring that system, began at the start of 1987 by opening government positions to people outside the Commu-nist Party and holding multicandidate elections by secret ballot for key posts. That was only a beginning. Gorbachev began trying to address some of the severe economic, cultural, and political contradictions of communism. Bob Gates, now the acting director of central intelligence, told Congress that the changes were creating tension and turmoil in the Soviet Union and its satellites, but the CIA didn't know the half of it: Gorbachev had told the leaders of Poland and the rest of the Warsaw Pact nations in a secret May 1987 meeting that the Soviets would never again intervene militarily to crush an uprising in Eastern Europe. And now the people of Poland were rising up again, as they had in 1944, 1956, 1968, 1970, 1976, 1980, and in centuries gone by. But this time no one could crush them.

The year 1988 brought the biggest strikes and protests in eight years. Starting with demands for better salaries, they grew into peti-tions to make Solidarity legal again, and they became running battles in the streets. General Jaruzelski realized the Red Army was not going to keep him in power. He saw that the Polish regime had to talk to its enemies. Before the end of the year, Wałęsa was debating the head of the communist trade unions on national television. And by January 1989, Jaruzelski was threatening to quit if the party didn't legalize Solidarity at once. Then Czesław Kiszczak, the interior minister, the commander of the secret police, and the second-most powerful fig-ure in the regime, began talking things over with the people he had long oppressed. On February 6, 1989, he convened the Roundtable group at a Warsaw palace. Fifty-five people gathered, half of them party leaders, the other half Solidarity members along with a handful of church observers. Jaruzelski soon joined in the talks, which con-

tinued until April 5, and he invited Wałęsa to join him. He saw that
the people he had despised as criminals and counterrevolutionaries
were his fellow countrymen.

This was a revolution of the mind. In *The Haunted Land*, the
journalist Tina Rosenberg wrote that it was hard, looking back, "to
remember how shocking the Roundtable was. In April 1989 a non-
Communist Poland was inconceivable. The Berlin Wall and the
Soviet Union still appeared indestructible." The government legal-
ized Solidarity that month, and it agreed to hold an election, and to
share power. The June 4 vote was not truly free: the party was guar-
anteed nearly two-thirds of the seats in the Sejm, the lower house.
But Solidarity won 160 of the 161 seats it contested and 92 of 100
seats in the newly created Senate. The warm talk of compromise had
led directly to a peaceful revolution. In August 1989 the two sides
created a coalition government. Solidarity now held real political
power. And it resolved to share that power with like-minded souls
throughout the Soviet empire. It linked up with independence movements in the Baltic states—Lithuania, Latvia, and Estonia—and the
Soviet republics of Ukraine, Belorussia, and Moldavia. It directly
supported striking Soviet coal miners. Its style, swagger, strategies,
and tactics inspired democracy movements from the mines of Siberia
to the capitals of Hungary and Czechoslovakia, and in the cockpit of
the cold war: the divided city of Berlin.

The CIA didn't see it coming, but the KGB did: days after the
Solidarity government took shape in Poland, the Soviet intelligence
service created a new directorate to combat "hostile elements that
are planning to bring about the forcible overthrow of the Soviet
government." A senior Soviet party official already had warned the
Politburo that "if you look at the 'experience' of Poland you can see
where our own country is heading"—and that was "toward disaster."
The Soviet embassy in Warsaw told the Kremlin that "Solidarity has
been actively playing up its experience and putting forth the 'Polish
model' as the most effective means of struggling against the 'obsolete

socialist system.'" A senior KGB officer added ominously that "Solidarity pursued this strategy, with American support, to undermine
socialism in Poland, and the Americans now want the Poles to do the
same in our country."

When the ripple effect of Solidarity's resistance to the Kremlin's
rule rose into a great wave and breached the Berlin Wall on November 9, 1989, it was the beginning of the end of the Soviet Union. On
that day, Vladimir Putin was a thirty-seven-year-old KGB lieutenant
colonel in Dresden, East Germany, working out of an elegant house
on Angelikastrasse, across a greensward from the local headquarters
of the Ministry of State Security, the Stasi, the loathed and feared
intelligence and security service. Soon the people of East Germany
turned their wrath on their oppressors. On January 15, 1990, some
two thousand protesters broke into the Stasi building at Dresden,
ransacking it. They then turned on the KGB station. Putin stood
between them and the secrets of the Soviets.

"All right, the Germans tore apart their own MGB [Ministry of
State Security]," Putin told his biographers a decade later, as he prepared to take power in Russia. "That was their own internal affair.
But we weren't their internal affair. Those crowds were a serious
threat. We had documents in our building. And nobody lifted a fin-
ger to protect us.

"After a while, when the crowd grew angry, I went out and
asked people what they wanted. I explained to them that this was
a Soviet military organization," Putin remembered. "And someone
shouted . . . 'What are you doing here, anyway?' It was if they were
saying, 'We know what you're up to.' . . . These people were in an
aggressive mood." Putin called his superiors and asked them to send
a contingent of armed soldiers to defend the building. "And I was
told: 'We cannot do anything without orders from Moscow. And
Moscow is silent.'

"After a few hours our military people did finally get there. And
the crowd dispersed. But that business of 'Moscow is silent'—I got

the feeling then that the country no longer existed. That it had disappeared."

Over the course of forty-five years, American political warfare had sought this victory. It was a time of triumph, and of glory, and a sense that anything was possible. But that was a transient impression, as fleeting as a Moscow summer. Putin would seek his revenge on America, and in the twenty-first century, he would have it.

CHAPTER 6

A VERY DIRTY GAME

Vladimir Putin was born in the shattered city of Leningrad, eight years after the German army nearly destroyed it. The suffering and death inflicted by Hitler's long siege had no equal in the annals of urban warfare, ancient or modern. One and a half million people had died in air raids, under attack by artillery, and from starvation. The number of the Russian dead and wounded in Leningrad was greater than all the American and British casualties of the war. By Putin's account, his mother, Maria, had been so close to starving to death that her neighbors laid her out with the corpses in the street until someone heard her moan.

The child of this broken world became a creature of the Leningrad KGB. He had wanted to join the spy service ever since he was in high school. It was the one sure path out of the tiny freezing apartment in his gray concrete building with its stink of cooking cabbage and communal toilets, the only way for a young man unacquainted with power and privilege to claw his way up the greasy pole of politics in Soviet Russia. It dominated everything.

Putin signed up in 1975, having made his desire to join clear to a KGB officer two years earlier. He trained at the 401st KGB school along the Okhta River, at the eastern edge of his birthplace, and spent almost all the next decade as a foreign intelligence officer in Leningrad. Many if not most of his working hours entailed spying on the Americans at the United States consulate, ceremoniously reopened in 1973, in the false dawn of détente between Washington and Moscow, fifty-five years after it was shuttered in the wake of the Russian revolution.

"Leningrad was a much tougher KGB town than Moscow, much," said G. Wayne Merry, a son of Tulsa, Oklahoma, who was a State Department political officer on the first of his three tours at the American embassy from 1980 to 1983. "I received more personal harassment in a total of about three months in Leningrad than I did in almost three years in Moscow. They conducted a series of near hit-and-run encounters with our consular staff. I was one of the targets and was very nearly hit by their car, with its license plates covered over. The Leningrad KGB were real sons of bitches." Six KGB officers conducted suffocating around-the-clock surveillance of each American diplomat in Leningrad on the supposition that he was a spy. The officers ran American diplomats off the road on the outskirts of the city with their children in the back seat of their cars. They broke into the Americans' apartments on a regular basis and rifled through their belongings. They telephoned them at 3 a.m. to let them know they were operating on KGB time. When they weren't harassing American diplomats, they went after American businessmen with sting operations. They were thugs whose talents lay in manipulating people, blackmailing people, extorting people. Putin was part of this culture from his mid-twenties to his mid-thirties, until he was posted to Dresden in time to see the Soviet Union start to collapse.

One of Putin's first official acts after he became the ruler of Russia at the turn of the century was to reinstall a commemorative plaque celebrating the life and work of Yuri Vladimirovich Andropov at the old headquarters of the KGB. He later commissioned a ten-foot-tall statue honoring his old boss. This was mete and fitting. Andropov had made him. Putin was his acolyte. He was the most successful graduate of the Andropov era at the KGB and Andropov's successor in every important regard, first as the chief of spies, and then the supreme leader of the nation.

As the Soviet ambassador to Hungary during the 1956 uprising, Andropov had watched as an enraged populace strung up members of the hated and feared secret police, and the experience of the uprising shaped him, just as the revolt against the Stasi and their Soviet commissars in Dresden shaped Putin. Andropov had coordinated the counterrevolution, the invasion by Soviet tanks and soldiers, the crushing of the Hungarian resistance, and the imprisonment and execution of the Hungarian prime minister, and this achievement catapulted him up the treacherous ladder of Soviet succession until he became the KGB's chairman in 1967. He led the most formidable intelligence service in the history of the world for fifteen years until he became the ruler of the Soviet Union in 1982. As KGB chairman, he was a kinder, gentler Stalin. He didn't murder millions of enemies of the state and send millions more to the Siberian gulag. He only arrested a few hundred thousand over the years and sent the most politically prominent and socially undesirable to imprisonment in so-called psychiatric hospitals. Outside of the Soviet Union and throughout the wider world, he made Moscow's methods of political warfare stronger and sharper. His lasting legacy is the enduring strength of the KGB school of political warfare.

The Russian-language version of political warfare is *aktivnyye meropriatia*—active measures. The two terms cover some of the same missions, but they are as different as Russians and Americans. American political warfare in the twentieth century was part of a strategy to win the cold war. Soviet active measures were a great grab bag of tactics aimed at mystifying, misleading, surprising, sabotaging, and on occasion killing political enemies. Deception was the weapon of choice in the battle to subvert the main enemy, America; it was the double helix in the Kremlin's DNA.

Andropov created an entire sector of the KGB—"Service A"—devoted to active measures. The CIA estimated that some 15,000 officers served in it, spending about $4 billion a year, in the early 1980s, making it roughly equal to the size of the entire clandestine service of the CIA. Every officer of the KGB's First Chief Directorate, the foreign intelligence division, had orders to spend 25 percent of his time conceiving and implementing active measures.

Americans who know nothing of Andropov may be nonetheless familiar with aspects of the work of Service A—as is anyone who has ever heard that the CIA killed President Kennedy, or that the FBI assassinated Martin Luther King, or that the army invented the AIDS virus in a germ-warfare lab, all falsehoods broadcast and published and perpetuated by Andropov's officers and agents. In the 1980s, they created thousands of stories like the 1984 report in TASS, the Russian-language service, one of the world's largest news agencies, that the United States was developing pathogens harmless to whites but mortal to people of color, and that these viruses were being tested on Africans in the prisons of apartheid South Africa and on Arab inmates in Israeli jails. They created globally circulated reports that the American government carried out the Jonestown massacre in Guyana, secretly maintained a massive biological warfare program, and supplied chemical weapons to the holy warriors fighting the Red Army in Afghanistan. All this and much more was carefully crafted disinformation intended to damage the image of the United States in the eyes of the world.

"The heart and soul of Soviet intelligence," the retired KGB major general Oleg Kalugin said after the cold war, was not espionage but subversion: "active measures to weaken the West, to [divide] NATO;

to sow discord among allies, to weaken the United States in the eyes of the people of Europe, Asia, Africa, Latin America, and thus to prepare the ground in case war really occurs."

The use of disinformation in Russia traces back at least as far as to the secret police of the czars and their creation of the infamous libel describing a Jewish conspiracy to rule the world, *The Protocols of the Elders of Zion*, a text beloved by Nazis and Saudis and American conspiracy theorists alike, still circulating on the internet today. Andropov's active measures department went far beyond that crude kind of work, though it was unusually adept at it. Andropov's KGB sought to change the course of history by rewriting it, to shape the policies of a foreign government and the thinking of its citizens by bending and warping them. It would steal an election when it was up for grabs, weaken the alliances of its enemies when it could, discredit foreign leaders and undermine their political institutions when it saw the opportunity. These stratagems were the core of the curriculum for Putin's education in the KGB.

If the great goal of intelligence is to know thine enemy, the object of active measures is to screw him. The KGB used political subversion and all manner of propaganda. It had agents of influence in proximity to the powerful. It had clandestine radio broadcasts. It used covert political and economic support for insurgent movements, opposition groups, and political parties. While the White House and CIA used many of the same instruments in the cold war, the Kremlin and the KGB had a bigger orchestra.

Allen Dulles had his friends at CBS News and *Time* magazine; he could nudge and cajole and on occasion co-opt them in the service of the CIA's interests. Yuri Andropov had the biggest global media outlets in the Soviet Union, *Pravda* and TASS, in the palm of his hand; they distorted the news and provided cover for thousands of spies serving overseas on a daily basis. Dulles controlled small publishing houses and little magazines. Andropov had a regiment of co-opted and compliant reporters and editors across Asia and Africa and more than a few in Western Europe as well. Dulles had the Congress for Cultural Freedom, which sponsored anti-communist literary conferences and political panels. Andropov had the World Peace Council, a staunch foe of American imperialism whose members included Jean-Paul Sartre and Pablo Picasso. The CIA did not fabricate documents to defame the Kremlin's leaders, though it had toyed with the idea of tweaking Khrushchev's secret speech in 1956. The KGB libeled American presidents, American ambassadors, and the American flag. Where the KGB truly excelled was in creating forgeries. It faked State Department cables showing that the United States was complicit in the attempted assassination of the pope, concocted American covert operations to support the racist white regime in South Africa, and counterfeited a U.S. Army field manual condoning genocide, not to mention its invention of top secret CIA reports and entire issues of *Newsweek* magazine.

Andropov joined the Politburo from his perch atop the KGB in 1973 and poured billions of rubles into political warfare. By the time Putin was serving in the Leningrad KGB, active measures constituted a crucial component of Soviet foreign policy. Andropov was riding high and thriving in his work against the United States. He had received a great boost from the CIA, first from the exposure of its misdeeds at the hands of the United States Senate in the mid-1970s, and foremost from his greatest nemesis, James Jesus Angleton.

Angleton was the Ahab of American intelligence, chasing the white whale of Soviet deception for two decades. He had single-handedly ruled the CIA's powerful and sovereign Counterintelligence Staff for two decades since 1954. An official historian at the CIA wrote this evocative portrait:

> He was tall, thin, and stooped; had a gaunt and pale face distinguished by a chisel nose and a wide mouth; wore oversized, heavy-framed glasses, black suits, homburgs, and floppy overcoats; and drove an old black Mercedes-Benz sedan. He arrived at the CI Staff's

suite late in the morning and left late in the evening. His curtain-
shrouded office was dimly lit, hazy with cigarette smoke, and full of
scattered files and papers. His lunch "hour" often lasted well into
the afternoon, spent at restaurants mainly in Washington with liaison partners, operational contacts, and professional colleagues. His
capacity for food (despite his wraith-like appearance) and liquor was
remarkable, and toward the end of his career he probably was an
alcoholic. . . . He was secretive and suspicious. Angleton enveloped
himself and his staff in an aura of mystery, hinting at knowledge of
dark secrets and hidden intrigues too sensitive to share.

Angleton had run counterintelligence out of the hip pockets of
his black suits; no one really knew what he was doing in his shrouded,
smoky lair. Fixated on the deceptions of the KGB, he had "largely
ignored the threat that the Chinese, Czechs, East Germans, and
Cubans posed. During his tenure, they either had agents in the CIA
or doubled all the spies the Agency thought it was running against
them." This continuous crisis in American counterintelligence lasted
long after Angleton's day was done.

He was one among very few Americans with an understanding of
Soviet active measures. But upon that rock he built a soaring church
of conjecture. Angleton believed that the KGB was manipulating
American perceptions of the military power of the Soviet Union by
commanding a company of moles within the CIA. He thought that
every Soviet defector who came to the CIA after 1961 was a double
agent working for Moscow. And he was convinced as a matter of
moral certainty that these moles and double agents were part of an
immense and monstrous plot. Their goal was to deceive the White
House, the Pentagon, and the American intelligence community; to
seduce American presidents into the delusions of détente, to shatter the solidarity of NATO, and to destroy the resolve of the West
to oppose Soviet power. His mole hunts damaged or destroyed the

careers of every senior officer in the Soviet division of the CIA's clandestine service. Then Angleton went to war against his own government. Détente was a sham. Arms control was suicide. William Colby, the director of central intelligence in the mid-1970s, was a KGB collaborator. Almost everything the CIA and its allied Western intelligence services knew about the Soviets—apart from what he knew—was wrong. "The bulk of information available to the West through Soviet Bloc contacts," he told the White House, "is, on the whole, spurious and represents little more than coordinated handouts which advance the interests of Soviet Bloc strategic disinformation." Only he understood the depths of this plot against America. And only he could save the nation. Angleton was fired at the end of 1974, after the *New York Times* reported that his staff had been opening Americans' first-class mail for twenty years and spying on the anti-war left in violation of the CIA's charter. He left in a drunken rage, and a trove of institutional knowledge went out the door with him. Angleton the mole hunter was half-crazy at best; the general consensus at headquarters was that he had gone mad. But as a dedicated analyst of active measures, he was at least half-right.

The revelations of CIA misconduct that began with Angleton's disgrace led directly to the congressional hearings that exposed the darkest chapters of the CIA's history. This proved a bonanza beyond imagining for Andropov. America had lost the Vietnam War, its military and intelligence services were in disarray, the reputation of the CIA was shattered, and a long heyday for his KGB was at hand. Seizing upon the Senate's disclosure of the attempted assassinations of Castro and Lumumba, he immediately launched a long-lasting disinformation campaign purporting to reveal CIA plots to kill forty-five foreign leaders over the past decade. In 1978, from his new sinecure at the Politburo, Andropov inaugurated the International Information Department of the Soviet Communist Party, which used the KGB to open a global propaganda offensive against the West. It worked in direct liaison with some seventy communist parties abroad, along with front groups and national liberation movements all over the world.

At the close of the 1970s, as active measures against the United States doubled and redoubled, the close study of Soviet deception was a second-echelon task for American intelligence. The work of thousands of KGB officers was the province of a handful of CIA analysts. But those analysts were good at what they did.

On February 6, 1980, six weeks after the Soviet invasion of Afghanistan, John McMahon, the chief of the CIA's clandestine service, testified about Soviet active measures at a closed-door hearing of the House Intelligence Committee, a discussion long overdue. "Given the importance of propaganda and covert action in its foreign policy implementation, the U.S.S.R. is willing to spend large sums of money on its programs," McMahon said, giving a rough estimate of $3 billion to $4 billion. "Furthermore, the Soviets have established a worldwide network of agents, organizations and technical facilities to implement its programs. That network is second to none in comparison to the major world powers in its size and effectiveness." He listed its ambitious goals:

> To influence both world and American public opinion against U.S. military and political programs which are perceived as threatening the Soviet Union; to demonstrate that the United States is an aggressive, colonialist and imperialist power; to isolate the United States from its allies and friends; to discredit those who cooperate with the United States; to demonstrate that the policies and goals of the United States are incompatible with the ambitions of the underdeveloped world; to discredit and weaken Western intelligence services and expose their personnel; to confuse world opinion regarding the aggressive nature of certain Soviet policies; to create a favorable environment for the execution of Soviet foreign policy.

McMahon went on to report a new and disturbing development in the Andropov era. The KGB was now producing "technically sophisticated falsifications" of a far higher quality than in the past. The new forgeries, he said, were "realistic enough to allow the Soviets to plant them in the western non-communist media with a reasonable expectation that they will be considered genuine by all but the most skeptical of recipients. . . . Furthermore, in two cases, Soviet forgers directly attributed false and misleading statements to the President and Vice President of the United States, something they had refrained from doing in the past." Not long thereafter, President Carter's press secretary called a news conference to display and denounce a forged top secret presidential memorandum that depicted a viciously racist Oval Office policy toward Africa. The KGB had produced a counter-feit National Security Council document and, through a cutout, sent it to an obscure African American newspaper in San Francisco. It ran under the headline: "Carter's Secret Plan to Keep Black Africans and Black Americans at Odds." TASS picked up the article and sent it to Soviet embassies, which redistributed it around the world. Though the White House press corps had never seen anything quite like it, it was a one-day story in the United States. But therein lay the origins of the first American attack against fake news from Moscow.

It began at the start of the Reagan administration in 1981. It took as its foundation a CIA study, classified above top secret, commissioned by Secretary of State Alexander Haig, signed by CIA director Bill Casey, and titled "Soviet Active Measures." The work's principal author was Dick Malzahn, an experienced clandestine-service officer in the Soviet/Eastern Europe division who went on to run the CIA's QR/HELPFUL operation in support of Solidarity. With the blessings of Casey and Haig, but without any coherent orders, a talented State Department official named Dennis Kux started up the Active Measures Working Group. Kux was fifty, a career Foreign Service officer, the deputy assistant secretary of state for coordination at the State Department's small but highly skilled Intelligence and Research bureau; his job included maintaining liaison with the CIA. He rounded up experts from the CIA (including Malzahn), State, the FBI, the Pentagon, the United States Information Agency, and the National Security Council. And they went to work, gathering the poison fruits of Service A from around the world.

"This was new," Kux recollected. "In the past, to the extent that the U. S. countered disinformation, it was handled by the CIA," exclusively, and in secret, without public knowledge or understanding. "The normal attitude in the State Department was: 'We don't want to dignify that kind of stuff with a comment. We won't comment on a forgery.'" He thought the United States needed an entirely new approach, combining facts laid out in public diplomacy with the force of political warfare to combat the Kremlin's ministry of untruth. Kux came up with a snappy acronym for the mission: *RAP*. First *Report*. American embassies and consulates overseas collected all the fake news and forgeries they could find. Then *Analyze*. That was done by the group's staff and the CIA. "We began to see patterns developing," Kux said. "We gradually developed a much better picture of what was going on. We also developed a new strategy to combat disinformation." And that was *Publicize*. "Unlike propaganda, disinformation is a lie ... done with the intent of misleading people through forgeries and planted false news stories," he said. "Journalists and media people were the main vehicle used by the Soviets to spread disinformation. We were going to try to sensitize people to the fact that this was going on by publicizing it. Also, we believed that the more noise we made the less likely that the Soviets would succeed. The more publicity that we could generate, the more successful we would be."

While 1984 was approaching in America, Kux argued, it was not yet *1984*, the Orwellian dystopia where the party commanded and controlled the perceptions of the people. In a time of mounting cold war tensions, he counseled his audiences to keep their cool: recognize disinformation as an attack on democracy, but reject the fear that the evil empire could afflict the American body politic, that it had strings to pull that were strong enough to stage a puppet show in the American political theater. Three decades passed before that apprehension evolved into a palpable reality.

On October 9, 1981, the group published fourteen thousand copies of its first report. "Soviet Active Measures: Forgery, Disinformation, Political Operations" was only four pages long, but it was a comprehensive and powerful document. "In late 1979," the report began, "agents of the Soviet Union spread a false rumor that the United States was responsible for the seizure of the Grand Mosque of Mecca." The Grand Mosque actually had been seized by a gang of messianic Saudis, forerunners of Osama bin Laden. But on November 21 of that year, a Pakistani radio announcer picked up and relayed the rumor blaming America during a broadcast of a cricket match between Pakistan and India, inflaming an Islamist student group in the Pakistani capital. The group stormed the American embassy in Islamabad, set it on fire, and killed a marine guard, two Pakistani employees, and an American contractor. Disinformation could be deadly when left unchallenged.

The *New York Times* and the *Washington Post* covered the group's work. Congress took notice. The House Intelligence Committee again held hearings on Soviet disinformation. Its chairman, Congressman Edward Boland of Massachusetts, and his colleagues praised Kux and his cohort. This in itself was something new. Interagency working groups are where good ideas go to die in Washington; the annals of American government are replete with their desultory proceedings, stilted reports, and stillborn recommendations. The Active Measures Working Group was starting a dynamic attack on secrets and lies.

Kux decided to take the show on the road, bringing the attack on disinformation directly to audiences around the world. In the spring of 1983, members of the group went to Latin America and to nations where the malign impact of fake news was greatest, including India, Egypt, Saudi Arabia, Kenya, Morocco, and Italy. "We went around the world with a little truth squad," Kux said, usually made up of himself, a State Department Kremlinologist, somebody from USIA, and a CIA analyst. They visited about thirty countries over three years, briefing intelligence officials, foreign ministries, and journalists.

They and their colleagues at the State Department and the National Security Council also had to try to counter an especially Orwellian lie that came not from the KGB but the Kremlin. On September 1, 1983, a Soviet warplane shot down Korean Air Lines Flight 007, en route from New York to Seoul, firing air-to-air missiles when the plane crossed into Soviet airspace over the Sea of Japan, killing all 269 people aboard. Among those passengers was an ultraconservative United States congressman from Georgia, Larry McDonald. The Soviets insisted that Flight 007 was a military spying mission and accused the United States of trying to start a war. Andropov wasn't in charge anymore when this outrage took place. He was still the ruler of the Soviet Union, but he had just entered a Moscow hospital suffering from kidney failure, and he would not come out alive.

In the summer and fall of 1983, the fear of nuclear war rose higher than at any time in more than twenty years, since the Cuban missile crisis. To the surprise and consternation of the Pentagon, Reagan had announced his vision for a "peace shield" that would revolutionize the world of nuclear weapons. The Strategic Defense Initiative—immediately renamed "Star Wars"—was a visionary concept of space-based lasers and particle beams that would knock out incoming Soviet intercontinental ballistic nuclear missiles in flight. Tens of billions of dollars went to waste during the 1980s in pursuit of this technological fantasy, but it served as a weapon of political and psychological warfare: it created terror in the Soviet Union. Andropov called it a manifestation of military psychosis. He believed that Reagan really was getting ready to fight and win a nuclear war. Nearly everyone within the Kremlin and the KGB thought that NATO and the United States could launch that war at any moment, without warning. American war games at NATO headquarters went on in November 1983, culminating in the simulation of a DEFCON 1 nuclear attack on the Soviet Union. The government of the United States was willfully ignorant of the intense panic these exercises for World War III engendered. They brought Washington and Moscow dangerously close to the edge of triggering an accidental Armageddon.

The war scare subsided somewhat after Andropov died in February 1984. The equally sickly leader of the Soviet Union for the next year was Konstantin Chernenko, a colorless factotum who was too ill to rule. In this interregnum, the most powerful man in the Politburo was the head of the KGB, Viktor Chebrikov. In the spring, he embarked on a powerful series of active measures and political influence operations designed to defeat Reagan in the 1984 presidential election. Remarkably, the White House saw the KGB coming, thanks in large part to John Lenczowski, a charter member of the Active Measures Working Group, who served as the National Security Council's staff director of European and Soviet Affairs. In August 1984, he sent a warning to his superior at the NSC, Admiral John Poindexter. The KGB's officers had planted anti-Reagan articles across Europe and India in 1976, during his failed bid for the Republican presidential nomination. Now they were at it again, but this time on a far greater scale, and in the United States as well.

"The Administration is harboring a growing concern about Soviet attempts to intervene in the American election process," Lenczowski wrote. "The Soviets devote a massive amount of resources to influence American voters. . . . Their activities not only constitute intervention into the internal affairs of our country, but have done a great deal to aggravate the international climate." That reporting never made its way out of the classified confines of the National Security Council, but it was a harbinger of things to come.

If the Active Measures Working Group had a blind spot, it was a failure to see that Soviet fakes were on occasion founded on facts, as the best disinformation always is. The KGB's propaganda painting Reagan as a warmonger was rooted in the reality that he was positioning intermediate-range American nuclear missiles in NATO's terrain, one thousand miles from the Kremlin. The group denounced a forged letter from the AFL-CIO's Irving Brown broadly implying a connection between Solidarity and the CIA—but Dick Malzahn, a core member of the working group, knew that deep secret to be true. The group condemned a second forgery, a letter supposedly sent by J. Edgar Hoover to the House Un-American Activities Committee in 1947, describing the FBI's links to the president of the Screen Actors Guild—Ronald Reagan—and Reagan's cooperation with the FBI in exposing communist infiltration of Hollywood. In fact, Reagan was at the time an FBI informant, complete with a code name: T-10.

As Soviet disinformation grew more sophisticated at outfoxing America and the world, the working group had to fight harder to ferret out its flaws. It won those battles more often than not by its meticulous attention to detail. Few Soviets had a fluent command of idiomatic American English; their intelligence officers had been schooled in the British tongue. When the Italian press ran with a forged American military memo describing NATO warplanes downing Italian civilian aircraft during training exercises, the group saw that the document used the British word *manoeuvre* rather than the American *maneuver.* Fake! They examined an official-looking letter purporting to prove that the Northrop Corporation, with the blessings of the Reagan administration, was selling fighter jets to South Africa in violation of an arms embargo. The letter used the un-American phrase "competent bodies"—a literal translation of *kompetentnyye organy*, KGB lingo for "state security services." Fraud! Kux and company used the same kind of linguistic forensics to expose the KGB's egregious efforts to tie the United States to the attempted assassination of the pope. "They had faked an Embassy Rome telegram," he said. "We had to take the fake telegram apart by pointing out the technical mistakes," including the bungled transliterations and the sclerotic syntax of the threadbare party line.

The working group's greatest coup came during the run-up to the

1984 Summer Olympics in Los Angeles. The Soviets secretly published two vicious pamphlets in the name of the KKK—or as the KGB put it, the "Ku-Klux Klan," the errant hyphen all but screaming out the sham. "AFRICAN MONKEYS! A GRAND WELCOME AWAITS YOU IN LOS ANGELES!" the first broadside began. "OUR OWN OLYMPIC FLAMES ARE WAITING TO INCINERATE YOU. THE HIGHEST AWARD FOR A TRUE AMERICAN PATRIOT WOULD BE THE LYNCHING OF AN AFRICAN MONKEY!" The leaflet featured a drawing of a chimpanzee dangling from a noose with a sign around its neck that read: "Hang the Nigger." It was mailed from outside Washington, D.C., to Olympic committees in ten African nations. A second, sent throughout Africa and to Japan, South Korea, Malaysia, and Hong Kong, read: "IF YOUR CURS DARE TO COME TO THE SUMMER OLYMPICS IN AMER-ICA THEY WILL BE SHOT OR HANGED. ALL OLYMPIC GOLD MEDALS TO THE WHITES ONLY! DEATH TO THE BLACKS AND COLOREDS!" The message of hate was picked up by TASS and blasted around the world. But in a matter of days, after an ironclad report from the Active Measures Working Group, Attorney General William French Smith publicly denounced the diatribes as Soviet disinformation.

The certitude came from the FBI's representative at the Active Measures Working Group, a counterintelligence agent named Jim Milburn. He had an impeccable source: a KGB officer at the Soviet embassy in Washington who was working in secret for the FBI. The man was Sergei Motorin, officially a low-ranking diplomat assigned to the information section but in reality a spy tasked with gathering political intelligence to help Moscow understand Washington's plans for fighting the cold war. He had been recruited by the FBI eighteen months before, by a combination of friendly persuasion and blackmail. And he had helped to write the racist tracts himself. Counterintelligence rarely produces such rapid results and clear-cut victories.

Eight months later, Motorin was betrayed by Aldrich Ames, an
alcoholic and embittered career officer at CIA headquarters who
had, incredibly, risen to the post of chief of the counterintelligence
branch of the Soviet division of the clandestine service. Ames was
the mole of Angleton's nightmares. He sold the identities of ten Soviets secretly working for the CIA or FBI in exchange for $2.5 million,
and all were tried for treason and summarily executed. He handed
over reams of secrets disclosing American military and intelligence
policies and plans. These in turn allowed the KGB to feed the United
States disinformation that distorted American perceptions of Soviet
military power, exactly as Angleton had feared twenty years before.
Milburn became one member of a team of FBI agents who finally
hunted down and arrested Ames—fully nine years after he had ran-
sacked the CIA's files on behalf of the KGB.

His continuing success at sabotaging American intelligence was in
part due to the CIA's collective failure to imagine that one of their own
officers could be a traitor. The agency missed many opportunities to
catch Ames, including two botched lie detector tests, a four-year failure to finish a financial inquiry into his newfound affluence, and a collapse in communications among CIA counterespionage officers when
they finally began to focus on him. Yet it was worse than that. How did
a man like Ames rise to a position where he held the keys to the kingdom? (The same question would be asked about Edward Snowden,
the twenty-nine-year-old systems operator with a high school education who stole terabytes of the most sensitive intelligence secrets from
the CIA and the National Security Agency, and who fled to find a
warm embrace in Putin's Russia in 2013.) Ames had a long history of
"no enthusiasm, little regard for rules and requirements, little self-
discipline, little security consciousness, little respect for management
or the mission, few good work habits, few friends and a bad reputation
in terms of integrity, dependability and discretion," the CIA inspector
general reported after his arrest. "Yet his managers were content to
tolerate his low productivity, clean up after him when he failed, find

well-chosen words to praise him and pass him on with accolades to the next manager." His laziness and drunkenness were tolerated, and that tolerance led to his promotion to a position "where he was perfectly placed to betray almost all of CIA's most sensitive Soviet assets."

Ames wasn't the only American spying for the Soviets in the 1980s. John Walker Jr., a navy warrant officer, led an espionage ring that sold Moscow the most sensitive information on American systems for secure military communications. Ronald Pelton turned over details of the National Security Agency's top secret programs for targeting the Soviets. Edward Lee Howard sold CIA secrets to the KGB and defected to Moscow. The United States was adept at calling out Soviet disinformation but seemingly powerless at countering Soviet espionage or stopping its American agents from spying before incalculable damage was done.

Having reached a high point of expertise and influence in 1984, the Active Measures Working Group fell on hard times. Kux had left for a classified State Department assignment, charged with protecting American embassies around the world from attacks by spies and terrorists. His replacement was a low-energy bureaucrat nearing an overdue retirement. And the CIA's Bill Casey had sent his own man to the White House, where he stole some of the group's talent and, for a time, much of its thunder. Walter Raymond was a twenty-eight-year CIA veteran with deep experience in covert operations and propaganda campaigns. Raymond had officially retired from the CIA in April 1983, but he continued to report to Casey. He held the titles of special assistant to the president for national security affairs and senior director of international communications and information at the National Security Council. He ran interagency task forces focused on public diplomacy, psychological operations, and political warfare.

Raymond created the Soviet Political Action Working Group, a squad of red-blooded Reaganauts who aimed to use the tools of disinformation to turn the tables on the KGB and undermine the Kremlin. The minutes of their first meeting, in December 1983,

reflected their shared belief that they had to "turn Soviet active measures back onto the Soviets—take the offensive—and make them pay
the price." Raymond's biggest champions and closest collaborators
were a gung ho marine on the NSC staff, Lieutenant Colonel Oliver
North, and a right-wing Cuban exile, Otto Reich, who was in charge
of the Office of Public Diplomacy at the State Department. Congressional investigators later labeled their work as propaganda aimed
primarily at Americans, not at the Soviets, seeking to achieve what "a
covert CIA operation in a foreign country might attempt—to sway
the media, the Congress, and American public opinion in the direction of the Reagan administration's policies" for political warfare in
Central America.

Reagan was single-mindedly devoted to supporting the contras,
the ragtag rebels backed by the CIA, as they sought to overthrow
the Soviet-supported leaders of Nicaragua, the Sandinistas, who
had toppled a four-decade dynasty of American-backed dictators in
1979. When Casey ordered the mining of Nicaragua's harbors, an act
of war, Raymond's spin machine sprang into action, telling reporters that the contras had done it themselves, proving their military
prowess. Reich's office leaked false stories to the American press,
like the bogus claim that the Sandinista government was receiving
Soviet MiG fighter jets. NBC News broke into its 1984 presidential
election coverage with that report, which spurred calls in Congress
for American air strikes. This was only one facet of a White House
disinformation program targeting the minds of an American audience, guided by Casey and overseen by Reagan's National Security
Council under the aegis of the president's mission to roll back Soviet
communism in Central America.

Raymond, Reich, and North, along with "senior CIA officials
with backgrounds in covert operations, as well as military intelligence and psychological operations specialists from the Department
of Defense, were deeply involved in establishing and participating in
a domestic political and propaganda operation," the House Foreign

Affairs Committee concluded in a report published at the close of the Reagan administration. The president and the director of central intelligence, through their offices and officers, were manipulating American public opinion with the tools of CIA tradecraft. They were waging political warfare against the American people, as Lyndon Johnson and Richard Nixon had done in their day; the difference was that Reagan used the national security system to lie to the people, where his predecessors used it to spy on them.

The effort on behalf of the contras, both covert and overt, went on for five years. It failed spectacularly. After Congress cut off funds for the "freedom fighters" in 1984, the CIA and the NSC, led by Casey and North and aided by a confederacy of spooks and swindlers, were caught trying to circumvent that legal ban. They had sold millions of dollars of weapons to the Iranian Revolutionary Guard, skimmed the profits, and backhanded them to the contras. No one could spin that fiasco, which broke the laws of the United States, violated American foreign policy, shattered the dictates of common sense, and set the Reagan administration reeling. The Iran-Contra story began to emerge in November 1986, eroding an elaborate White House cover-up, engulfing the Reagan administration in infamy, and exposing its political warriors to investigations and indictments. (Six years later, a lame-duck president George H. W. Bush, counseled by Attorney General William P. Barr, who returned to that high office under President Trump, issued pardons to five senior CIA, NSC, and State Department officials convicted in the case, along with Reagan's secretary of defense, Caspar Weinberger, who was awaiting trial. With that, the cover-up was complete.)

Three days before the Iran-Contra firestorm erupted, *Pravda* ran a crude cartoon showing a mad scientist handing a huge test tube to a grinning American general in exchange for a fistful of dollars. The vial was filled with floating swastikas and bore a large label: "AIDS virus." The caption above read: "The AIDS virus, a terrible disease for which up to now no known cure has been found, was, in the opinion

of some Western researchers, created in the laboratories of the Pentagon." An elaborate story went with it. The disinformation campaign
had gone on undetected and uncontested for more than a year while
the original Active Measures Working Group sputtered and its NSC
counterpart concocted falsehoods for Americans.

The KGB had sent a directive to its allied spy services in Eastern Europe in September 1985: "We are conducting a series of active
measures in connection with the appearance in recent years in the
USA of a new and dangerous disease, 'Acquired Immune Deficiency
Syndrome—AIDS' ... and its subsequent, large-scale spread to other
countries, including those in Western Europe. The goal of these measures is to create a favorable opinion for us abroad that this disease is
the result of secret experiments with a new type of biological weapon
by the secret services of the USA and the Pentagon that spun out of
control [and] is the result of yet another Pentagon experiment with
a new type of biological weapon"—specifically, genetic engineering
experiments at Fort Detrick.

The Soviet weekly *Literaturnaya Gazeta*, read by the Russian cultural elite, had published an article headlined "Panic in the West or
What Is Hidden Behind the AIDS Sensation" in October 1985, and
the story gradually seeped into the minds of millions. The East German spy service, the Stasi, sent out a global bulletin to Soviet-affiliated
agencies headlined "Combatting the USA's Policy of Confrontation
and Arms Build-Up." It said that "Operation 'DENVER' had the goal
of exposing the dangers to mankind arising from the research, production, and use of biological weapons ... to strengthen anti-American
sentiments in the world and to spark domestic political controversies
in the USA." The East Germans would "deliver a scientific study and
other materials that prove that AIDS originated in the USA, not in
Africa, and that AIDS is a product of the USA's bioweapons research."
The Bulgarian spy service handled the distribution of the disinformation in the United States, Western Europe, and the Third World.

The story spread around the world. It was picked up by the London tabloid *Sunday Express,* the Madrid magazine *Interview,* and the Argentine daily *Diario Popular,* among other publications; TASS then replayed the *Diario Popular* piece, making the newspaper look like the original source. It immediately ricocheted into India, Pakistan, Indonesia, the Philippines, New Zealand, and Nigeria. The KGB's hand in this had gone unseen; the service laundered disinformation like a mafia laundered money. By the end of 1986, the story had surfaced in at least sixty nations, very much including the United States. Twenty-first-century polls suggest that millions of Americans still believe it to be true.

The big lie helped to rejuvenate the Active Measures Working Group. The group rebounded under a new leader, Kathleen Bailey, a feisty thirty-seven-year-old Texan, a political scientist by training, who had two years' experience as the deputy director of the United States Information Agency and strong ties to the American intelligence community from her previous work on nuclear proliferation. She took command at the end of 1985. "To be honest, I didn't know the Active Measures Working Group existed before I took it over," Bailey said. "It was not something on my radar. The group had all but vanished during 1985. My job was to stand it up again." It had faltered due to a lack of leadership, wavering support from the top echelons of the State Department, and the poaching of its talent and energy by Raymond and his covert propaganda campaign. "I viewed Walt Raymond and his work at the NSC as an outlaw operation," she said. "'Let's do active measures ourselves' was not to me legitimate. I don't believe the United States government should be involved in active measures short of warfare. Unless we're trying to overthrow somebody, I don't find it acceptable. The Russians have dedicated bureaucracies for deception. We don't." She went to several meetings Raymond chaired at the NSC and came away with a feeling of foreboding. "He was very influential in the Reagan administration and

with Ronald Reagan himself," but she conscientiously kept her dis-
tance from his work at the White House.

The KGB's AIDS deception appalled her. "I was aghast," she said.
"It made me angry. It seemed so slimy to me. I was particularly struck
by the cartoon. It was brilliant. Absolutely brilliant. Every word carried an impact. Every aspect—the general, the swastikas, the money
changing hands. . . . We decided to go whole hog and publicize it
ourselves and say the Soviets were playing a very dirty game."

The *Pravda* cartoon was the cover and the centerpiece of the
group's biggest counterpunch against the KGB, a highly detailed
101-page compendium of lies and propaganda published in August
1987. The forgeries it exposed included a bogus NSC memo detailing
the Reagan administration's pursuit of a first-strike nuclear strategy
against the Soviets, an invented American propaganda campaign
exaggerating the fallout from the Chernobyl nuclear power plant
disaster, and a fake report from General Mobutu about American
support for anti-communist guerrillas across Africa. It meticulously
recorded the almost daily repetition of the AIDS hoax by print and
broadcast outlets around the world. It reported on the Soviets'
worldwide broadcasts of disinformation about biological warfare
by the United States. "Pentagon bacteriologists are provoking epi-
demics," including "hemorrhagic fever in Korea, dengue in Cuba
[and] viral encephalitis in Nicaragua," one such fake news item read.
Another incendiary falsehood detailed CIA support for RENAMO,
a vicious African guerrilla army created by the white racist regimes
of South Africa and Rhodesia in the 1970s, whose senseless violence
killed hundreds of thousands of civilians. The CIA didn't back REN-
AMO, despite the strong desires of Director Casey, due in great part
to the insistence of American ambassadors in Africa. But countless
Africans and millions of Americans thought it did. One chapter in
the report included an interview with Stanislav Levchenko, who
had been a KGB major assigned to active measures while posing as a

Soviet journalist in Tokyo when he defected to the United States in 1979. "The Soviet Union has been tricking the West for almost 70 years," he said. "Without any doubt, both in Europe and the United States there are still a significant number of people who remain naïve" about that fact, he added, but "the number of people who are completely naïve is gradually diminishing."

The report found many readers among the American public, the Congress, the White House, and the Kremlin. Among them was Mikhail Gorbachev.

The last of the Soviet leaders had been in power since March 1985, and over the following two years, it had become apparent that he was something new under the sun. Though he had risen rapidly through the ranks of the Soviet system in the 1960s and 1970s, a rise accelerated by Andropov's political support and personal friendship, he seemed to differ from his predecessors in almost every significant regard. He stopped to talk to people in the streets. He encouraged new ideas and open debate in the Politburo. He was socialism with a human face. By the start of 1987, he had met with Reagan in Geneva and in Reykjavík. He was negotiating nuclear weapons deals with the United States, preparing to pull the Red Army out of Afghanistan, and trying to change the rancid politics and starveling economics of his country through his policies of *glasnost*, or openness, and *perestroika*, or reform.

What he hadn't done was to alter the KGB's use of active measures. In October 1987, Secretary of State George Shultz and National Security Adviser Frank Carlucci were in Moscow, in the grandeur of Saint Catherine's Hall at the Kremlin, discussing the fate of nations with Gorbachev, Foreign Minister Eduard Shevardnadze, and Communist Party secretary Anatoly Dobrynin, when, to the Americans' astonishment, the subject of the American counterattack against Soviet disinformation suddenly came up.

The meeting had started on a high note. A grinning Gorbachev

offered a hearty "So, we go forward!" But midway through a four-and-
a-half-hour session dealing with issues including strategic arms reduction talks and the Iran-Iraq War, the Soviet leader turned sour. "He
had with him an interesting document," read the American minutes,
declassified in 2016. "He had decided he must raise it with the Secretary. Holding up a copy of the State Department publication, *Soviet
Intelligence Activities: A Report on Active Measures and Propaganda,
1986–87*"—the recent work of Bailey and her team—"Gorbachev
alleged that it contained 'shocking revelations.' Specifically, he noted
the pamphlet's treatment of a 'Mississippi Peace Cruise,' which Gorbachev had commended to President Reagan during the Geneva summit as an example of the kinds of people-to-people activities they had
agreed to expand. Now, it turned out, the U.S. had discovered that
these same agreements—and this same cruise—were being used by
the Soviets to deceive Americans. Gorbachev asked if the example he
had given the President had been chosen on purpose for inclusion in
the study."

Shultz, taken aback, said he was unfamiliar with the report, which
he was, and he asked if he could keep it. Gorbachev said it was his
only copy. He had raised the issue, he said, because he wanted to
improve relations across the board. "There was no interest in Moscow
in nourishing hatred for the U.S," he said. "Could the U.S. not live
without portraying the Soviet Union as an 'enemy'? Was it a 'must'
to do so? What kind of a society would need such an approach?" He
wondered aloud whether the Soviet Union still really was seen as an
"evil empire" by the White House, and if so, "how could the Secretary of State negotiate with people he considered 'enemies'?" Then he
struck a low blow. He said Shultz's own State Department had itself
"developed active measures which portrayed two years of progress
in expanding exchanges as KGB penetration." Shultz, now reeling,
tried counterpunching with the time-honored technique of what-
aboutism, long practiced by Soviet propagandists, trying to discredit
Gorbachev as a hypocrite without disproving his argument. What

about the Soviet occupation of Afghanistan? Shultz said. What about the downing of KAL 007? Gorbachev fired back: How much had the American government paid for the military pension of the pilot who flew the doomed plane? "The Secretary said he would not dignify the comment with a response. Gorbachev said he would ignore the Secretary's remarks as well." A cold shadow fell across the glittering room.

Shultz tried to recoup. He said he thought there was no more important task than improving relations between Moscow and Washington. But Gorbachev was still furious. Waving the working group report, he asked how it could have been published: "Did documents like this one produce confidence? There had been some improvement in contacts between the two countries, and the Soviet side welcomed this. But the U.S. seemed to be afraid of it. How weak the U.S. must be to react so. Gorbachev said he would like to conclude this sharp exchange on the note with which he had begun—a desire to improve relations. The desire was there on the Soviet side. The U.S. should reflect on this. The Secretary said he agreed. Gorbachev said, 'Good. Let's forget it.'"

It wasn't forgotten. When Shultz returned to Washington, he wanted the Active Measures Working Group abolished. He was furious that Gorbachev had blindsided him and that the sandbagging and the ensuing confrontation had come close to derailing the delicate negotiations. His anger was misplaced. The report was in his briefing book before he arrived in Moscow. He simply hadn't taken time to read it. "I was very unhappy with George Shultz," Bailey said. "He should have read the report and he should have taken Gorbachev to task and supported us."

Gorbachev visited the White House seven weeks later, floating on a sea of popular acclaim from Americans, met by cheering crowds in the streets of Washington chanting, "Gorby! Gorby!" But active measures were on the agenda again. Gorbachev and his team had a ninety-minute working lunch at the White House with Reagan, Bush, Shultz, Carlucci, Colin Powell, and the U.S. Information Agency director

Charles Wick on December 10, 1987. Unprompted, Wick chimed in
to say that he had met with the heads of TASS and two other Soviet
news agencies, and they had agreed "that there would be not only arms
reduction, but also an end to disinformation." Gorbachev pondered
this. "In other words," he said, "both sides spoke against psychological
warfare." The transcript records that "Shevardnadze joked that disarmament would come faster than agreement on this." He was dead
right on that point.

The Soviets did ease up on the most aggressive active measures
against the United States; the CIA attributed that, in part, to the
efforts of the Active Measures Working Group. But the United States
stepped up political warfare operations in the Soviet Union, as the
CIA reported to the White House in November. "Our enhanced program is designed to exploit the current Soviet policy of 'glasnost' and
the revolution in electronic communications, two phenomena which
offer an unprecedented opportunity for our covert action program to
impact on Soviet audiences," the agency's Soviet division noted. "Last
year, some 500,000 books, periodicals, audio cassettes, and video cassettes were distributed inside the Soviet Union and Eastern Europe."
There was more to it than that. A still mostly classified readout of
a covert-action review at a July 1988 White House Situation Room
meeting shows that CIA director William Webster told the president,
Carlucci, and Powell that the agency had been using many of the same
tools, such as clandestine electronics and computer publishing, that
it had used in support of Solidarity, and wielding them against the
Soviets. He showed Reagan a "Russian-language propaganda pamphlet, ostensibly written by the Communist youth organization," but
produced by the CIA. "Six thousand copies were infiltrated into the
Soviet Union, claiming to support Gorbachev's reform program, but
demanding democratic reforms well beyond what the regime will
tolerate," he reported. "The pamphlet was openly circulated and triggered a KGB investigation. We recently learned that students called
in for questioning by the KGB claimed they supported the pamphlet's

message." Perhaps they had escaped imprisonment; on this point the record is silent.

The Active Measures Working Group began to fall apart as the Reagan administration came to an end, in no small part due to the animus of the secretary of state. Bailey went to the Arms Control and Disarmament Agency. Her best staffers returned to their full-time jobs at the CIA and the FBI. The bureau's Jim Milburn devoted his life to hunting down Aldrich Ames. The FBI agent sent to replace Milburn was a dour and taciturn man, a counterintelligence veteran who presented a personality so colorless that some members of the group couldn't recall him clearly in years to come, though he sometimes chaired its meetings and served as a principal author of its final report to Congress.

His name was Robert Hanssen, and he had been spying for the Soviets from inside the FBI since the late 1970s. Like Aldrich Ames, Hanssen had betrayed almost every Soviet agent who worked in secret for the FBI and the CIA, and the double proof provided by the two turncoats sent each one to their deaths. The FBI had assigned Hanssen to study all the known and suspected Soviet penetrations of the bureau, in order to find the man who had unmasked Sergei Motorin and two of his KGB colleagues. Hanssen was looking for himself, so his study proved maddeningly inconclusive, and it turned the trail cold. Having covered his tracks, Hanssen saw a clear field for his trysts with Moscow's spies. As a counterintelligence supervisor entrusted with an unsurpassed ability to tap into the FBI's computer systems, he delivered to the KGB, among other treasure troves, a complete list of double-agent operations being run by the FBI, a warning that the bureau was tunneling into the basement of the new Soviet embassy in Washington, a detailed technical description of the National Security Agency's ability to decode Moscow's communications, a line-by-line reading of the CIA's budget requests for the next five years, and a great deal more. Hanssen was not arrested until the twenty-first century, twenty-two years after his treason first took shape.

Moscow's spies and agents had made a clean sweep of their American enemies in the first years of the cold war. They had done so in the last years, even as the final battles of the long struggle came to a close. And they would do so once again after a veteran of the Leningrad KGB took power in the Kremlin.

CHAPTER 7

"THE DECEITFUL DREAM
OF A GOLDEN AGE"

After forty-five years of struggle, the decline and fall of the Soviet Union seemed like the triumph of American political warfare. The United States now felt free to export the twin pillars of its principles, American capitalism and American democracy, across the domain of the vanishing empire and everywhere on earth. Two American presidents saw the chance to make liberated Soviet satellites and states part of the West, and they took it. By 1999, the United States, still triumphant in its role as the world's sole superpower, had incorporated Poland, the Czech Republic, and Hungary into NATO, making them military allies; nine more nations once under Soviet domination were preparing to join them. Warsaw, Prague, Budapest, once capitals of communism, were now in America's sphere of influence, which would reach from the Baltics to the Black Sea. And Moscow itself was still up for grabs.

That projection of power was seen as the American foreign policy masterstroke of the decade, embraced by a broad political consensus in Washington, by hawks and doves alike. But not by all. Bob Gates, the CIA director under President George H. W. Bush, thought the United

States was playing with fire. "At a time of a special humiliation and difficulty for Russia, pressing ahead with expansion of NATO eastward,
when Gorbachev and others were led to believe that wouldn't happen, at least in no time soon, I think probably has not only aggravated
the relationship between the United States and Russia but made it
much more difficult to do constructive business with them," he said in
2000, shortly after Putin took power. "We have really antagonized the
Russians in a major way." And George Kennan, at the age of ninety-
three, warned that "expanding NATO would be the most fateful
error of American policy in the entire post-cold-war era. Such a decision
may be expected to inflame the nationalistic, anti-Western and militaristic tendencies in Russian opinion; to have an adverse effect on the
development of Russian democracy; to restore the atmosphere
of the cold war to East-West relations, and to impel Russian foreign policy in directions decidedly not to our liking." He feared it
could be the beginning of a new cold war, and in this he was prophetic.
Kennan knew that empires do not vanish into thin air.

Every Russian leader from Gorbachev onward, each with escalating degrees of anger, believed that the United States had achieved the
expansion of NATO into the old Soviet domain more by deception
than diplomacy. Boris Yeltsin directly addressed Bill Clinton shortly
after the American strategy came to light. "Why are you sowing the
seeds of mistrust?" he thundered. "History demonstrates that it is a
dangerous illusion to suppose that the destinies of continents and of
the world community can somehow be managed from one single capital." Dmitry Medvedev, Putin's junior partner in power, said: "We
were assured . . . that NATO would not expand endlessly eastwards
[as] a military bloc whose missiles are pointed towards Russian territory." Putin thought the Americans "wanted a complete victory over
the Soviet Union. They wanted to sit on the throne in Europe alone."

He saw the American push as a cold war stratagem disguised in
new-age camouflage—"a serious provocation," as he said at the Munich
Security Conference in February 2007. "And we have the right to ask:

against whom is this expansion intended? And what happened to the assurances our western partners made?" He has sought revenge ever since. He believed that the United States had moved the Berlin Wall east to Russia's borders. And he began to push back. Only in the past few years have some of the key American records of the 1990s been declassified, and now that we can read them, we can begin to understand the origins of Putin's assault on America.

The cold war had started after America and Russia could not reach a peace that satisfied Stalin in July 1945; three years later, he had cemented his control of Poland, Hungary, and Czechoslovakia, along with the rest of Eastern Europe and the Baltics. In response came containment, the inauguration of American political warfare, the Marshall Plan, and the creation of NATO. Four decades thereafter, the rebels of the Solidarity movement took power in Poland, the Hungarian government dismantled the electric fence at its border with Austria, the poets and political theorists and students who created the Velvet Revolution forced the Communists from power in Czechoslovakia. After the Berlin Wall was breached on November 9, 1989, tens of thousands of East Germans voted with their feet to join the West. "The strength of NATO has made possible these changes in Eastern Europe," President Bush told the West German chancellor, Helmut Kohl, in a telephone call shortly before the wall came down. The tide of history was sweeping a divided Germany to reunite. And Germany reunited within NATO was the great prize of the cold war.

It also was "the Soviet Union's worst nightmare," National Security Adviser Brent Scowcroft told Bush on November 29. It would "rip the heart out of the Soviet security system." Would the Red Army move to stop the tide? Could it start World War III? Bush's national security team weighed that terrible threat as the German people tore down the wall with sledgehammers. But the team soon concluded that they could dictate their decision to Gorbachev and the Soviet Union. Germany once again would be one nation.

This prospect did not gladden hearts throughout the world. "We

beat the Germans twice, and now they're back," British prime minister Margaret Thatcher told European heads of state with more than a
touch of alarm. French president François Mitterrand said to Thatcher
over lunch at the Élysée Palace that a reunited Germany would have
more influence and power than Hitler had ever wielded. "Every other
leader, East and West, was against it," Gates said. "The French were
against it, the British were against it, the Soviets were against it, the
Poles were against it, the Czechs were against it, the Hungarians were
against it, the Italians were against it. We were totally isolated." At
the start of December 1989, Bush met Gorbachev on a storm-tossed
ship off the coast of Malta. A year had passed since the Soviet leader
had made a momentous speech at the United Nations renouncing the
rationale for the cold war. "Life is forcing us to abandon traditional
stereotypes and outdated views, and free ourselves from illusions," he
said. "Today a new world is emerging, and we must look for a different road to the future." But for the Bush White House, it had been
in many ways a lost year. For months after he took office, Bush had
dithered, mistrusting his counterpart in Moscow, failing to see clearly
that a new world really was emerging from the collapse of Soviet communism, balking at a different path than the one he had trodden since
1945, embarking instead on a painstaking and painfully slow review
of each facet of American foreign policy. He had been looking in the
rearview mirror while, out the windshield, the world was changing
forever.

Now, finally, he engaged directly with Gorbachev. "Talking eye to
eye, we discussed the problem of the reunification of Germany," Bush
told the Soviet delegation aboard the rocking boat. "We are aware
how much of a delicate, sensitive problem this is." After all, when unified, Germany had killed upward of twenty million Soviets. "We do
not at all want the reunification of Germany done on the model of
1937–1945 which, obviously, concerns you," Secretary of State James
Baker said, treading less lightly than his president. "The Germany of
that time had nothing in common with Western values." Gorbachev

bristled at this. Why, he asked pointedly, were democracy and openness *Western* values? Weren't those precisely his highest goals, too? He cut to the chase: what were the two sides to call their common ground? Bush fumbled for the right words. Baker stepped in: "Could we possibly say as a compromise that this positive process is proceeding on the basis of 'democratic values'?" And there the transcript tantalizingly ends.

In February 1990, Baker went to Moscow to appease Gorbachev. "We fought alongside with you; together we brought peace to Europe. Regrettably, we then managed this peace poorly, which led to the Cold War," Baker told the increasingly embattled Soviet leader. "Now, when rapid and fundamental changes are taking place in Europe, we have a propitious opportunity to cooperate in the interests of preserving the peace. I very much want you to know: neither the president nor I intend to extract any unilateral advantages from the processes that are taking place." And he said explicitly: "We understand that not only for the Soviet Union but for other European countries as well it is important to have guarantees that if the United States keeps its presence in Germany within the framework of NATO, not an inch of NATO's present military jurisdiction will spread in an eastern direction."

Not an inch eastward. The United States gave "categorical assurances" on that point, said Jack Matlock, the American ambassador in Moscow under Reagan and Bush. Gorbachev heard them clearly, and he heard them repeatedly. He responded: "Any extension of the zone of NATO is unacceptable." He trusted but did not verify: he never got America's assurances in writing.

Kohl came to Camp David to brainstorm with Bush two weeks later and they had a meeting of the minds. They agreed to impose the terms of reunification on Moscow. The West Germans had no military power. But they had immense economic leverage; they were the largest sources of capital investment and joint ventures in the Soviet Union. The two men agreed that Kohl could in essence purchase

East Germany, infusing it with capital, paying the Soviets to leave the country, and bringing a unified Germany into NATO. Baker gleefully saw this grand gambit as the greatest leveraged buyout in history. Gates later called it a plan to bribe the Soviets out.

"We are going to win the game," Bush told Chancellor Kohl at Camp David, "but we must be clever while we are doing it." Their conversation was suffused with Bush's sense that he was in the saddle and riding history.

"The Soviets are not in a position to dictate Germany's relationship with NATO," Bush said. "To hell with that. We prevailed and they didn't. We can't let the Soviets clutch victory from the jaws of defeat."

"Of course," Kohl said, "they will want to get something in return."

"You've got deep pockets," said the president of the United States.

Kohl would shoulder the lion's share of the costs for extracting 546,000 Red Army troops from Germany—an exodus requiring fifty troop trains a day, fifty-five cars each, for more than three years—and building bases to house them once they were home. The immediate cost of the buyout, or the bribe, was measured in tens of billions, then hundreds, a spectacular use of economic power in political warfare. Its immensity matched the importance of the moment. Over time, the bill for unification would come to more than two trillion dollars.

The withdrawal of the Red Army from the center of Europe would change the way American leaders viewed their mission in the world. They looked out over the horizon and saw a new dawn, in which the authority and influence of the Kremlin retreated all the way back to Russia's frontiers, to be replaced by American power and principles. "Beyond containment lies democracy," Baker proclaimed in a speech on March 30. "The time of sweeping away the old dictators is passing fast; the time of building up the new democracies has arrived. That is why President Bush has defined our new mission to be the promotion and consolidation of democracy. It is a task that fulfills both American ideals and American interests." The promotion of democracy would be a defining force of American political warfare for the rest of the century.

While the earth moved under their feet, Bush and Baker continued to reassure Gorbachev that the great tectonic shift was not an earthquake. "I wanted to emphasize that our policies are not aimed at separating Eastern Europe from the Soviet Union. We had that policy before. But today we are interested in building a stable Europe, and doing it together with you," Baker told the Soviet leader in Moscow on May 18. But Foreign Minister Eduard Shevardnadze had a very different view: he warned that "if united Germany becomes a member of NATO, it will blow up perestroika. Our people will not forgive us. People will say that we ended up the losers, not the winners."

At a Washington summit on May 31, Bush insisted to Gorbachev that "we are not pushing Germany towards unification. And of course, we have no intention, even in our thoughts, to harm the Soviet Union." Though that was a half-truth, Gorbachev felt he had to believe in the good faith Bush professed. With his will and ability to preserve the crumbling architecture of Soviet power almost exhausted, he gave in a few days later. (He later told Kohl that after he fully realized the consequences, he felt like he had fallen into a trap, albeit one well baited with cash and credits.) The settlement reached in principle at the summit cemented the entrance of a unified Germany into NATO—and let the military alliance expand not by an inch but by forty-two thousand square miles, eastward to the borders of Poland and Czechoslovakia. It was the glorious culmination of a half century of political warfare against Soviet communism, and the greatest thrust of one nation against another in Europe since Eisenhower's troops and Stalin's soldiers crushed the fascist forces of Nazi Germany. It happened without a shot being fired, and it brought an epoch to an end.

"For months, the President's speechwriters had included a phrase in speeches saying 'The Cold War is over,'" Scowcroft said years later.

"And routinely I crossed it out and crossed it out and crossed it out. After this meeting, I came to the conclusion that this time I could leave it in."

Bush was more than just the last president to preside over the grinding tensions of the cold war. He was the last president to have served in World War II, the last to have seen combat in any theater of war, the last whose views of the world and America's role in it were formed in the 1940s and 1950s—the last Eisenhower Republican, the last whose strategic mind-set was shaped by Kennan and his concept of political warfare. And he was the last to lead the United States into battle backed by an international alliance.

After Saddam Hussein invaded Kuwait in August 1990, the planning and execution of the war to drive him out was more than a display of America's military might. Thirty-eight countries combined to face the Iraqi Army in combat, and they all fought and flew on NATO signals when the war was launched in January 1991. Six kinds of warplanes with pilots from eight nations flying up to four thousand sorties a day were woven together on NATO wavelengths. Nothing like it had happened before, and nothing like it has happened since. The war was a striking demonstration of the power the alliance possessed when harnessed by the United States. The lesson was not lost within the high councils of the Soviets.

The Kremlin was disintegrating into warring fiefs by the time the genial alcoholic Boris Yeltsin was elected president of the Russian republic of the Soviet Union in June 1991. Yeltsin led a delegation to visit NATO headquarters in Brussels at the end of that month. He met with the secretary general of NATO, the former West German defense minister Manfred Wörner, who told Yeltsin in no uncertain terms that he and the great majority of his member states were dead set against including Poland, Hungary, and Czechoslovakia in their ranks. They did not want to isolate Russia from Europe. Yeltsin, sorely in need of international allies, had thought he had made a friend he could trust in Wörner. That hope became clear a few weeks later, in August, when the old guard of the Soviet Union, led by the KGB chairman Vladimir Kryuchkov and the defense minister Dmitry Yazov, tried to mount a coup to topple Gorbachev and save Soviet communism from certain death. The Russian White House, the seat of the republic's government in Moscow, came under armed attack.

"As the sun went down the first day, the outcome of the coup attempt against Gorbachev was an open question," remembered Wayne Merry, the political officer at the American embassy in Moscow. "There were a number of very strange things about this *putsch*. First, there was nothing up in the sky. There were no helicopters. They didn't have control of army aviation. The very fact they were conducting a coup in the middle of the massive metropolitan area that is Moscow and there were no helicopters in the sky was a fairly strong indication that not everything was under control. Second, the telephones were still working in the White House. Yeltsin had telephones. What the hell kind of a coup is it when you can't control who's got a telephone land line?"

An urgent call from Moscow got through to NATO headquarters in Brussels, where Wörner and his assistant secretary general, the American philanthropist Philip Merrill, were running an all-hands meeting of the sixteen member nations, several hundred people all told. "The one phone at the head of the table rings," Merrill recounted. "It is for Wörner."

"Boris? Boris who?"

"Boris Yeltsin, you idiot."

"Boris. Nice to hear your voice. What can I do to be helpful?"

"I've got kind of a problem."

"What's the problem?"

"I'm here in the White House in my office, surrounded by a bunch of army troops. I'm not sure which way they are going to go. I need some help from NATO."

Wörner put the phone down and said: "What are we going to do?"

The coup collapsed quickly, and that was the beginning of the end for the Soviet Union. The next evening, Merry went out walking to Lubyanka Square, in front of the KGB headquarters. A jubilant crowd had gathered there. "They were taking down the huge statue of Felix Dzerzhinsky, the creator of the Soviet secret police," he said. "There were fireworks in the sky. We went down to the Communist Party headquarters building on Old Square, where a number of Yeltsin's associates had taken possession of the building, so the files couldn't be taken away or destroyed. There is a street that looks past the Communist Party headquarters and into Red Square, along which you can see the flagpole on top of what's called the Senate building inside the Kremlin. Instead of the red flag with the hammer and sickle on it, there flew the white, blue and red Russian tricolor."

Bush and his national security team, almost to a man, and almost to the last, thought that Gorbachev would ride out the storm. They all were overtaken by the flood of events sweeping the Soviet Union away. A small example of how quickly the experts had to rethink the unthinkable: in late October 1991, George Kolt, the preeminent Soviet specialist at the CIA, told the White House that Ukraine—a Soviet republic with fifty million people and the world's third-largest nuclear arsenal—might become an independent country within five years. His counterpart at the National Security Council, Ed Hewett, thought that impossible. A fierce argument ensued. Five years or never? It happened in five weeks.

The last American ambassador to the Soviet Union was a smart, and smart-mouthed, former Democratic National Committee chairman named Robert Strauss; he told Bush and his national security aides that he soon would be the first American ambassador to Russia. No one believed him. But the hammer and sickle went down over the Kremlin for the last time on Christmas Day, marking the end for Gorbachev and the Soviet Union—and Bush would be out of power a year later. Ambassador Strauss had "a great metaphor," Merry said, "which was that we—including Russia's leaders—were all like a pissant riding on a log in a river going downstream imagining it determines the direction the log is going and its destination." The fall of the Soviet Union undermined some of the certitudes of American national security. How could America be a great nation without a great enemy? Why did we need an immense military establishment built to fight the Third World War against a nation that no longer existed? And what *was* NATO supposed to do? As Yugoslavia imploded and the bloodiest conflict in Europe since 1945 began to ravage the Balkans, NATO and the rest of the West stayed out of the fray.

Into this swirl of uncertainty stepped the next president of the United States, the governor of Arkansas, Bill Clinton. "The Cold War is over," Clinton had proclaimed at the Democratic National Convention in July 1992. "And our values—freedom, democracy, individual rights, and free enterprise—they have triumphed all over the world." His speech ran to 4,000 words, 141 of which dealt with America's role abroad. He had by all accounts thought little about foreign policy, perhaps less than any commander in chief of the twentieth century. As president, he believed he could deal with the immense problem of Russia by the force of his good nature, befriending and cajoling Yeltsin, calling him a democrat though he ruled by decree, and doing everything he could to support him. At the same time, he became the singular force for expanding NATO, and that push eastward was certain to subvert Yeltsin. These were profoundly contradictory positions, but Clinton was a supremely gifted politician, charming and seductive, at times a silver-tongued liar, and so he was sure he could do both things at once.

He began to advocate enlarging the alliance at the urging of his national security adviser, Tony Lake, whose job required the resolution of contradictions. Lake was a rare bird in Washington, a moralist, or at least far less amoral than most of his peers and his new boss. He had been a highly regarded Foreign Service officer in Vietnam in the early 1960s, before the arrival of American combat troops. Among the lessons Vietnam taught him was that good intentions can lead to "a war of murderous naivete." He had joined Henry Kissinger's National Security Council staff in 1969; he had resigned on principle after Nixon invaded Cambodia in 1970; Kissinger had wiretapped him when President Nixon set out on a futile search for leakers. Under President Carter, he had held Kennan's post as director of policy planning at the State Department. Under Presidents Reagan and Bush, he taught college students and raised cattle in western Massachusetts, a cerebral professor and a gentleman farmer, just like Kennan after his days at State were done. Now he held Kissinger's old job. And it was up to him, more than anyone else in Washington, to determine how to project American power after the end of the cold war; Clinton for all his talents lacked the experience and intellectual capacity to do it. Lake thought the foreign policy of the United States could be both realistic and idealistic, thoughtful and muscular, perhaps even virtuous. "I think Mother Teresa and Ronald Reagan were both trying to do the same thing—one helping the helpless, one fighting the Evil Empire," he once said. "One of the nice things about this job is you can do both at the same time and not see them as contradictory." He served his president well in that regard, holding two opposing ideas in his head and trying to make them one. His intentions were excellent.

But no one, particularly the president, knew what the foreign policy of the United States was supposed to be after the cold war. This created what one of Lake's aides called the "Kennan sweepstakes"—a contest to find a guiding principle that could replace Kennan's strategy of containment, preferably one that could fit on a bumper sticker. Lake won by default with a speech in September 1993 espousing the principle of "democratic enlargement." He said America would expand the map of the world's market democracies, and the best way to do that was to add new nations to NATO. "During the Cold War, even children understood America's security mission; as they looked at those maps on their schoolroom walls, they knew we were trying to contain the creeping expansion of that big, red blob," Lake said. Now, he said, America's mission was to enlarge the blue blob of market democracies by expanding NATO:

> For half a century NATO has proved itself the most effective military alliance in human history. . . . [But] unless NATO is willing over time to assume a broader role, then it will lose public support, and all our nations will lose a vital bond of transatlantic and European security. That is why, at the NATO summit that the President has called for this January, we will seek to update NATO so that there continues behind the enlargement of market democracies an essential collective security.

In advance of that summit, the State Department's top international security and policy planning officials had proposed admitting Poland, Hungary, and the Czech Republic to NATO in 1998; then the Baltic states of Latvia, Lithuania, and Estonia in 2000. They had a more ambitious agenda for the twenty-first century that included Ukraine. And they were clear-eyed about the underlying rationale. It had less to do with expanding democracy and more to do with confronting the Kremlin. "The challenge for NATO over the next generation," they wrote, was "containing and coopting Russian power." But how to convince the Russians to cooperate with their own containment? No one knew. "Obviously, this is tricky," they wrote, "but we do need to coopt the Russians."

An immediate objection to this thinking came from General John Shalikashvili, NATO's supreme allied commander in Europe, who became the chairman of the Joint Chiefs of Staff in October 1993. Born to a Polish mother in Warsaw, the son of a military officer from the Soviet republic of Georgia and the grandson of a czarist general, he and his family had fled to Germany from Poland, running for their lives before the westward advance of the Red Army half a century before. He argued that the Russians would see an expanding NATO as an existential threat.

The question of where the Russians might fit into the new map of the world remained enormous and unanswered, as was the equally thorny question of how to co-opt them. Yeltsin's conduct did not inspire confidence in the idea of Russian democracy. His vision was often blurred. He had seen Clinton for the first time at a summit in Vancouver back in April 1993 (the first of their eighteen meetings, nearly as many as all their cold war predecessors combined). One pleasant afternoon, they went on a boat ride. "We were barely away from the dock before Yeltsin had downed three scotches," wrote Strobe Talbott, Clinton's close friend and his administration's top Russia hand. He drank his dinner, too. "Yeltsin's speech grew sloppy, his message sappy ('Beeell, we're not rivals—we're *friends!*')." Clinton, raised by an alcoholic stepfather, looked on the bright side: Sure, ol' Boris was a drunk, he said, but he wasn't a *mean* drunk, and in any case Yeltsin intoxicated was better than most of the alternatives sober.

Lech Wałęsa, Poland's leader, turned Yeltsin's weakness to his advantage. Wałęsa had leapt at the thought of joining NATO as a bulwark against Russia, though the offer had not been made yet. He had invited Yeltsin for dinner in August, and a river of vodka flowed. In his cups, Yeltsin agreed in principle that Poland was a sovereign nation and could join the alliance if it chose—and then, sobering up after sleeping it off, he tried to take it all back. Under the influence of his advisers, he wrote to Clinton that he was deeply uneasy at the prospect that nations once within the Warsaw Pact might become part of NATO. He argued that "the spirit" of the German unification treaty "precludes the option of expanding the NATO zone into the east." In Russia, he warned, expansion would be seen by hard-liners and moderates alike as a continuation of the cold war, with all the dangers that implied.

Tony Lake, unlike Clinton, had calculated this risk carefully. He had reasoned: "If Russia went south, as it were, and did not become democratic, then at that point, if it was five years, ten years, twenty years down the road, certainly Poland, the Czechs, the Balts—who I've always argued passionately should be involved in this—are going to clamor for Western protection," as he recounted a decade later. "So it's better to do it now." He had downplayed the effect expansion might have on the Kremlin, though an encounter with his Russian counterpart had given him pause. "It was a reception in Moscow at the time of an anniversary of the end of World War II. He'd had something to drink. I'd had something to drink. We had been talking about the 25 million Russians who had died in World War II, and he said, 'You know, we made that sacrifice in World War II and we're prepared to make that sacrifice now against NATO enlargement.' I remember thinking: *This is really good vodka.*"

On September 21, 1993, the same day Lake made his speech about the burgeoning blue blob of democracy, anarchy struck Moscow. Yeltsin, his hold on power slipping in the face of rising political opposition from nationalists and neofascists, resolved to dissolve the Russian legislature. This violated the constitution, so the legislators moved to impeach and replace him. Street protests erupted, with hordes of demonstrators carrying Soviet flags and portraits of Stalin. Violent clashes followed; 187 people died in the streets of Moscow over the course of the next ten days. On October 3, Yeltsin ordered the shelling of the parliament to break the back of the resistance, blowing a hole in the Russian White House. And on the same day, Somali rebels brought down a Black Hawk helicopter over Mogadishu, killing eighteen Americans whose humanitarian mission had morphed into counterinsurgency, and dragging the charred corpses of the fallen soldiers through the streets. The split-screen disasters struck a blow at the hope that American democracy would shape the world. On October 6, Clinton told Talbott: "Boy, do I ever miss the cold war!"

Less than a year after his election, Clinton was reeling, his popularity plummeting, his administration faltering. He faced a world that would not easily be remade in America's image. He keenly wanted a foreign policy victory in the name of American democracy, something looking to a new era, beyond the cold war. His calendar for the start of the new year included the NATO summit in Brussels, a

meeting in Moscow with Yeltsin, and a conference in Prague with
the leaders of Poland, the Czech Republic, and Hungary. He wanted
to offer the three leaders membership in NATO—though by now
he was well aware that saying so could blow up relations with Russia.
Was it worth that risk? The Pentagon and a good part of the State
Department thought not. They promoted an alternative: the Partnership for Peace. First conceived in 1990, after the deal sealing reunification of Germany, the partnership would establish military-to-military
contacts with Russia and the seven former Warsaw Pact states, inviting them to sit in on NATO councils without being allowed to join
the alliance, sharing information but not power, and requiring their
armies to have civilian control, a transparent budget, and a doctrine
based on defense, not offense. Clinton would try to have it both ways,
as was his wont. It would require a measure of duplicity to sweet talk
Yeltsin into the partnership while making a pact with Warsaw, Prague,
and Budapest behind his back.

Secretary of State Warren Christopher and Talbott flew to Russia
after reading a sobering memo from the American chargé d'affaires in
Moscow, James Collins, warning that the NATO issue was "neuralgic to the Russians. They expect to end up on the wrong side of a new
division of Europe if any decision is made quickly. No matter how
nuanced, if NATO adopts a policy which envisions expansion into
Central and Eastern Europe without holding the door open to Russia, it would be universally interpreted in Moscow as directed against
Russia and Russia alone." On October 22, they took a helicopter to a
dacha in the forest, once Stalin's hunting lodge. They walked into an
overheated sunroom filled with stuffed trophy animals. Yeltsin, who
had beaten back a coup by blunt force barely three weeks before, was
in bad shape. He reeked of booze.

Christopher told him that Russia would have "full participation
in the future security of Europe." The Partnership for Peace would
include all the former Soviet and Warsaw Pact states, and "there
would be no effort to exclude anyone." Yeltsin wanted to make sure

that he understood: was it partnership for all, not NATO membership for some? "That is the case," said Christopher. "A brilliant idea,"
Yeltsin responded, "a stroke of genius! This serves to dissipate all
of the tension which we now have in Russia regarding East European states and their aspirations with respect to NATO. It would
have been an issue for Russia, particularly if it left us in a second-
class status. Now, under your new idea we are all equal." Yeltsin was
delighted. "Really great," he exclaimed. "Tell Bill I am thrilled."

But not for long: on January 12, 1994, Clinton conferred with
the Poles, the Czechs, and the Hungarians at Prague Castle and
emerged to announce that the game had changed. He said: "Now
the question is no longer whether NATO will take on new members
but when and how." *Not whether but when* was the near-opposite of
not an inch eastward.

Wayne Merry was handling the political reporting at the American embassy in Moscow. In one hand he held a State Department
readout of what Clinton and Christopher had told Yeltsin. In the
other he held the Warsaw embassy report of what the president had
told the Poles. "The contrast was quite stark, as was our duplicity,"
he said. "The Poles and others publicly trumpeted their achievement
of quick entry into NATO, so the Russians knew we had, more or
less, lied to them. I never understood why we did this. It would have
been much better to tell Yeltsin the truth and work with Moscow
on how to manage the issue to improve ties between NATO and
Russia. I think it was a characteristic of the Clinton Administration,
especially in its relations with Russia, to believe it could have its cake
and eat it too, that we could blatantly deceive the Russians about a
matter of great importance to them without some loss of credence
on their part in our word and in our intentions. Good diplomacy is
not lying for your country, as is often said. Good diplomacy is being
known as true to your word."

The last man among half a million Russian soldiers, a huge pro-
portion of them officers, and many thousands of them having been

billeted in boxcars or in tents with their wives and their children
for years, now had retreated eastward from Germany into Mother
Russia. The Soviet victory over Nazi Germany, the Red Army ram-
paging toward Berlin half a century before, now ran like a movie in
reverse. The culmination of this crucial phase of rolling back the Russians came in Berlin on August 31, 1994, at a formal ceremony led by
Helmut Kohl. The chancellor made solemn remarks about the Soviets' suffering in the war. Yeltsin, drunk again, wandered off to snatch
a baton from the conductor of a military band serenading the troops,
grabbed a microphone, and attempted to lead the audience in song. It
was a mortification for the Russian nation. And the humiliation was
about to deepen.

The Clinton administration had been deceiving the Russians, but
it was also deceiving itself. "NATO expansion will, when it occurs,
by definition be punishment, or 'neo-containment,' of the bad Bear,"
Talbott wrote to Christopher. "Our current position is based on the
proposition that an expanded NATO will not be directed at Russia," he pointed out. But did "we really, or at least entirely, believe
this? Certainly the Poles and Czechs don't." The historian Mary Elise
Sarotte obtained the declassification of these and other secret documents from the twenty-five-year-old diplomatic record and published them in the journal *International Security* in July 2019. Among
them were Talbott's musings on the state of play with Russia. Talbott, who held the rank of deputy secretary of state for seven years
under Clinton, was a journalist, not a diplomat, by trade; he had
been *Time* magazine's chief correspondent on Soviet-American relations in the Reagan and Bush years and had written four hefty books
in that time. He deeply admired Kennan and, like him, he threw his
weight around with words. "We and the Soviet Union didn't meet
each other halfway" at the end of the cold war, "and we and Russia
aren't going to do so either," he now wrote. "Russia is either coming
our way, or it's not, in which case it's going to founder, as the USSR
did." He rejected Vice President Al Gore's statement to Yeltsin that

relations between the United States and Russia would emulate the docking of the American space shuttle with the Mir space station, matching orbits as they moved to merge in synchrony: "It's Russia that must move toward us, toward our way of doing things." This might seem to be "an obnoxious confirmation of our doctrine of 'exceptionalism.'" And if so? "Well, tough. That's us; that's the U.S. We are exceptional," wrote the Russia hand.

The doctrine of exceptionalism was a deeply held faith that America was the last, best hope of earth, in the words of Abraham Lincoln. But another current of thought ran even deeper. Alexander Hamilton wrote in 1787 that America would not be an exception to the history of clashing empires, a chronicle of war as old as Christendom, centuries of folly marked by flashes of glory. "Have we not already seen enough of the fallacy and extravagance of those idle theories which have amused us with promises of an exemption from the imperfections, weaknesses and evils incident to society in every shape?" he asked. "Is it not time to awake from the deceitful dream of a golden age, and to adopt as a practical maxim for the direction of our political conduct that we, as well as the other inhabitants of the globe, are yet remote from the happy empire of perfect wisdom and perfect virtue?"

Blinking in the light of a false dawn, America's leaders saw their nation as that wise and virtuous empire. The rest of the world had to become more like America, like it or not.

Talbott wrote to the secretary of state that he saw the United States as a lighthouse, illuminating the true course for the Russians toward "democratic elections, free press, pluralism, open markets, civil society, rule of law, independent judiciary, checks and balances, respect for minority rights." And that light should guide "the rickety, leaky, oversized, cannon-laden Good Ship Russia, with its stinking bilge, its erratic, autocratic captain, and its semi-mutinous crew" to a harbor on the horizon. If the United States was to be the indispensable nation in the remaking of a new world, Clinton made Yeltsin an irreplaceable partner in that quest, though his personal conduct might be irredeemable and his political course indefensible.

The commodore of the Russian rust bucket had joined the Partnership for Peace, and he was set to arrive for his first formal meeting at the White House at the end of the summer of 1994. Clinton had been telling his aides that he was sick and tired of talking about the "post-cold war era," defined by what had gone past and not what lay ahead. He wanted to look forward, but he didn't see a clear blueprint for a bridge to the twenty-first century. He felt that his administration was on autopilot as it approached an uncertain future, and the greatest uncertainty, he told his foreign policy brain trust, was "the big mess in Russia, which has got everybody afraid that things are going to fall apart." Yeltsin arrived in Washington on September 26, stumbling off his plane. He stayed at Blair House, across Pennsylvania Avenue from the executive mansion, and that night, by Talbott's account, he was "roaring drunk, lurching from room to room in his undershorts," and emerging on a landing, shouting "Pizza! Pizza!" Then, over lunch in the White House, Clinton told Yeltsin the unpleasant truth: NATO would head east. "We're going to move forward on this," he said. He insisted in the next breath that "NATO expansion is not anti-Russian." And he promised that someday Russia could join, too—a false hope, since you had to be a democracy to get into the club, and Russia wasn't one. Yeltsin had little to say of substance on the issue. But out of the blue, at day's end, he asked Clinton to attend a fifty-two-nation conference in Budapest in December, where and when, as it turned out, he would give his reply.

A few days before the Budapest conclave, NATO ministers met in Brussels, and the alliance resolved to expand as America wished. Yeltsin responded with a frosty letter to Clinton warning that the move "will be interpreted, and not only in Russia, as the beginning of a new split of Europe."

Clinton hadn't focused on this as he prepared to fly to Budapest. He was preoccupied: The Democratic Party had suffered a historic drubbing in the November elections, as voters punished Clinton for his failed domestic health care initiatives and his foreign policy fiascoes; the Republicans had won control of the House of Representatives for the first time since 1952, and won it overwhelmingly. With it, they sought to implement their conservative "Contract with America," which notably included the integration of the former Warsaw Pact nations into NATO in its highly hawkish text. One of the first orders of business for the new Congress would be the NATO Expansion Act, explicitly inviting Poland, Hungary, and the Czech Republic into the alliance. That reinforced Russia's sense that American leaders wanted to cage the bear and poke it in the eye for good measure.

Clinton had told Yeltsin that together they could create "the first chance ever since the rise of the nation-state to have the entire continent of Europe live in peace." The cold war was over, as Clinton had declared on a dozen occasions, and with that glorious achievement would come an end to the wars of the twentieth century; now war-fighting would become peacekeeping, carried out by the United Nations, NATO, and perhaps one day by the Partnership for Peace.

That vision—and the very idea of the prospective partnership—overlooked some cold hard facts.

The great wars of the twentieth century all had started in the center of Europe, each leading inexorably to the next, world war to world war to cold war, each igniting after the winners and losers had failed to make a lasting peace, and the peace at the end of the cold war had proved fleeting there as well. The breakup of the former Yugoslavia in 1991 had engendered the bloodiest battles in Europe since the death of Adolf Hitler. The Serbian leader Slobodan Milošević had so pitilessly attacked the predominantly Muslim cities and villages of Bosnia that two million out of four million people were driven into refuge, wounded, or killed. Yeltsin unswervingly supported his fellow Slav, Milošević; Russia unfailingly blocked and tackled for the Serbs in the United Nations Security Council.

America and NATO had fiddled while the Balkans burned and innocent civilians died. NATO airpower would have deterred the Serbs and saved countless lives. But to the enduring shame of the Americans and the Europeans, neither Bush nor Clinton nor the leader of any NATO nation had had the will to take action. Throughout 1993 and 1994, NATO had contributed a pittance—not much more than logistical support—to a UN peacekeeping mission whose robust military rules of engagement were routinely annulled at UN headquarters in New York. Now Clinton and his national security team rebuffed all pleas for action. "I wanted us to use air strikes, and they didn't want to do that," said Warren Zimmermann, the American ambassador to Yugoslavia under Bush, who resigned in protest as the director of the State Department's refugee bureau under Clinton. "Not only did they not want to do it, but they used deception and subterfuge to pretend that we had a tough policy when we really didn't." He had calculated that bombing the Serbs could have protected one hundred thousand civilians from certain death. "And so it continued: week in and week out," Talbott wrote, "the Serbs brutalized the Muslims in Bosnia while the West issued warnings and Russia did everything it could to make sure that nothing came of our threats."

After flying all night to Budapest on December 5, 1994, a bleary Clinton fumbled his speech to the security conference. "As NATO expands," he said, "so will security for all European states, for it is not an aggressive, but an offensive organization." He must have meant to say defensive. Yeltsin then took to the stage. He said the Russians would not tolerate being isolated. They would not be excluded from a new world order in Europe. The expansion of NATO was a divisive force driven by a cold war logic. And then he let Russia's old enemies have it: "Europe, even before it has managed to shrug off the legacy of the Cold War, is risking encumbering itself with a cold peace." A few hours later, back aboard Air Force One, Clinton fumed as he flew home, saying he'd been blindsided, stabbed in the back. He now knew that *cold peace* was the bumper sticker that would adhere to his era.

But he kept up his courtship with Yeltsin at a May 1995 meeting in Moscow marking the fiftieth anniversary of the end of World War II. Yeltsin warmed up to his wooing and cajoling. They were geopolitical codependents: Yeltsin needed America's political and financial support to win reelection in 1996, and Clinton desperately wanted Yeltsin to win, to keep the communists and neofascists out of the Kremlin—and for his own political future. Talbott said: "We had to be careful not to let a Yeltsin defeat be seen as a Clinton defeat." Clinton knew that if Yeltsin fell, he himself would face a who-lost-Russia hellfire on the campaign trail when he sought a second term. Bill sorely wanted his pal Boris to say yes to NATO, though Yeltsin and his ministers all said *nyet* with increasing intensity.

"For me to agree . . . would constitute a betrayal on my part of the Russian people," Yelstin told him flatly. "I see nothing but humiliation for Russia if you proceed." He proposed a way out: "You and I are heading for elections. The extremists and hardliners are exploiting this issue for their own purposes—on both sides. I am being attacked from both the right and the left on this. . . . So let's postpone any change in NATO until 1999 or 2000."

Clinton tried to reason with him: "The question is, does the U.S. at the end of the Cold War still need a security relationship with Europe along with a political and economic relationship?"

"I'm not so sure you do," said Yeltsin.

"Let me be clear, Boris: I'm not bargaining with you," Clinton said, while driving his bargain harder.

Clinton gave him unequivocal and unwavering personal and financial support, the first and only American president to campaign openly for his Russian counterpart. He depicted Yeltsin as the embodiment of Russian democracy, a declaration that fell outside diplomacy, lying somewhere in the realm of magical thinking. As

Russia's military slaughtered thousands of civilians in the secessionist republic of Chechnya, Clinton stood by Yeltsin's side in Moscow and, incredibly, compared him to Abraham Lincoln in the American Civil War. He helped to arrange for the International Monetary Fund to pump billions into Russia—money intended to prop up his man in Moscow and reinforce the illusion that a free-market economy was working in Russia. It wasn't. The Russian people felt like lab rats, living in an economic experiment cooked up by political scientists playing God. American leaders preached that capitalism brought democracy, and free markets begat freedom surely as dawn followed the dark of night. But this proved to be a fantasy. The American dream that a strong dose of unfettered capitalism would engender the rule of law helped guarantee that political racketeers emerged as the winners of the struggle for post-Soviet Russia.

Yeltsin had been blunt about his need for cold cash and plenty of it. He asked Clinton to use his influence with the IMF "to perhaps add a little—from nine to thirteen billion dollars—to deal with social problems in this very important pre-election situation." Clinton did that. In March 1996, the IMF approved $10.2 billion for the Russian government over three years, with $4 billion front-loaded in the first year, a last-minute increase of $1.2 billion over what had been contemplated a few weeks before. And then Yeltsin haggled for more in May: "Bill, for my election campaign, I urgently need for Russia a loan of $2.5 billion." It's hard to say whether Yeltsin got his hands on a great windfall in time to grease his political machine. More important was the perception among the populace that he could provide for Mother Russia in a time of continuous crisis. Most crucially, Clinton averted his gaze as Yeltsin embarked on his corrupt "loans-for-shares" program, in which Russia's new oligarchs received ownership of state energy and mineral industries and, in turn, gave Yeltsin political and financial support. If this was free-market capitalism, it was a kind not seen in the United States since John D. Rockefeller and J. P. Morgan and the rest of the robber barons built their empires in the late nineteenth century. The disastrous privatization scheme helped to spur the death of reform. Under Yeltsin, the nation's economic wealth decreased by more than 40 percent; the collapse was twice as large and lasted three times longer than the Great Depression in the United States. Russia wasn't on the road to democracy, but to a thieves' paradise where the Kremlin's favorite gangsters extracted the nation's treasure, laundered it, and turned it into overseas luxuries.

When Yeltsin won in a runoff in July 1996, defeating the communist candidate, Clinton told the Russian deputy foreign minister that there was dancing in the White House. His support for Yeltsin at all costs had been a centerpiece of his foreign policy. But within days, Yeltsin was dancing with death; at his inauguration in August, he was barely able to walk or talk. His heart was failing. He disappeared from view before he underwent a seven-hour quintuple bypass in November, and he was out of the picture for months thereafter.

Clinton won a second term in November—the first Democrat reelected as president since FDR—with notably strong support from ethnic Catholic voters who had roots in Central Europe. The Polish diaspora in particular helped him win Wisconsin and Michigan. In Detroit, two weeks before election day, he had inhaled stuffed cabbage, pierogis, and sauerkraut for lunch at the Polish Village Cafe. And he proclaimed in public on that day, for the first time, that by 1999, on the occasion of NATO's fiftieth anniversary and ten years after the fall of the Berlin Wall, the alliance would embrace its old Warsaw Pact enemies.

In Moscow, Yevgeny Primakov steeled Russia for this reality. He was Yeltsin's minister of foreign affairs and in time would be his prime minister. Primakov had worked as a KGB spy, undercover as a radio journalist and as a foreign correspondent for *Pravda*, from 1956 to 1970, executing espionage missions in the United States and the Middle East. He had run the Russian foreign intelligence service for five years under Yeltsin, the leader of a cadre of veteran KGB officers gaining political sway over the country. On January 31, 1997,

Primakov told the speaker of the Duma, the Russian parliament, that "our position with regard to NATO expansion remains invariably negative . . . especially the possibility of moving NATO's military infrastructure to the East." He said the decision would "define the European configuration for decades in the future," and "politicians who are in power today will bear historic responsibility" for its consequences.

The relationship between Clinton and Yeltsin was sustained in 1997 by American flattery. Clinton offered him entrée into glittering institutions of Western power like the Group of Seven, comprised of the world's leading industrial nations, which commanded half of the world's gross domestic product. It would now become the Group of Eight, and so it remained until it expelled Russia after Putin's military seizure of the Crimean Peninsula from Ukraine in 2014. Russia had no business belonging to the club; its economy was about one-fifth the size of California's. Though the offer delighted Yeltsin, his warm feelings soon began to cool, and the issue was, inevitably, NATO.

At the start of 1998, the Serbian strongman Slobodan Milošević was on the warpath once again, fighting the latest battle of a six-century war between the Serbs and the Kosovars. Kosovo was part of the Ottoman Empire until 1912; it was now incorporated into Serbia, and its 1.5 million people wanted out. They were ethnically Albanians and culturally Muslims, though irreligious ones: they drank wine and ate pork, and they did not pray five times a day, if at all. Milošević nonetheless painted them as Islamic terrorists, and Yeltsin went along with that libel. When the self-styled Kosovo Liberation Army attacked Milošević's forces, he started a massacre; more than a million people were driven into exile as they ran from his campaign of ethnic cleansing, and more than ten thousand would die before it ended. NATO was trying to keep the peace in Kosovo during 1998, but it was not holding. Clinton called Yeltsin from the Oval Office on June 15 and tried to find a common ground. He couldn't. The use of force by NATO was inadmissible, Yeltsin said. Clinton, taken aback, said maybe something could be worked out at the United Nations. That hope did not take hold.

The fortunes of both men plummeted in the fall of 1998. Russia was in the grip of a crippling financial crisis, and Yeltsin lacked the acumen to solve it. His political standing would never recover. The Russian people had become weary of his weakness, tired of failed flirtations with free markets, fed up with America's efforts to impose democracy upon them. Clinton's own trouble was self-inflicted. His unfaithful relationship with the truth had ensnared him; he had been caught lying under oath about his sexual liaisons with a White House intern. The House of Representatives opened hearings on October 8 and impeached Clinton on counts of obstruction of justice and perjury by a narrow partisan vote on December 19. (The hypocrisy of the Republican leadership was profound: House Speaker Newt Gingrich was engaged in adultery, as was his designated successor, Representative Robert Livingston; both men resigned in early 1999. The next Republican Speaker, Representative Dennis Hastert, became the highest-ranked American politician in history to go to prison after he was convicted of crimes stemming from his long history of molesting teenage boys.) The Senate acquitted Clinton on February 12, 1999, and by the time the political circus in Congress struck its tent, his popularity was headed to an all-time high.

One month later, on March 12, Secretary of State Madeleine Albright and the foreign ministers of Poland, Hungary, and the Czech Republic convened at the Truman Presidential Library in Independence, Missouri, where the ministers signed the documents sealing their nations' accession into NATO. Bulgaria, Estonia, Latvia, Lithuania, Romania, Slovakia, and Slovenia, all once part of the Soviet empire, were next in line, with Ukraine waiting in the wings. Albright, who was born in Prague and fled with her family after the Communist takeover in 1948, declared that the alliance now would do "for Europe's east what NATO has already helped to do for Europe's west: steadily and systematically, we will continue erasing—without replacing—the line drawn in Europe by Stalin's bloody boot." Erasing without replacing was a diplomatic way to encapsulate nine years of America's efforts to enlarge its global influence and power.

The first mission of the newly expanded NATO would be launched in eleven days. It was an act of war in the name of peace: the bombing of a European capital, with the goal of stopping the continuing onslaught of Milošević and the Serbs. Three and a half hours before the first bombs struck Belgrade, Clinton called Yeltsin. One thousand NATO warplanes, most of them American, were at the ready; the German Air Force was about to launch its first combat operations since World War II.

"We have to launch airstrikes against military targets in Serbia soon," Clinton told him, without saying how soon, since the Russians had not been consulted. "It will be your decision if you decide to let this bully destroy the relationship we worked hard for six and a half years to build up. . . . I know this is a political problem for you at home, and I will do everything I can to put it right and restart the diplomacy at any point in this. I'd give anything not to have to make this telephone call today, but we have no choice. I hope between the two of us we will not let it destroy all the bigger issues before us and the world."

Yeltsin was enraged. "In the name of our future, in the name of you and me, in the name of the future of our countries, in the name of security in Europe, I ask you to renounce that strike," he said. "Our people will certainly from now have a bad attitude with regard to America and with NATO. . . . I remember how difficult it was for me to try and turn the heads of our people, the heads of the politicians towards the West, towards the United States, but I succeeded in doing that, and now to lose all that. Well, since I failed to convince the President, that means there is in store for us a very difficult, difficult road of contacts, if they prove to be possible. Goodbye." He hung up on Clinton, something he had never done before.

The NATO bombing went on for eleven weeks, killing more than one thousand combatants, before Milošević raised a white flag. The attack was not without fatal errors. NATO jets struck a convoy of refugees, and fifty died. And an American B-2 stealth bomber, the most expensive warplane ever built, flying its first combat missions in the ten years since its creation, hit the Chinese embassy in Belgrade, using coordinates supplied by the CIA, which had identified the building as Milošević's military procurement headquarters. Three innocents were killed, joining some five hundred unintended casualties of the war and outraging the Chinese. Milošević survived politically, but not for long; the United States openly worked to defeat him in the next election, with the State Department and American political consultants advising his opponents and providing millions of stickers with a clenched fist symbol and the slogan "He's finished" in Serbian. He would be charged with war crimes by an international tribunal, and would die in prison.

All of this fiercely infuriated the Russians: Milošević was a murderous son of a bitch, but he was their son of a bitch. The military and political campaign to crush him confirmed every fear, and fueled many conspiracy theories, about what the expansion of NATO foretold for Russian influence and power in the world. And now America was once again bombing Iraq, Russia's longtime ally in the Middle East, this time in an effort to knock out what it believed to be Saddam Hussein's weapons of mass destruction. Throughout the 1990s, "it sometimes seemed to Russian generals and Duma committee chairmen that every time they turned on CNN there was another briefing from the Pentagon announcing that the U.S. had yet again dispatched its aircraft carriers and launched its cruise missiles," Strobe Talbott observed. "And even when the U.S. wasn't striking against targets in Russia's neighborhood if not its front yard, it was expanding its capacity to do so through the enlargement of NATO. . . . Some of those generals and politicians believed that it was only a matter of time before Russia itself would be in the crosshairs of America's unchecked military power."

Among them was the next leader of Russia. In August 1999, Yeltsin fired his entire cabinet; it was the fourth time in eighteen months he had sacked his prime minister. The new man for that job was a mysterious figure, little known in Moscow and less so in Washington, who had risen from obscurity to become chief of the FSB, the main Russian intelligence service, in July 1998; then, in March 1999, the new head of the Russian national security council. "I would like to tell you about him so you will know what kind of man he is," Yeltsin told Clinton in passing during a phone call on September 8. "It took me a lot of time to think who might be the next Russian president in the year 2000. Unfortunately, at that time, I could not find any sitting candidate. Finally, I came across him. . . . I explored his bio, his interests, his acquaintances, and so on and so forth. I found out he is a solid man. . . . I am sure you will find him to be a highly qualified partner." A Russian presidential election was set for the coming March, but the outcome was a foregone conclusion; Russian democracy was now a contradiction in terms. Yeltsin had privately determined to step down on New Year's Eve, six months before his term of office ended, and cede his power to his handpicked successor, who would then run as an incumbent president, with all the power that entailed.

Vladimir Putin's very first act after taking office as president of Russia was guaranteeing his predecessor immunity from prosecution. As the intelligence czar, Putin had protected Yeltsin and his family from charges of corruption being investigated by Russia's prosecutor general, Yuri Skuratov. Yeltsin's chief of staff had summoned Skuratov to the Kremlin and showed him a videotape that purported to show him cavorting with two prostitutes. The prosecutor insisted that the tape was a fake, but he resigned nonetheless. The Russian parliament summoned him to testify, but hours before he was set to appear, the sex tape was broadcast on a Russian television station. Putin apparently delivered it in person. Then he went on TV himself to announce that the man on the grainy surveillance tape was definitely Skuratov. It was a classic case of *kompromat*, the use of compromising material for blackmail, a technique honed by Stalin's secret police in the 1930s, perfected by the KGB, and by now a permanent part of Russia's political culture.

Clinton asked Yeltsin who was going to win the election during their last tête-à-tête, at a security conference in Istanbul on November 19, 1999. "Putin, of course," came the reply. "I will do everything possible for him to win—legally, of course. And he will win." In the course of this conversation, Yeltsin made an extraordinary statement that in one stroke evoked the imperial ambitions of the nineteenth-century czars and foreshadowed how a new czar might rule in the twenty-first century. In retrospect, it could be inferred that Putin had become his patron's Rasputin.

"I ask you one thing. Just give Europe to Russia," he told Clinton. "Russia is half European and half Asian."

"So you want Asia too?" an incredulous Clinton responded.

"Sure, sure, Bill. Eventually we will have to agree on all of this."

"I don't think the Europeans would like this very much."

"Bill, I'm serious," insisted Yeltsin, who for once was sober. "We have the power. . . . Russia has the power and intellect to know what to do with Europe."

Their last conversation lasted ten minutes. It was New Year's Eve. The American intelligence community was on high alert, both from forebodings of a terrorist attack and fears that computers everywhere would crash if their software reset to 1900 instead of 2000. Yeltsin was counting down to the end of his tumultuous reign. Clinton called him from the Oval Office.

"Boris, I believe that historians will say you were the father of Russian democracy," Clinton said, praising him for his decision to cede power.

"Thank you, Bill," said Yeltsin. "Of course, this was not an easy decision for me, and you, as no one else, can understand that. But I want to support Putin 100 percent and now I've given him three months, three months according to the constitution, to work as president, and people will get used to him for these three months. I am sure that he will be elected in the forthcoming elections; I am sure about that. I am also sure that he is a democrat, and that he is a person with a big soul."

It was three hours to midnight and the dawn of a new millennium.

CHAPTER 8

THIS UNTAMED FIRE

Ever since the end of World War II, exporting democracy had been a principle of American political warfare. Now it was the polestar. Every president had espoused it, each in his own way, some with less faith or force than others, but always with the hope that America would project its predominant power and prevail across the earth. The means and methods were sometimes ugly. The United States had supported more than a few dictators in its struggle against the Kremlin. But its record on human rights beat the Soviet Union's by any standard, and the ideals of the Declaration of Independence were stronger than the ideas of the Communist Manifesto, when the United States lived up to them. Two decades after a long, dark passage—the retreat and defeat of American forces in Vietnam, the decline and fall of President Nixon in the face of impeachment— America appeared ascendant, trailing clouds of glory, and the world was going its way.

At the start of the new century, it seemed the American flag might be planted almost everywhere. Small green shoots of liberty had sprouted in cracked streets once ruled by security forces in steel-toed

jackboots and watched over by pitiless commissars surveilling the citizenry. American pressure had helped create some of the fissures and
flowerings. The number of democratic nations around the world had
increased, slowly but steadily throughout the cold war, and then rapidly after the fall of the Berlin Wall, until, by the summer of 2001, the
numbers of autocracies and democracies on earth were roughly equal.
Nothing like that had ever happened in the history of the world. The
arc of justice seemed strong and true and the trend toward freedom
irreversible. It was not so.

Five years later, democracy had fallen into a long global recession. It has not recovered since. The rule of law, free and fair elections, freedom of expression, freedom of association, and free and
independent voices in the media flatlined and declined all over the
world. As American political warfare gave way to the war on terror,
the image of the United States as a force for truth and justice began
to dim, and the polarities of global power began to shift away from
American dominion.

"Much depends on health and vigor of our own society," George
Kennan had cabled in the Long Telegram of 1946. "The greatest
danger that can befall us in coping with this problem of Soviet communism is that we shall allow ourselves to become like those with
whom we are coping." The awful truth was that American democracy
began to face that danger in the new century. A disputed presidential
election was decided by a politically governed 5-to-4 decision in the
Supreme Court. Civil liberties and political rights eroded and the
scope of government surveillance grew after 9/11. Economic inequal-
ity expanded; the richest 1 percent now owned more wealth than all
of the middle class. Public trust in American government plummeted
to 17 percent, a historic low. And as America embarked on a military
crusade to impose democracy upon the Islamic world, it subjected
captured enemies to medieval tortures in secret dungeons. The voice
of America turned into an angry rasp, a command barked at gunpoint; the face of America was no longer the kind soldier handing out

candy, but the leering prison guard at Abu Ghraib. The squandering of America's power and principles was the enduring legacy of our field marshal in the march of folly, the forty-third president of the United States, George W. Bush.

In June 2001, Bush set off for his first transatlantic trip since his election, a chance to show the world that he had a semblance of the strategic skills his father had possessed. In Warsaw, he said that NATO should admit the Baltic states of Lithuania, Latvia, and Estonia as soon as possible. The Soviet Union had violently seized those nations during the dark days of the devil's bargain between Stalin and Hitler. Every Western nation deemed the Kremlin's annexation and occupation of the Baltic states illegal; none had ever seen it as anything but armed conquest. Bush went on to say that NATO now should be open to "new democracies from the Baltic to the Black Sea," a front line for American influence stretching fourteen hundred miles across the entirety of Russia's western frontier. "NATO's promise," he proclaimed, "now leads eastward and southward, northward and onward," encompassing former Soviet republics from Estonia down to Georgia and Ukraine.

The next day, Bush met Putin for the first time, at a five-hundred-year-old mansion in Slovenia. The president of the United States said, famously: "I looked the man in the eye. I found him to be very straightforward and trustworthy. We had a very good dialogue. I was able to get a sense of his soul." Putin passed no such judgment on what he had seen in Bush, or how he sized up the leader of the free world and the commander in chief of the most powerful country in the history of Western civilization. He did have a few choice words on the subject of NATO. "'Look, this is a military organization," he said. "It's moving towards our border. Yes, it's moving towards our border. Why?"

Bush spent the month of August chopping brush at his ranch in Texas, and he paid scant attention to his CIA director's reports that something terrible might be about to happen, in great part because no one could say with an iota of confidence when or where the attack might strike. It came out of a clear blue sky in September. A systemic breakdown of American government from the CIA to the customs, immigration, and aviation agencies contributed to the success of the attacks. The fatal errors of American intelligence, whose highest calling had been to prevent another Pearl Harbor, were compounded by breakdowns at the National Security Council and in the Oval Office of the White House, all cascading into a catastrophic failure of vision. America had been flying blind. As the World Trade Center crumbled and the Pentagon burned, the American century, which had started in August 1917 when the United States went to war to make the world safe for democracy, came to an end. The hinge of history swung wide, and the world was once again in arms. America has spent more than a trillion dollars on intelligence since that bright September day, now a generation gone. The CIA and the FBI and the NSA threw everything they had at their command into fighting the real and perceived threats of terrorism. But as they wielded those powers with a single-minded focus, they became half-blind to what was happening in the rest of the world. American intelligence became an instrument of the war on terror, so much so that the nation's capacity to conduct espionage, analyze information, and coordinate political warfare to confront the Kremlin and project its power in the wider world was compromised.

Osama bin Laden was hiding in a cave in Afghanistan and facing a crushing assault from the United States Air Force and the CIA's commandos in December 2001. The Taliban had vanished. Bush had declared victory. And then bin Laden escaped, the Taliban came down from the mountains to fight, the war went on and on, and a black hole lay at the end of the tunnel. Eighteen years later, more than 2,300 Americans were dead and 20,000 wounded in Afghanistan; the toll among Afghan civilians ran far higher. "We were devoid of a fundamental understanding of Afghanistan—we didn't know what we were doing," Douglas Lute, the three-star Army general who was the

Afghan war czar in the Bush and Obama administrations, reflected at a lessons-learned session at the Pentagon in 2015. "We didn't have the foggiest notion of what we were undertaking."

President Bush, Vice President Dick Cheney, and Secretary of Defense Donald Rumsfeld had turned away from Afghanistan to make war against Iraq. Starting in January 2002, their deputies met in utmost secrecy to plan that attack, and throughout the summer and fall of 2002, the president and his aides prepared the battlefield of the American mind with apocalyptic warnings about Saddam Hussein's weapons of mass destruction: Baghdad had chemical and biological weapons, and it could build a nuclear weapon in a few years. The alarms were terrifying, and utterly false. The cause for war was an illusion.

Bush, Cheney, and Rumsfeld had no plan for what would happen after Baghdad fell and no strategy for their wider war around the world. American intelligence knew little about Iraq, and much of what it knew was wrong. The CIA didn't begin to imagine that Saddam could be overthrown and then operate from underground, nor did it foresee the insurgency that followed, and the ripple effect of that fighting, inspiring jihadists across the Middle East and North Africa. The consequences of that ignorance have been immense. Roughly half a million people have died, including fifteen thousand American combatants and contractors, in the name of the war on terror. Estimates of the financial toll run from $3 trillion to $6 trillion; in today's dollars, World War II cost about $4 trillion. And in Iraq, the only winners of the war have been Iran, whose military commanders gained political power and prestige in Baghdad while working with jihadists to kill American troops, and Russia, which has forged a regional alliance of convenience with the Iranians.

By March 2003, as the war was imminent, Putin called it a political blunder that could destabilize the world. He warned of the dangers of American warmongering, and he called on the Russian military to be ready to defend the nation. As America bombed Baghdad, the

Russians reacted less with shock and awe than with fear and loathing, but that soon turned to reflections on a key aspect of the attack. They saw that the blows against Saddam had been inflicted not only by cruise missiles and tanks but with information warfare. Not only had the White House bludgeoned the world into thinking the war was justified, American aircraft and ships had bombarded Iraqi military and civilian leaders with broadcasts, emails, faxes, and cell phone calls. They were dropping leaflets, running psyops, deceiving computer networks—influencing the enemy, getting inside his head. Information could shape a battlefield of thought, perception, consciousness, and decision-making.

On May 1, 2003, Bush stood under a banner proclaiming "Mission Accomplished" on the deck of the aircraft carrier *Abraham Lincoln* and announced that America was going to bring the blessings of democracy and peace to Iraq and the Middle East. That ambition was news to his generals and spies. Rumsfeld and his top aides at the Pentagon looked up at CNN and returned their focus to their chosen mission: they were creating a military internet for the wars of the future and preparing to spend hundreds of billions of dollars to build it. Their World War Web would weaponize information and intelligence in ways few had imagined. They sought a moving picture of all foreign enemies and all the threats on earth, a God's-eye view of the global battlefield. They wanted to know "everything of interest to us, all the time," said Steve Cambone, the undersecretary of defense for intelligence. "What we are really talking about," said Art Cebrowski, director of the Pentagon's Office of Force Transformation, "is a new theory of war." That theory exponentially expanded the idea of information warfare. In the late twentieth century, information warfare meant an attack on the computers supporting an enemy's communications networks and power grids. By the early twenty-first century, the concept was evolving into a broadly defined form of political warfare targeting an enemy's government, military, and civilians: the battle space of the mind. In the new theory of war, it was an essential element of establishing American dominion over the earth.

Moscow's military and intelligence officers had been watching, listening, taking notes, and thinking hard. As one who rose to become chief of the Russian General Staff wrote: "For the first time in the history of warfare, relying on information as the fundamental element in the conduct of armed conflict, the collective West managed to imbed... the idea that the United States had the exclusive right to world governance." The military theorist Vladimir Slipchenko put it more succinctly: "Information has become a destructive weapon just like a bayonet, bullet or projectile." The president of the Russian Academy of Military Sciences, Makhmut Gareyev, a retired general who had served in the Red Army from 1941 to 1992, was highly attuned to the power of disinformation as an instrument of war: "The systematic broadcasting of... partially truthful and false items" could create "mass psychosis, despair and feelings of doom, and undermine trust in the government... creating a fruitful soil for actions of the enemy."

Russian political analysts who longed for Putin to revive their old empire enlarged mightily on this kind of thinking. Igor Panarin, a KGB veteran who became dean of international relations at the diplomatic academy of Russia's Foreign Ministry, was among the most influential. Regarded by many as a visionary, and by some as half-mad, he became the father of information warfare doctrine in Russia. Panarin presaged a new American attack on the Kremlin, a sequel to the cold war, and proposed that Moscow needed new swords and shields. He argued that Andropov's mind-altering measures of media manipulation needed to be harnessed to mass media and multiplied a millionfold. From 2003 onward, he pushed to revive "the mechanism of foreign political propaganda which was completely destroyed in the 1990s" and to magnify its force with a satellite television network to broadcast Moscow's messages around the world. These ideas engendered and empowered RT, Putin's television news and propaganda service, established in 2005.

Within a decade, RT was reaching hundreds of millions of households with its blend of infotainment and disinformation, garnering tens of millions of Facebook followers, driving traffic to its platforms with a clever mix of clickbait and conspiracy theories.

Panarin called for Putin to establish "the Information KGB," a secret government center to train intelligence cadets and civilian computer wizards in the dark arts: manipulating facts to create falsehoods, turning misinformation into disinformation, using fabricated realities for everything from political lobbying to blackmail, spearheading secret operations to manipulate the media, shaping public opinion, influencing the behavior of political leaders, ultimately exerting a tidal pull on the course of human events. Those ideas would come to full flower during the American presidential election of 2016.

The idea of the Information KGB was more than a brainstorm; it was a way of seeing Putin's Russia, and a key to understanding Putin's thinking about political warfare, beyond the observation that his practice of judo informed his geopolitical conduct. The Information KGB could create a factory of facts that were not facts. It could make Russian politicians, plutocrats, soldiers, spies, think tanks, journalists, judges, scholars, and students in varying walks of life sing in harmony to music played by Putin's orchestra. The idea made perfect sense if you listened to Panarin's argument—and he argued at great length, with great force, as an article of faith, in the paranoid tradition of conspiracy theorists in general and Russian intelligence officers in particular—that American information warfare led by the CIA had caused the rise of Gorbachev and the fall of the Soviet Union. He had identified the six leading "directors of the information war against the USSR: A. Dulles, G. Kennan, D. Rockefeller, H. Kissinger, Z. Brzezinski, R. Reagan."

V. Putin strongly suspected Russia was still in America's crosshairs, and he wanted a battle plan for a new generation of political warfare. He began to urge his people to join in a great patriotic struggle.

He gave his military, intelligence, and political aides a multifaceted task: research, develop, and test weaponry for twenty-first-century battles—beginning with information warfare. Instead of grand strategies, he had grand ambitions. He wanted his nation to be seen as a global power, as it had been at the height of the cold war. He wished to reestablish his influence in the nations of the old Soviet Union, to make that influence felt around the world, and to contain and constrain the power of the United States. He needed a new kind of bomb.

The containment of America and the West was the ultimate goal as the doctrines of twenty-first-century Russian political warfare developed. Putin saw his strongest counterforce as information warfare, which the Russian defense ministry defined as the power to "undermine political, economic, and social systems; carry out mass psychological campaigns against the population of a state in order to destabilize society and the government; and force a state to make decisions in the interest of their opponents." He sought to master and marshal that force. He wanted to make Russia great again.

Putin told the Russian people that the collapse of the Soviet Union was the greatest political catastrophe of the twentieth century, greater than the two world wars, greater than the deaths of millions in Hitler's concentration camps and Stalin's gulags. He believed that American political warfare intended to undermine the Soviet Union had been far bigger, bolder, and more powerful than it really was; he was equally convinced that it never ceased after the cold war ended. (He has said with a straight face that the internet was a "CIA project" aimed at subverting Russia.) He saw the Yeltsin years as a grinding humiliation, the Bill-and-Boris act as a Punch-and-Judy show in which America constantly clobbered the Kremlin and Russia continually capitulated, as American consultants drafted the new Russian constitution, and the White House dictated the way of the world and the Kremlin's place in it. "At all turns," wrote Fiona Hill, America's most astute Kremlinologist after Kennan, "Putin saw U.S. and European institutions as actively fomenting dissent" against him and his country: first in Poland, where

American political warfare had achieved a singular success; then in East Germany, where he had seen it with his own eyes; then throughout Eastern Europe, in the Baltic states, and cascading into the Soviet Union itself. He thought that "Russia was clearly in their sights. The United States and its allies had openly discussed their intent to transform the Russian political system since the 1990s."

Putin believed that the CIA, the State Department, NATO, the European Union, the Western media, international nongovernmental organizations, and the Open Society Institute, financed by the Hungarian American billionaire George Soros, all were conspiring to wreck his plans to rebuild Russia's influence and power. He himself had sleeper agents sent by Russian intelligence who were living in the United States, trying to burrow their way into American think tanks and NGOs. So naturally he thought the same stratagems were arrayed against him. He saw the hidden hand of the United States at work in the popular revolutions that overthrew his allies and installed new leaders with democratic aspirations in Georgia and Ukraine.

In Georgia, President Eduard Shevardnadze, the aging and increasingly autocratic ruler who once had been Gorbachev's foreign minister, had rigged the November 2003 parliamentary election. The opposition, led by the thirty-six-year-old reformer Mikheil Saakashvili, a Columbia Law School graduate with connections in the State Department, rose up to demand an honest vote. Georgia's independent TV station gave voice to the rebellion. So did Soros's backing for pro-democracy groups and young activists clamoring for change. When Shevardnadze tried to seat the fraudulently elected parliament on November 22, Saakashvili and his supporters burst into the legislature, bearing roses in their hands, demanding that he step down. Shevardnadze's bodyguards hustled him away, and he resigned the next day. Saakashvili won a presidential election in January 2004, and his followers gained control of parliament in March.

So went the Rose Revolution, which the world saw as a democratic leader toppling a corrupt regime tied to the Kremlin, and which Putin regarded as a political nightmare, a replay of the 1989 uprisings in Poland, Hungary, Czechoslovakia, and East Germany. His anger deepened days later when Bulgaria, Estonia, Latvia, Lithuania, Romania, Slovakia, and Slovenia joined NATO in a formal ceremony at the Treasury Department in Washington, the biggest expansion of the alliance into the post-Soviet realm. The European Union soon incorporated seventy-three million people in Poland, Hungary, the Czech Republic, the Baltic states, and four other nations, another affront in Putin's eyes. The West was inexorably marching east to Russia's borders.

In Ukraine, the Orange Revolution soon followed. President Leonid Kuchma, a crooked old Communist Party chief, had picked his successor, the thuggish Viktor Yanukovych, a former coal trucking director twice convicted of assault in his youth. Their strategies and tactics had included propaganda spewed by government broadcast networks, covert support from the Kremlin, elaborate electoral fraud, the jailing of opponents, and the killing of a muckraking journalist; three high-ranking intelligence officers eventually were convicted of that murder. Their opponent was the popular former prime minister, Viktor Yushchenko, whom Kuchma had fired to forestall his rise to power. Orange was the new rose, the signifying color of his campaign. Russian media, widely broadcast in Ukraine, portrayed him as a crypto-fascist, a creature of the United States, and a puppet controlled by his American wife, who once had worked at the Pentagon.

When Putin's favorite son, Yanukovych, couldn't steal enough votes to win on the first ballot, he and his allies went to Washington for help. They hired a famously amoral American political consultant whose long client list had included an array of pro-American dictators, notably General Mobutu. Their man in Washington was Paul Manafort, the future Trump campaign chairman, and his role, the American embassy in Kyiv reported, was to perform an extreme makeover of Yanukovych and his allies, trying to change their image from a mafia family into a legitimate political party. That was a tall order:

a month before a court-ordered runoff election set for the end of December 2004, Yushchenko suddenly became horribly ill, his body wracked with pain, his face disfigured with lesions and half-paralyzed. Someone, likely a Russian intelligence officer, had used a huge dose of dioxin, a hard-to-detect cancer-causing compound, to poison his food.

The old regime tried to steal the runoff election. Yushchenko had called on his supporters to rally at the Maidan in Kyiv (*maidan* means "town square," but the word quickly came to signify independence itself). Soon several hundred thousand people were there around the clock, shivering through the long nights in a tent city. The vocal backers of their democracy movement had included a multitude of nongovernmental groups, the American embassy, and Secretary of State Colin Powell. More subtle American and European political and financial support had been flowing to the cause. A widely read online news outlet, *Ukrainska Pravda*, which had first exposed the old regime's corruption, survived through foreign financial support. So did the hope for a free and fair election. The ideas and technology for defeating election fraud—exit polls, ballot tabulations, vote monitors—were financed by Americans. It made a difference, if only in the margins; counting votes was not the same as voting. At the end of the struggle, the people spoke, and they defeated the Kremlin's candidate.

To the West, the color revolutions in Georgia and Ukraine looked like rays of hope. To Putin, they were part of a pattern of subversion and sabotage conducted by American intelligence against Russia, camouflaged as support for democracy. The United States, he said on December 4, 2004, was pursuing a "dictatorship of international affairs . . . wrapped up in a beautiful package of pseudo-democratic phraseology."

The victory of the Orange Revolution came a few hours before Bush ascended the steps of the Capitol to deliver his second inaugural address on January 20, 2005. The audience included his aged father, Presidents Carter and Clinton, and the American citizenry. He set forth a new goal for American political warfare: the Freedom

Agenda. "It is the policy of the United States to seek and support the growth of democratic movements and institutions in every nation and culture, with the ultimate goal of ending tyranny in our world," Bush proclaimed. "Because we have acted in the great liberating tradition of this Nation, tens of millions have achieved their freedom. And as hope kindles hope, millions more will find it. By our efforts, we have lit a fire as well, a fire in the minds of men. It warms those who feel its power. It burns those who fight its progress. And one day this untamed fire of freedom will reach the darkest corners of our world."

The president's speech had a messianic tinge. He invoked God, "the Maker of Heaven and earth," as the true creator of his policy to engender democracies and destroy tyranny: "History has an ebb and flow of justice, but history also has visible direction, set by liberty and the Author of liberty. . . . Renewed in our strength, tested but not weary, we are ready for the greatest achievements in the history of freedom."

He was upending the foundations of American foreign policy since World War II in favor of a crusade. America would spread freedom everywhere on earth as an existential struggle. The survival of liberty in the United States, Bush said, depended in great part on the expansion of democracy throughout the world. This was a foolish idea. James Madison had warned in 1787 that "democracies have ever been spectacles of turbulence and contention . . . and have in general been as short in their lives as they have been violent in their deaths."

Perhaps history was not a line ascending to enlightenment but a wheel turning back to brutality.

The great global democratic recession began in full as Bush put forth his Freedom Agenda, and it gathered and deepened thereafter. Perhaps it started with the revelations of the tortures in the CIA's secret prisons, the worst of which had taken place in Poland, or with the NSA's illegal surveillance of American citizens and its Orwellian overtones. Possibly Bush had gotten it precisely backward, and the expansion of democracy in the world depended on the resilience of liberty in the United States. Probably it was the ways in which Bush expanded American military and intelligence alliances with dictators in nations such as Saudi Arabia and Pakistan. Maybe it was when, in the first free and fair parliamentary election ever held by the Palestinian people, the militant Hamas party won and the United States refused to recognize the results. Surely it was the way the war in Iraq was going; the crusade to inject democracy into the Islamic world at gunpoint had gone haywire. His resplendent rhetoric aside, a truer expression of the way Bush saw the world came in the recounting of Lt. Gen. Ricardo Sanchez, who had been the top American commander in Iraq. As the war descended into chaos in the spring of 2004, the general wrote, Bush had shouted: "Kick ass! If somebody tries to stop the march to democracy, we will seek them out and kill them!"

Bush kept trying to will his vision into existence. In June 2005, he sent the new secretary of state, Condoleezza Rice, to the American University in Cairo, where she vowed: "The day is coming when the promise of a fully free and democratic world, once thought impossible, will also seem inevitable." His administration spent billions through the State Department, the Agency for International Development, the National Endowment for Democracy, countless consultants, and numberless nongovernmental organizations, all of them trying to package and export American democracy in the Arab world. They were pounding sand. The head of the State Department's Middle East Partnership Initiative, a deputy assistant secretary of state named J. Scott Carpenter, told the *Washington Post* reporter David Finkel at the end of 2005: "We don't know yet how best to promote democracy in the Arab Middle East. I mean we just don't know."

Bush had no strategy for the Iraq War once his army of liberation became an army of occupation. "We didn't know anything about Iraq," said Eric Edelman, his undersecretary of defense for policy. "Not only was the strategy not working, but we couldn't explain to anybody what it was we were trying to do," said Condoleeza Rice, his secretary of state. By March 2006, Bush was "bordering on despair" about the war, said John Negroponte, his director of national intelligence. Instead of facing reality, Bush burrowed deeper into the bunker of his ideology, increasingly disconnected from the realities of the world he was creating, the captain of a sinking ship. Iraq was in a state of civil war, its cities had become killing fields, 1.6 million of its people were internal refugees, 1.8 million had fled the country, and the Iraqi Interior Ministry's death squads were driving around Baghdad murdering people. Yet that month Bush extolled the triumphs of his Freedom Agenda in a formal National Security Strategy statement, claiming to have established democracy in Iraq and applauding the rise of political freedoms and civil liberties throughout the Middle East. Right after that litany, Bush listed the victories of the color revolutions in Georgia and Ukraine as his own. He asserted that they had brought hope for liberty and justice across all of Eurasia, the continent bordered by the Atlantic, the Pacific, the Arctic, the Mediterranean, and the Indian Ocean, the greatest part of which was Russian soil. He cautioned Putin "to move forward, not backward, along freedom's path."

The soaring language of the Freedom Agenda asserted that America was "leading a growing community of democracies" while in fact their number was shrinking all over the world. Many newly emerging democracies had been born into harsh terrain, and some failed to thrive. Nations that had spent a thousand years under tyrants did not transform into free republics overnight because the United States wished them to do so. Elections alone did not a democracy make; they could bring strongmen to power and keep them there. Democracy, as it developed, could not be easily exported; it was not a commodity like soybeans or sneakers but an ideal that lived in the mind. Bush and Cheney spoke of democracy on the march, crushing dictatorships, but they displayed an authoritarian streak in their actions. As the president gazed upon the nations of the world, mouthing platitudes about freedom in televised addresses, it was as if a chyron with the words of Larry Devlin's cable from the Congo were running underneath his face: "If we to be realistic, must be satisfied with democratic façade."

Putin had dropped that façade. He saw Bush failing in his role as the leader of the free world. He was rebuilding the Russian intelligence services to secure his power at home and strike back against America abroad. He had once told his former colleagues at the FSB, the KGB's main successor: "A group of FSB operatives, dispatched undercover to work in the government of the Russian federation, is successfully fulfilling its task." This was no joke. He had often said that there was no such thing as a former Chekist. He had installed Russian intelligence officers throughout the Kremlin, its key ministries, the media, the oil and gas industries that drove the economy, banking and finance companies, universities, and television stations. His *siloviki*—something between "security officers" and "power brokers"—were running Russia now. And beyond its borders, they sought to subvert and sabotage its enemies. They were creating a smash-and-grab world owing much to the political philosophy of Stalin and the czars and the business principles of the Mafia but above all to the traditions of the KGB.

Russia's intelligence and security services, television stations, hackers, and trolls were learning how to weaponize the powers of the internet and the vocabularies of social media to disrupt foreign governments and discredit democratic institutions. Putin started spending hundreds of millions of dollars creating and running government-funded think tanks, foundations, and thinly disguised nongovernmental organizations, establishing branch offices for information warfare throughout Europe, seeking to shape public opinion and to co-opt Western experts, academics, and politicians. The Kremlin began cultivating relationships with right-wing political activists in Austria, Hungary, Italy, France, Germany, Britain, and across the Atlantic in America. It would support the far right and the far left simultaneously, so long as they were fighting one another or attacking a common enemy. To divide and conquer was a glorious goal—but to divide would do.

Putin had fabricated a new intelligence state out of the rubble of the Soviet Union, and he was readying it for a re-inauguration of political warfare. He offered the new Russia—his corrupt and authoritarian nation—as the alternative to liberal democracy and a bulwark against political disorder and moral decay. After years of patient planning, he took vengeance on those who had opposed the power of the Kremlin, and launched the first of an escalating series of attacks against democracy in twenty-seven nations over the course of the next decade. And soon he would set his sights on the United States itself.

CHAPTER 9

THE FIRST CASUALTIES

For a generation, from the rise of Solidarity onward, the global power of the Kremlin had eroded like a sand castle lapped by the waves of the sea. In the spring of 2007, Vladimir Putin began fighting to turn back the tide.

On June 4, a secret cable from the American embassy in Estonia reported an epochal event with an eye-popping headline: "WORLD'S FIRST VIRTUAL ATTACK AGAINST NATION STATE." "Estonia has been the victim of the world's first coordinated cyberattacks against a nation state and its political and economic infrastructure," the embassy report began. "For over a month, government, banking, media, and other Estonian websites, servers, and routers came under a barrage of cyberattacks. . . . Experts cite the nature and sophistication of the attacks as proof of Russian government complicity."

This assault was the sixth time over the course of a millennium that the Russians had attacked the people of Estonia, whose capital, Tallinn, lay two hundred miles from Putin's birthplace, no longer called Leningrad, but once again Saint Petersburg, as its founder, Peter the Great, had christened it three centuries before.

The Soviet wartime reign in Estonia had been marked by rape, murder, the forced conscription of men and boys as slave laborers for the Red Army, and mass deportations to Siberia. One-third of the citizens had been killed or exiled. After the war, the Kremlin had ordered hundreds of thousands of Russians to colonize the country and consolidate the Kremlin's control. At the end of the cold war, Russians were roughly a third of the population of Estonia, constituting a state within a state; they ran key industries, organized-crime gangs, and money-laundering rings; they watched Russian television and socialized with their fellow Russians. Clinton had had to strong-arm Yeltsin to withdraw Russian military forces from the country. The Kremlin resisted for many months before Congress authorized $50 million to buy them out. They left behind a war memorial that stood over the remains of twelve Red Army troops in downtown Tallinn, a six-foot statue known as the Bronze Soldier; the last contingent of the living had headed east on August 30, 1994.

"It was quite a day," said Keith Smith, the chargé d'affaires at the new American embassy. "I remember walking around town and asking Estonians what they thought about it. I thought they'd be delirious. To a person, they said, 'they'll be back.'"

The Estonians found a unique way to liberate themselves from Russian economic, political, and social influence after they joined NATO in March 2004, having established a working democracy in a nation that had never known government by the people. By 2006, they had created an international exemplar of interconnectedness. Estonian software engineers had not only created Skype; they were helping to build a new society, where the only rituals requiring you to show up in person and present a document were marriage, divorce, and buying property. Everything else was online—government, banking, finance, insurance, communications, broadcast and print media, the balloting for elections. Wi-Fi was strong, ever present, and free. People began to call their homeland e-Estonia. They had created the first country whose political and social architectures were framed by an internet infrastructure—and perhaps the most technologically sophisticated nation on earth.

In April 2007, the authorities in Tallinn decided to move the Bronze Soldier from its pedestal to a military cemetery. Estonian patriots found it offensive, Russian nationalists came to Estonia to rally around it, and the statue became a flash point of confrontation. Russia's foreign affairs minister, Sergey Lavrov, called the decision disgusting; he warned of serious consequences for Estonia. An angry mob of Russians ran riot in the capital. In Moscow, young thugs laid siege to the Estonian embassy and forced it to shut down. And then Putin waged political warfare in a way that made Estonia's strength its weakness.

The first wave of the attacks started on April 27; its targets included the websites of Estonia's president, prime minister, parliament, and its foreign affairs and justice ministries. The initial barrage was carried out by an online mob spewing an avalanche of spam and fake news on Estonian networks, urged on by Russian-language chat forums that furnished downloadable software tools to carry out the vandalism. One hacker posted a forged letter from Prime Minister Andrus Ansip on government websites, apologizing for ordering the removal of the Bronze Soldier. Another posted a militant mission statement on a public forum: "Take Estonnet the fuck down :)."

On April 30, the cyber riot became a war. A series of coordinated distributed denial-of-service attacks struck Estonia. A multiplicity of malevolent systems flooded the nation's bandwidths, a DDoS blitzkrieg driven by Russian botnets, hundreds of thousands of computers hijacked by hackers overseen by the Kremlin's military and intelligence agencies. The onslaught came from internet service providers based in seventy-five nations around the world—including the United States, Russia, Canada, Germany, Belgium, Egypt, Turkey, and Vietnam. Its intensity reached ninety megabits per second (five Mbps is plenty for streaming high-definition videos on a home computer). As the flood swamped the nation's computer systems, Estonia went down. The attacks crashed not only the government's systems but those serving banks, businesses, telecommunications, and the media; Estonians couldn't use cash machines, pay their bills, or see the news. Russia also conducted economic warfare, cutting off oil deliveries and impeding over-the-road commerce between the two nations. The costs to Estonia, a country of 1.3 million people, were estimated at well over half a billion dollars. "They've basically been brought to their knees because of these attacks," said Howard Schmidt, who was by turns the White House cybersecurity adviser and a chief security officer at Microsoft.

Web War I peaked on May 9, 2007, the Russian anniversary of the end of World War II. On that day, after reviewing a parade of seven thousand Russian troops in Red Square, Putin came close to endorsing the attacks: "Those who are trying today to . . . desecrate memorials to war heroes" were vandals, bent on "sowing discord and new distrust between states and people." The lessons that the United States and NATO learned from the cyberwar were stark, though slow to take hold. "The potential exists for capabilities that are much more destructive," said Deputy Secretary of Defense William Lynn. "History will tell you that somebody will take it to the extreme." The greatest lesson was this: "What they do to us we cannot do to them," said Toomas Hendrik Ilves, the president of Estonia from 2006 to 2016. "Liberal democracies with a free press and free and fair elections are at an asymmetric disadvantage. . . . The tools of their democratic and free speech can be used against them."

The knowledge Russia reaped from the attack built on ideas established at the start of Putin's long reign. Before Estonia, the thrust of Russia's twenty-first-century political warfare had been defensive, as befitted a nation whose deepest historical memories were the invasions of Napoleon and Hitler, and whose leader perceived America's promotion of democracy in Russia during the Yeltsin years as insidious subversion. The first "Information Security Doctrine" that Russia promulgated under Putin established a need to "counter propagandistic information and psychological operations from a probable enemy." The threat was broadly defined as spiritual—*dukhovnyi*—especially when it came from "mass media use by foreign special services" to spread disinformation and undermine the Russian state.

After Estonia, retired major general Ivan Vorobyev, a former defense minister and, at the age of eighty-five, a grand old man of Russian military theory whose work was widely read by the political elites, wrote that it was time to go on a global offensive. He put forth a three-part shock doctrine: deceiving the enemy, getting inside his head to skew his thinking, and attacking his computers to disorient or disable his ability to command. Vorobyev wasn't only talking about the military, but about foreign policy and geopolitics: he said Russia needed above all to manage the perceptions of foreign leaders and the people they governed. Like his spiritual ancestor, Clausewitz, he saw all politics as warfare and warfare as the continuation of politics by other means.

The United States, Putin had said at the 2007 Munich Security Conference, wanted to create "a world in which there is one master, one sovereign." It ceaselessly preached democracy to Russia and the rest of the world—"but for some reason those who teach us do not want to learn themselves." He continued: "Today we are witnessing an almost uncontained hyper-use of force—military force—in international relations, a force that is plunging the world into an abyss of permanent conflicts. . . . The United States has overstepped its national borders in every way. This is visible in the economic, political, cultural and educational policies it imposes on other nations. Well, who likes this? Who is happy about this?"

In April 2008, NATO convened in Bucharest, and the alliance announced that it was open to admitting Georgia and Ukraine in the future, a move Bush endorsed in full. Putin was enraged. Those countries had been vitally important Soviet republics, and they held strategic and spiritual value for millions of Russians. Georgia was Stalin's birthplace, and its Black Sea resorts were playgrounds for the wealthy; to its south lay Turkey, Syria, and Iraq. More crucially, the roots of Russian empire had lain in Ukraine for more than a thousand years. When the Russians controlled it, they were a superpower; but without Ukraine, Russia was just another country. The republic had been the Soviet Union's breadbasket, Odessa its great trading port; it was now the largest nation in Europe, albeit one of the poorest.

"Trying to bring Georgia and Ukraine into NATO was truly overreaching," Bush's new secretary of defense—Bob Gates—wrote six years later. "Were the Europeans, much less the Americans, willing to send their sons and daughters to defend Ukraine or Georgia? Hardly. So NATO expansion was a political act, not a carefully considered military commitment, thus undermining the purpose of the alliance and recklessly ignoring what the Russians considered their own vital national interests." Gates had a good idea of how Putin would respond. He, too, had looked into Putin's eyes. He said he had seen a stone-cold killer—and a man haunted by lost empire, lost glory, and lost power.

In no way would Putin allow these two nations to align with the West. He was going to change the colors of their revolutions. "NATO was created at a time when there were two blocs confronting each other," Putin had told reporters in Bucharest, where NATO had let Russia look on as an outside observer. "Let's not get into the question of who were the good guys at the time. But it is obvious that today there is no Soviet Union, no eastern bloc and no Warsaw Pact."

Putin continued:

We have withdrawn our troops deployed in eastern Europe, and withdrawn almost all large and heavy weapons from the European part of Russia. And what happened? A base in Romania, where we

are now, one in Bulgaria, an American missile defense area in Poland
and the Czech Republic. That all means moving military infrastructure to our borders. Let's talk about it directly, honestly, frankly, cards
on the table.

He started laying down his hand.

He put plans for an attack on Georgia in motion days after he
left Bucharest. He had two goals from the outset: to test Russian
capabilities for information warfare, and to start a counterrevolution
in Georgia that would stop the expansion of NATO once and for
all. That spring, and into the summer, RT and other Russian media
painted Georgia's President Saakashvili as an unhinged warmonger
and an American stooge. Putin deployed *spetsnaz*, Russian special-
operations soldiers posing as peacekeepers, in the long-disputed
Georgian enclaves of Abkhazia and South Ossetia, where loyalties to
Russia and resistance to Saakashvili were strong. He signed decrees
establishing political and economic ties with those separatist regions
as if they were independent states, and the Kremlin issued Russian
passports to their residents.

His talking heads and internet trolls beat the war drums by assert-
ing that Moscow had to intervene to prevent an impending slaughter. Their theme was that NATO, led by the United States, was the
real aggressor in Georgia, arming and training Saakashvili's troops;
therefore Russia was compelled to defend innocent people fighting a
powerful enemy backed by the imperialist West. Putin launched military maneuvers on nearby Russian terrain. He sent warplanes aloft,
a thousand miles south of Moscow, flying into Georgia's air space to
fray the government's nerves. And before he made his move, he flew
in fifty handpicked Russian reporters whose fealty to the Kremlin
was unquestioned.

On July 29, 2008, paramilitary forces in South Ossetia began
shelling Georgian villages. On the night of August 7, the government
panicked. The Georgian military launched artillery into the enclave's

provincial capital. And then the Russians struck after midnight. Putin's tanks and troops rolled south, the first Russian military invasion of a sovereign nation in nearly thirty years, after Afghanistan in 1979, Czechoslovakia in 1968, and Hungary in 1956. The story quickly fell off the front page, another not terribly significant tragedy in a place few Americans could find on a map. But it was a watershed in the history of warfare.

Georgia was hit with a massive coordinated cyberattack in the first minutes of the war. It immediately struck fifty-four websites in the capital of Tbilisi, obliterating news and information. In a few hours, one-third of the nation's computer networks went down, including the official sites of Saakashvili, his government, and his ministries of defense and foreign affairs. The Russians leaped into the information void with terrifying tales of war crimes committed by Georgian soldiers in South Ossetia—the killing of pregnant women and children, the spearing of the wounded with bayonets, the slaughter of the innocents. Russian television inflated the actual figures of civilian deaths and refugees in South Ossetia by thousands.

"Putin Accuses Georgia of Genocide," read the headlines on RT on the second day of the war. He had flown from the Beijing Olympics to the edge of the war zone to conduct a staged television interview with two women who played the roles of terrorized refugees:

FIRST WOMAN: They burned our girls when they were still alive!
PUTIN: *Alive?*
FIRST WOMAN: Yes, young girls! They herded them like cattle
into a house and burned them. . . .
SECOND WOMAN: They stabbed a baby, he was one and a half.
They stabbed him in a cellar. . . .
PUTIN: I cannot even listen to this.
SECOND WOMAN: An old woman with two little kids—they
were running and a tank drove over them.
PUTIN: They must be crazy. This is genocide.

Governments around the world found these reports so disturbing that they doubted the wisdom of lending diplomatic support to Georgia. Human rights groups launched investigations into Russia's reports of pitiless atrocities. It was fake news, but it took time to prove its falsity, and while the fact-checkers tried to disprove one story, the Kremlin put out two more. Russia proved that it could use television and the internet as weapons, launching barrages of disinformation and demonization—aiming, as one analyst put it, to "dismiss the critic, distort the facts, distract from the main issue, and dismay the audience." Russia's war in Georgia revived an old joke among the bloggers of Moscow. Hitler comes back from the dead and reviews the annual May Day parade of Russia's tanks and missiles. A silent smile plays on his lips. A Russian general leans over and says: "Bet you're thinking if you had those weapons you wouldn't have lost the war." *Nein*, says Hitler: "I was just thinking that if I had a newspaper like your *Pravda*, no one ever would have found out that I did!"

In the twentieth century, when the Kremlin invaded a sovereign nation, the West had reacted with horror and outrage. Now, there were expressions of concern followed by silence. The military campaign was over in five days, and while the Russian army did not distinguish itself in battle, its soldiers split Georgia into two by seizing its east-west highway. Today Russian forces still occupy a fifth of the country, two hundred thousand people driven from their homes have not returned, and Georgia remains a wounded nation, frozen in a state of conflict, sundered and isolated. Putin's goal had not been conquest. It was to show the world that he could marshal a counterforce against the West, contain its expansion of power, and control its perceptions.

The information war was more important than the war itself. Putin had given new meaning to the old saying that the first casualty of war is truth. Truth was the main enemy now.

Putin had launched "a new form of warfare" in which the human mind was the main battlefront, a comprehensive assessment by the Modern War Institute at West Point concluded a decade later. Using disinformation and deception, "Russia created the time and space to shape the international narrative in the critical early days of the conflict." The West Point study saw four essential elements of Russian information warfare on display in Georgia and thereafter: "First, and most benignly, it aims to put the best spin it can on ordinary news; second, it incites a population with fake information in order to prep a battlefield; third, it uses disinformation or creates enough ambiguity to confuse people on the battlefield; and fourth, it outright lies." The overarching Russian strategy was "to degrade trust in institutions across the world." As Mikhail Zygar, the former editor in chief of TV Rain, the only independent Russian national television network, wrote: "Russian television doesn't suggest that Russian leaders are any better or less corrupt, or more honest and just, than Western leaders. Rather, it says that everything is the same everywhere. All the world's politicians are corrupt. . . . All elections are falsified. Democracy doesn't exist anywhere, so give it up."

Americans didn't give much thought to a small war in a faraway place as it flickered across their screens that summer. The United States was teetering on the edge of a disastrous recession sparked by fraud and greed, and Senators Barack Hussein Obama and John McCain were contesting a presidential election in which the rest of the world looked insignificant next to saving the American economy from disaster. But Obama was looking beyond the borders of the United States in a way that transfixed the world's attention. The forty-seven-year-old first-term senator with the highly inconvenient name had captured the nomination in June, decisively defeating Hillary Clinton in the campaign primaries. In July 2008, before the Democratic convention, he set out for Afghanistan, Kuwait, Iraq, Israel, the West Bank, Britain, France, and Germany. By the time he got to Berlin, where he spoke to a crowd of two hundred thousand people gathered at the Victory Column in the city's central park, the Tiergarten, he was running for the vacant position of leader of the free world.

He invoked the memory of the 1948 Berlin Airlift, when American planes ferrying food had broken the Soviet blockade of the divided and desperate city:

> In the darkest hours, the people of Berlin kept the flame of hope burning.... Hundreds of thousands of Berliners came here, to the Tiergarten, and heard the city's mayor implore ... "People of the world, look at Berlin!"
>
> People of the world—look at Berlin!
>
> Look at Berlin, where Germans and Americans learned to work together and trust each other less than three years after facing each other on the field of battle.
>
> Look at Berlin, where the determination of a people met the generosity of the Marshall Plan and created a German miracle; where a victory over tyranny gave rise to NATO, the greatest alliance ever formed to defend our common security....
>
> When you, the German people, tore down that wall—a wall that divided East and West; freedom and tyranny; fear and hope—walls came tumbling down around the world....
>
> People of Berlin—people of the world—this is our moment. This is our time.... We are heirs to a struggle for freedom. We are a people of improbable hope. With an eye toward the future, with resolve in our hearts, let us remember this history, and answer our destiny, and remake the world once again.

Healing the world would prove harder than raising its hopes. No president ever had been left a more dismal legacy by his predecessor. Untamed fire had scorched the earth at home and abroad. Obama inherited a howling recession that wiped out millions of Americans' jobs and savings; two wars, with 161,000 American troops in Iraq and 38,000 more in Afghanistan, some on their third and fourth tours of duty, their commanders with no clear goal in sight nor any glimmer of light at the end of the tunnel; and an American political warfare machine that now resembled a rusting 1948 Cadillac resting on cinder blocks. Bush had run it off the road.

Having come to power from farther on the left than any president before him, Obama tacked sharply to the center in the realm of national security. He asked the old cold warrior Bob Gates to stay on as secretary of defense, chose the four-star marine general Jim Jones as his national security adviser, and after twisting her arm made Hillary Clinton his secretary of state. Clinton's six years on the Senate Armed Services Committee—she never missed a meeting—had made her something of a hawk. She had supported, while Obama had opposed, Bush's resolve to go to war in Iraq, which now looked like the worst foreign policy decision any president had ever made, and on the campaign trail, she had called Obama's stated willingness to talk to America's most strident enemies as "irresponsible, and frankly naïve." At her confirmation hearings, she said she would use "all elements of our power—diplomacy, development, and defense"—and the fourth *d* of democracy was mentioned only in passing. "While our democracy continues to inspire people around the world," she said, "we know that its influence is greatest when we live up to its teachings ourselves."

America had not done that. Its influence had fallen to a seventy-year ebb under Bush, and the inspirational rhetoric of Obama could not revive it. Promoting democracy and pushing back against Putin were not in the first rank of the new president's priorities. He now was in charge of the war machinery of the Pentagon and the CIA, the lethal weapons of counterinsurgency and counterterrorism, and as Obama sent more troops into Afghanistan and deployed a barrage of Predators and special-operations forces to hunt and kill America's enemies abroad, the greatest part of the foreign policy of the United States was not executed by diplomats and democracy advocates but by soldiers and spies. "It too often became surge surge surge, drone

drone drone," said Harold Hongju Koh, the Yale Law School dean
who had left to serve as Clinton's legal adviser at the State Department.

Political warfare lived, though barely, and it was often incoherent
at best. Obama's vainglorious envoy Richard Holbrooke tried to fix
the 2009 presidential election in Afghanistan, but he did it brazenly,
and he failed miserably. Bob Gates later called that effort "our clumsy
and failed putsch." At a meeting of the NATO defense ministers, the
UN high representative, Kai Eide, leaned over to Gates and whispered: "I am going to tell the ministers that there was blatant foreign
interference in the Afghan election. What I will not say is it was the
United States and Richard Holbrooke."

Obama had a highly centralized power structure at the White
House, but he handed the Russia portfolio to Clinton. She, too, had
scoffed at Bush's claim to have formed a spiritual bond with Russia's
leader. "This is the president that looked in the soul of Putin," Clinton
had said during the primaries. "He was a KGB agent. By definition
he doesn't have a soul. . . . This is nonsense, but this is the world that
we're living in." The world, on the surface, had changed. Putin had
been barred by Russia's constitution from a third consecutive term,
so he became the prime minister and, on paper, ceded the presidency
to Dmitry Medvedev, a good-looking young Saint Petersburg politician who served as the velvet glove for Putin's iron fist. While Putin
still called the shots, Medvedev and Foreign Minister Sergey Lavrov
handled diplomacy with the United States. Clinton set out to reset
American relations with Russia, writing Lavrov to propose that they
work together on START, a new strategic arms reduction treaty, as
well as Afghanistan, Iran, and the Middle East. Their first meeting
started off on a false note. In March 2009, at a news conference in
Geneva, Clinton gave Lavrov her best smile and handed him a big
red button mounted on a yellow box and labeled with the word *reset*
in English and the word *peregruzka* in Russian. "We worked hard to
get the right Russian word," she told him. "Do you think we got it?"

"You got it wrong," Lavrov said. Someone at the State Department had screwed up: *peregruzka* means "overload." Despite the awkward beginning, over the course of more than a year, the Americans and the Russians cooperated as Clinton had proposed. They agreed at the United Nations to impose harsh economic penalties that coerced Iran into negotiating limits to its nuclear program. They worked to reduce their teeming nuclear weapons stockpiles. The Russians let American military planes use their airspace to resupply soldiers in Afghanistan. Obama invited Medvedev to the White House, and they set the date for June 18, 2010. The day before Medvedev landed, an urgent meeting took place in the Situation Room, led by Obama, Vice President Joe Biden, Bob Gates, FBI director Robert Mueller, and CIA director Leon Panetta, an intelligence novice who had served sixteen years in Congress and four years as President Clinton's chief of staff.

Mueller told the president that the United States urgently needed to extract a highly valued intelligence source from Moscow. The source had identified a ring of ten "illegals"—an underground network of sleeper agents working for the Russian Foreign Intelligence Service. They had been living in the United States for a decade, since the start of the Putin era. They had come to the United States with fake passports and invented identities, and they worked as teachers, real estate brokers, travel agents. They included married couples with young kids who didn't know their parents' true names. And they couldn't be charged with espionage—because they hadn't done any actual spying yet, as far as the FBI could tell. The role of a sleeper is to await orders to awake and act. One of them was going back to Moscow, signaling something big was afoot. So now the FBI wanted to round up the whole web at once, and that, in turn, could expose the source. Medvedev probably didn't even know this Russian underground existed. But Putin surely did.

Obama exploded. "Just as we're getting on track with the Russians, this? This is a throwback to the Cold War. This is right out of John le Carré. We put START, Iran, the whole relationship with Russia at risk for this kind of thing?" Gates, the intelligence veteran, told the president to play political hardball: confront Medvedev, really stick it to him—is *this* your idea of a reset, Dmitry?—and drive a wedge between him and Putin. Panetta, the political pro, advised the president to follow the cold war intelligence playbook— deport the sleepers and swap them for four Russians imprisoned by Putin for spying for the United States and Britain. Obama took his advice. Putin gave the sleepers a hero's welcome when they returned. Their story became a popular television series, *The Americans*, and the White House moved on to the next crisis, which at any given moment was usually fifteen minutes away.

The men in the Situation Room that day, along with Hillary Clinton, Director of National Intelligence James Clapper, and Obama's counterterrorism chief, John Brennan, were sitting "at the bottom of the huge funnel pouring problems from Pandora's global trove into Washington . . . dealing daily with multiple problems, pivoting on a dime from one issue to another . . . then making decisions, always with too little time and too much ambiguous information," Gates wrote, "and that is a problem in its own right: exhausted people do not make the best decisions." This human factor helped to fuel a terrible choice Obama made after the uprisings of the Arab Spring gained force in 2011.

In February, immense demonstrations in Cairo forced the aging strongman Hosni Mubarak to end his thirty-year reign in Egypt, a move openly endorsed by Obama. Four days later, protesting lawyers and students took aim at Muammar Qaddafi, the half-mad dictator who had ruled Libya since 1969. Qaddafi started massacring them, igniting an armed rebellion in which some of his own security forces sided with the people. The opposition took control of the sprawling city of Benghazi, and Qaddafi sent his soldiers to take it back, threatening a bloodbath in which thousands would die. Obama said Qaddafi had to go. The question was how. Clinton wanted to use military force to stop him from slaughtering civilians, by bombing his military bases and command headquarters, including his residences. Biden, Gates, and Brennan were adamantly against starting another war in the Middle East. On the campaign trail, Obama had argued that a president could not launch a military attack absent an actual or imminent threat to the United States. As commander in chief, he chose force, backed by the Republican-led Congress, a NATO coalition, and a UN Security Council resolution, which passed with Russia abstaining, a last result of the reset. Putin denounced that vote. Borrowing Qaddafi's own words, he said the resolution resembled medieval calls for a Christian crusade.

The NATO military campaign—fueled by American warplanes, bombs, missiles, drones, intelligence, and reconnaissance—destroyed the regime. And when it dissolved, Libya swiftly descended into a war of all against all, with rival militias backed by Saudi Arabia and Turkey killing one another, and a million migrants trying to flee the chaos, all going down a road to hell paved by the best humanitarian intentions. Obama later called this debacle the worst choice of his presidency. It was the death of America's militant drive to remake the Middle East in the name of democracy.

On October 20, 2011, the rebels overran Qaddafi's last stronghold, found him hiding in a drainpipe, sodomized him with a bayonet, and killed him, capturing his last moments on video. Putin watched that tape over and over again, probably thinking that this was what happened when America wanted to change a regime— Milošević dead in a prison cell, Saddam with a noose around his neck, Qaddafi on the wrong end of a spear.

Four weeks before, the United Russia party, created by Putin for Putin and his power, had held a convention in a stadium outside Moscow. The Russian-born American journalist Julia Ioffe was there taking notes. "Medvedev takes the stage, and he says, 'I've done a lot of thinking,'" she recounted. "And immediately people can tell something's wrong. He looks like he's been up all night, either drinking

or crying. He doesn't look good. And then people start listening to
what he's saying. Nobody usually listens to what he's saying. . . . And
he says, 'I've decided that I think Vladimir Putin should run for the
presidency in 2012.' And jaws drop."

United Russia retained control of the Russian parliament in
December 2011. The election was entirely fraudulent: Putin's appa-
ratchiks harassed the opposition, stuffed ballot boxes, manhandled
poll watchers, and launched cyberattacks on the websites of election
observers. "Russian voters deserve a full investigation of electoral fraud
and manipulation," Secretary Clinton said in a speech in Lithuania a
few days later. "The Russian people, like people everywhere, deserve
the right to have their voices heard and their votes counted. And that
means they deserve fair, free, transparent elections and leaders who are
accountable to them." Thousands of Russian citizens now took to the
streets. Putin accused Clinton of inciting them. The demonstrations
grew, the biggest since the fall of the Soviet Union. "Putin is a thief!"
protesters chanted. "Russia without Putin!" The specter of the Arab
Spring demonstrations haunted the Kremlin. Putin said, louder this
time, that hundreds of millions of dollars in foreign money was influencing Russian politics and that Clinton was the opposition's puppet
master, working in secret to subvert him. "She set the tone for certain actors inside the country; she gave the signal," he insisted on
December 8. "They heard the signal, and with the support of the
U.S. State Department began active work." He issued an ominous
warning to anyone who would dare to influence Russian politics on
behalf of the United States.

After his preordained reelection as president in March 2012, Putin
cracked down on Russian news outlets that didn't dance to his tune.
"The Kremlin successfully erodes the integrity of investigative and
political journalism, producing a lack of faith in traditional media," the
Soviet-born author Peter Pomerantsev wrote as the noose tightened on
what remained of the free press in Russia. He saw "new propaganda"
emerging, and he said its goal was "not to convince or persuade, but

to keep the viewer hooked and distracted, passive and paranoid." RT, which received more than $1 billion a year from the Kremlin, began to fine-tune its English-language shows, targeting the fringes of the American political spectrum on the right and the left. After the BBC, it was now the most popular foreign news source in the United States, reaching millions of viewers in the United States. Its mission, as Putin put it in an interview with RT, was to "break the monopoly of Anglo-Saxon global information streams."

Putin repressed or expelled an array of international human rights groups. Under intense pressure from the Kremlin, the United States Agency for International Development shut its doors after two decades of trying to support democracy and the rule of law in Russia. Putin forced dozens of nongovernmental organizations out of the country and created in their stead state-sponsored NGOs that served as propaganda platforms. They became "a real-world equivalent of the Internet troll armies that insecure, authoritarian, repressive regimes have unleashed on Twitter," as an American ambassador to the Organization for Security and Co-operation in Europe put it. "They use essentially the same tactics as their online counterparts—creating noise and confusion, flooding the space, using vulgarity, intimidating those with dissenting views, and crowding out legitimate voices."

Shortly after Putin began his third term, a shadowy organization called the Internet Research Agency, a troll farm in Saint Petersburg financed by a Kremlin oligarch, began planning to target American voters, using techniques of disinformation and deception that it was already testing on Russian citizens and their neighbors in Eastern Europe. At the same time, the CIA, the National Security Agency, and private security firms detected a growing wave of cyberespionage attacks conducted by the Russian military intelligence service, the GRU, and the foreign intelligence service, the SVR. They were stealing information to gain a strategic advantage for the Kremlin. They often used spear-phishing emails with malicious attachments crafted to attract their targets' interest. And their targets included governments, embassies, militaries, political parties, think tanks, international and regional defense groups, and media outlets from the United States to Ukraine. The information they stole was ammunition stockpiled in a virtual arsenal.

On February 26, 2013, a justly obscure Russian newspaper called the *Military-Industrial Courier* reprinted a speech that General Valery Gerasimov, chief of the General Staff of the Armed Forces of the Russian Federation, had given at the end of January. It might have gone unnoticed in the West but for the efforts of Rob Coalson, a talented reporter at Radio Free Europe/Radio Liberty, who translated it and posted it. Months later, Mark Galeotti, a prolific Kremlinologist, picked it up and published it online with a snappy title, "The Gerasimov Doctrine." As Galeotti later noted with chagrin, after it had gained worldwide attention and stirred considerable alarm, it was neither a doctrine nor a declaration of war on the West. But it was a deep look into how the Russian military saw the color revolutions and the Arab Spring as anarchic creations of American intelligence, and it was a foreshadowing of how Moscow might fight back against the power and influence of NATO and the United States without using tanks and missiles.

"In the 21st century we have seen a tendency toward blurring the lines between the states of war and peace," Gerasimov began. "Wars are no longer declared and, having begun, proceed according to an unfamiliar template. . . . A perfectly thriving state can, in a matter of months and even days, be transformed into an arena of fierce armed conflict, become a victim of foreign intervention, and sink into a web of chaos, humanitarian catastrophe, and civil war." He continued:

> The very "rules of war" have changed. The role of nonmilitary means of achieving political and strategic goals has grown, and, in many cases, they have exceeded the power of force of weapons in their effectiveness. . . . All this is supplemented by military means of a

concealed character, including carrying out actions of informational conflict and the actions of special-operations forces. The open use of forces—often under the guise of peacekeeping and crisis regulation—is resorted to only at a certain stage, primarily for the achievement of final success in the conflict.

All war now depended on political warfare in the eyes of the Kremlin.

Putin fixed on his next target: Ukraine, bordering Russia to its east, the warm waters of the oil-rich Black Sea to its south, four NATO allies to its west. The imprint of seven decades as a Soviet republic lay deep in its soil. A statue of Lenin still stood on one end of the main street of the capital, Kyiv, and another in the image of Felix Dzerzhinsky, the father of Soviet spies, graced a town named after him. No one had dared to tear them down. The power of the Kremlin still resonated.

When the Soviet Union dissolved, it had left 2,000 strategic nuclear warheads and 2,500 tactical nuclear weapons in Ukraine; the unstable and insecure country possessed the world's third-largest nuclear arsenal. The threat of loose nukes haunted Washington. Bill Clinton and Boris Yeltsin had cut a deal with Ukraine in December 1994. It would send the weapons to Russia to be destroyed with American know-how. Ukraine received promises in exchange for giving up that power: Russia would respect its sovereignty and its borders, forswearing "the threat or the use of force" against its independence, and the United States would protect it against Russian aggression through the United Nations. The Ukrainian people would soon find out how ironclad these assurances were.

The corrupt Viktor Yanukovych had returned to power in the last election, thanks to the efforts of the equally crooked political consultant Paul Manafort, whose office manager in Kyiv, Konstantin Kilimnik, had deep ties to Russian intelligence. Their paymasters included tycoons enmeshed with both organized crime and the Kremlin.

Manafort collected many millions in fees from Yanukovych, laundering them in offshore accounts, and attracting the attention of the FBI, which began wiretapping him in a foreign intelligence investigation. Manafort also cut business deals with the country's richest and most odious oligarchs, including Dmytro Firtash, a Putin crony and a prominent associate of Russian organized crime indicted on federal corruption charges in Chicago in October 2013. Firtash was the Ukrainian middleman for Gazprom, the Russian state-run natural gas giant. Putin used the company as an instrument of statecraft and an engine of corruption. Firtash bought gas from Gazprom at a steep discount. He marked it up threefold when he sold it to Ukraine, pocketing $3 billion and paying pro-Russian politicians, chiefly Yanukovych, to do the Kremlin's bidding. Through the oligarch's largesse, the president paid Manafort his millions.

Mirroring Manafort's outrageously expensive tastes, Yanukovych had built a $250 million mansion north of Kyiv with marble staircases and golden toilets and a zoo stocked with peacocks and wild boars, all with funds stolen from his nation's treasury. These two men personified the corruption and greed that had permeated the country's political and economic systems.

In the fall of 2013, Manafort urged his client to strike a free-trade agreement with the European Union, linking Ukraine to the West and corporate America. Yanukovych openly embraced the deal. Public opinion overwhelmingly favored it. But Putin didn't. He would no more let Ukraine associate with the EU than he would allow it into NATO. He believed it was his country: a core element of Russia itself. (At the sidelines of the 2008 NATO summit in Bucharest, he had tried to make Bush grasp this idea in simple language: "You don't understand, George. Ukraine is not even a state. What is Ukraine? Part of its territories is Eastern Europe, but the greater part is a gift from us.") The greatest gift was the Crimean Peninsula, home to Russia's Black Sea Fleet, and a land that Russia had controlled since the eighteenth century, until Khrushchev had transferred it to Ukraine in 1954, in atonement for Stalin's genocidal repression of its people.

Putin met with Yanukovych twice, in late October and again in early November 2013, and he threatened him in no uncertain terms, as a KGB case officer would talk to a deeply compromised recruited foreign agent. He had two ways of making him balk. Russia could, and would, inflict deep economic pain on Ukraine, or it could loan it billions. And Russian intelligence had gathered an encyclopedia of *kompromat* on Yanukovych that it could unleash at any time. An EU summit was set for November 28 in Lithuania, and everyone expected that Yanukovych would sign the pact. But he pulled out. One thousand protesters marched down the streets of Kyiv to the Maidan that night. Three nights later, there were one hundred thousand. Soon there were hundreds of thousands. They weren't waving orange banners, but the blue flags of the European Union. Russian media depicted them as a rabble of neo-Nazis. Yanukovych forced a law against the protests through the Ukrainian parliament and tried to add Putinesque clauses to the constitution. The demonstrators now wanted two things: their country in Europe and their president out of office.

The United States pressed the European Union to midwife a power-sharing pact between Ukraine's president and his political opponents, but the EU's ministers were dithering, nervous about picking a fight with Putin. On January 27, 2014, the assistant secretary of state for Europe and Eurasia, Victoria Nuland, telephoned the American envoy in Ukraine, Geoffrey Pyatt. Nuland held the highest diplomatic rank in the Foreign Service, career ambassador, and the relationship with Russia was part of her portfolio; she had dealt with the Russians in one way or another for thirty years.

She thought it was high time to get the United Nations involved in brokering a change in the government of Ukraine.

"That would be great," Nuland said, "to help glue this thing and to have the UN help glue it and, you know, fuck the EU."

"Exactly," Pyatt said. "I think we've got to do something to make it stick together because you can be pretty sure that if it does start to gain altitude, that the Russians will be working behind the scenes to try to torpedo it."

Russian spies were monitoring and taping the call, in which the American diplomats discussed whom among Yanukovych's opponents to support. A few days later, the eavesdroppers posted the conversation on YouTube for the world to hear. "They hadn't put a phone call on the street publicly in twenty-five years," Nuland later observed. "Putin knew exactly what we were doing. . . . It was later very useful to him to make me and us the poster child for interference in another country's affairs."

This theft of strategic information was part of a bigger Russian campaign in Ukraine that had been going on for months. "Operation Armageddon," a persistent cyberespionage program aimed at disrupting the effort to link up with the EU, targeted Ukrainian government, law enforcement, and military officials. While Putin was proudly presiding at the 2014 Winter Olympics in Sochi, six hundred miles southeast of Kyiv—Russian athletes won at least fifteen medals at the games with the aid of a state-sponsored doping program overseen by intelligence officers—his minions were bombarding Ukrainian TV stations, news outlets, and politicians with repeated distributed denial-of-service attacks.

On February 18, Yanukovych's soldiers and snipers began using live ammunition to slaughter protesting civilians; they killed one hundred people over the course of three days. His political allies began to abandon him. Five days later, in an evacuation overseen by Putin, he fled to Russia. The Russian media went into high gear: a fascist junta had taken power in Kyiv, in a coup ordered by the United States and the EU, ousting a democratically elected president by force. As Yanukovych went underground, Putin led the closing ceremonies in Sochi and ordered Russian special-operations forces and troops based at the headquarters of the Black Sea Fleet to seize Crimea's airfields and its regional parliament. Thousands of Russian soldiers, their uniforms bearing no insignia, took control of the peninsula. Putin insisted that they were local militias. Defense Minister Sergei Shoigu denied that Russian troops were in Crimea even as Ukrainian soldiers surrendered to them. The Ukrainians started calling the invaders "little green men," evidently from outer space.

The Russians cut Ukraine's fiber-optic cables and attacked the national telecommunications company, which lost its connections between the peninsula and the rest of Ukraine; mobile, landline, and internet access were all afflicted. The main Ukrainian government and media websites were knocked out by DDoS attacks and the cell phones of Ukrainian parliamentarians were hacked. Putin summoned Yanukovych to his home and ordered him to sign a backdated letter asking Russia to invade Ukraine. On March 18, he walked into the Kremlin and announced to thundering applause that Crimea was reunified with Russia.

Putin had broken the rules, treaties, and understandings about the sovereignty of nations and the inviolability of borders that had kept the peace in Europe since World War II. No nation on earth had taken another's land like this since Saddam Hussein invaded Kuwait in 1990. And the Russians hadn't fired a shot. Cyberwarfare, media manipulation, and psyops had done the trick. It was twenty-first-century political warfare at its most potent.

And Putin wasn't finished. In southeastern Ukraine lived thousands of people who spoke Russian and identified with the Soviet Union. On April 17, Putin referred to this land as *Novorossiya*—New Russia—as it had been in the eighteenth century under Catherine the Great. Official websites in that name had already been registered. Within days, new battalions of little green men took municipal and regional government buildings and proclaimed the establishment of the People's Republics of Donetsk and Lubansk. The outgunned Ukrainian army struggled to mobilize throughout the spring and into the summer as Putin sent tens of thousands of soldiers without uniforms and many tons of arms and ammunition into the region, all the while insisting that they weren't there. Ukraine would lose more than thirteen thousand soldiers fighting the Russians over the next five years; the war created millions of refugees and left four million more stranded in the separatist republics. The stakes of the conflict were great. "If Ukraine succeeds in breaking free of Russian influence, it is possible for Europe to be whole, free, democratic, and at peace," said William B. Taylor Jr., the American ambassador to Ukraine from 2006 to 2009. "In contrast, if Russia dominates Ukraine, Russia will again become an empire, oppressing its people, and threatening its neighbors and the rest of the world."

On May 25, Ukraine held a presidential vote. The Russian military intelligence service unleashed its most potent malware against it. The American security firms CrowdStrike and FireEye had already identified the cyberespionage weapon that ran the operation. CrowdStrike nicknamed the malware's masterminds Fancy Bear. FireEye reported a few months later that the operation had "a government sponsor—specifically, a government based in Moscow," and that similar cyberweapons had been targeting government, military, and security organizations since at least 2007. Fancy Bear enabled Russian hackers to get inside the Ukrainian election commission's computers, compromise them, destroy their tally of votes, and post results on the commission's website showing that a right-wing Russsophile fringe candidate had won the presidency. Russian television networks reported the fake news. It took forty minutes before the commission detected the attack and corrected the facts. It wasn't long before Fancy Bear and its cousin, Cozy Bear, started burrowing into the government of the United States.

On July 17, Putin's troops shot down a civilian plane, Malaysia Airlines Flight MH-17, bound from Amsterdam to Kuala Lumpur, over southeastern Ukraine, killing all 298 people on board. He insisted Russia had nothing to do with it. "Of course not!" he said indignantly. To counter the harsh facts, the Kremlin put a conspiracy theory out on the internet. "I saw people claiming the CIA had put dead bodies inside a plane and purposely shot it down to create propaganda against the Russian government," said Sri Preston Kulkarni, the campaign director for the Ukraine Communications Task Force. "People were repeating that story again and again. . . . And I realized we had gone through the looking glass at that point and that if people could believe that, they could believe almost anything." It took more than three years before the Dutch and Australian governments published an official report holding Russia responsible for shooting down the aircraft.

The fog of war was now a toxic miasma of disinformation spewing from Russian television and social media. Russian talking heads and internet trolls peddled all manner of conspiracy theories and shameless concoctions. The brave separatists of New Russia were being slaughtered. Ukrainian soldiers had tortured and crucified a three-year-old boy in a public square. The government in Kyiv was building concentration camps financed by the European Union. It had filled the forests with neo-Nazi assassins. It had poisoned the region's water supply. And the United States and NATO were aiding and abetting all of it. On September 4, General Philip Breedlove, NATO's top military commander, said this cascade of lies was an aspect of "the most amazing information warfare blitzkrieg we have ever seen." The message from the Kremlin was that reality could be bent to its will, because objective truth did not exist, and thus falsehoods could trump facts. As Kennan had written in the Long Telegram back in February 1946: "The very disrespect of Russians for objective truth—indeed, their disbelief in its existence—leads them to view all stated facts as instruments for furtherance of one ulterior purpose or another." Now the internet could magnify their clandestine ambitions a millionfold.

The United States did little in direct response to Putin's war on truth. "We had a massive information gap," Ambassador Nuland said. "We didn't have the kind of intelligence assets where we could prove that he was lying about Russian involvement. We knew internally, we knew as a matter of policy debate, but we weren't doing well in the court of public opinion."

The Russians' information warfare attacks now began striking at the heart of American government. By August 2014, Cozy Bear was prowling in the Pentagon; the Joint Chiefs of Staff's unclassified email system was hacked. In October, the White House discovered that the Kremlin's spies were reading Obama's unclassified emails and collecting the addresses of his correspondents. In November, the National Security Agency found the Russians rooting around in the computer archives of the State Department, likely seeking dirt on Hillary Clinton, already the unannounced front-runner for the next presidential election. Richard Ledgett, the NSA's deputy director, later described a weekend in which his cybercommand fought "hand-to-hand combat" against a Cozy Bear attack within the State Department's networks. Instead of disappearing when detected, the hackers battled back. "We would take an action; they would then counter that," he said. "It was about a 24-hour period of parry-riposte, parry-riposte, measure, countermeasure. That was new. That's a new level of interaction between a cyber attacker and a defender." It was as if the Russians wanted the president of the United States and his presumptive successor to know they were lurking in the shadows, looking over their shoulders in silence.

When Putin invaded Ukraine and seized Crimea in the name of a resurgent Russia, Obama had been at a nuclear security conference in The Hague, where he disdainfully disparaged his rival as the embattled leader of a second-rate nation. "Russia is a regional power that is threatening some of its immediate neighbors—not out of strength but out of weakness," Obama had said. "They don't pose the number-one national security threat to the United States. I continue to be much more concerned when it comes to our security with the prospect of a nuclear weapon going off in Manhattan."

But Putin had another kind of weapon at the ready, and its long fuse was about to be lit. He wanted to undermine democracy in America, and how better to achieve that aim than to elect a dangerous demagogue as president?

CHAPTER 10

DEMOCRACY
IN AMERICA

The Internet Research Agency set out to alter the mind of the American body politic in the spring of 2014. Working at the direction of the Kremlin and in concert with Russian intelligence, the IRA became the Information KGB.

Financed by an oligarch, Yevgeny Prigozhin, a convicted pimp who became a close confidant of Putin's, the IRA began to assemble a workforce of four hundred trolls working twelve-hour shifts at a four-story building in Saint Petersburg; many were hipsters in their twenties and thirties, sporting stylish clothes and cool haircuts. Marat Mindiyarov, an unemployed teacher who lasted four months at the IRA, said the job required him "to write that white is black and black is white. Your first feeling, when you ended up there, was that you were in some kind of factory that turned lying, telling untruths, into an industrial assembly line."

The IRA created a new branch: the American Desk, also known as the Translator Department. It vetted its new hires for their fluency in American English, which was often slightly imperfect, and their feel for the nuances of American political discourse, which was

usually quite impressive. It trained its internet-savvy young employees to understand the issues that divided Americans—gun rights, gay
rights, immigration, the Confederate flag and its racist connotations.
They learned how to argue online in ways that could deepen the frac-
tures in the American political system. Aleksandra Krylova, the IRA's
third-ranking employee, and Anna Bogacheva, a new hire who oversaw the IRA's data analysis, ran a coast-to-coast reconnaissance mission through the United States in the summer of 2014, making stops
in California, Nevada, New Mexico, Colorado, Illinois, Michigan,
Louisiana, Texas, and New York, gathering insights and intelligence
along the way. Another operative, posing as an American and chat-
ting with a member of a grassroots organization in Texas, gained the
insight that they should focus on politically fractious "purple states"
like Florida, where the 2000 presidential election had been decided
by a few hundred disputed ballots.

The IRA studied Americans to understand what made them
angry, to learn how to think and speak and write like them and, in the
fullness of time, to spearhead a new kind of political warfare against
the United States. "Our task," one of the Saint Petersburg trolls later
told a Russian reporter, "was to set Americans against their own government: to provoke unrest and discontent." From the outset, the
mission was to incite a civil war within the American political system.
As a report released by the Republican-led Senate Intelligence Committee put it, the Russians sought to "blur the lines between reality
and fiction, erode our trust in media entities and the information
environment, in government, in each other, and in democracy itself."
It took years before Americans understood this. Neither the president
of the United States nor any of his military and intelligence services
had the slightest warning of the attack as it was looming early in 2015.
By then, the United States had all but withdrawn from the realm of
political warfare, while the Russians ran rampant.

American democracy was already in trouble, its strength
sapped by self-inflicted wounds. As a consequence, the American

government's promotion of democratic ideals had arrived at death's door. "Perhaps the most worrisome dimension of the democratic recession has been the decline of democratic efficacy, energy, and self-confidence in the West, including the United States," Larry Diamond, a prominent American political sociologist, wrote in January 2015. "There is a growing sense, both domestically and internationally, that democracy in the United States has not been functioning effectively." Voter turnouts were sinking. The cost of election campaigns was crushing. The role of dark money in politics was surging. Public trust in government was fading. Comity, courtesy, the consideration that the other person might have a point, were dying. Conspiracy theories were trending. Talking heads were shouting. Everyone was arguing with everybody else. The political discourse of Congress and cable news and Facebook and Twitter was growing coarser by the hour. Putin and his state-run media reveled in America's travails, mocking democracy, promoting autocracy. "The world takes note of all this," Diamond warned. The democratic recession let "autocrats perceive that the pressure is now off: They can pretty much do whatever they want to censor the media, crush the opposition, and perpetuate their rule."

On June 16, 2015, one of the coarsest public figures in America announced that he was a candidate for president of the United States. Only someone "really rich"—like himself—could "take the brand of the United States and make it great again." On the threat of jihad—"Islamic terrorism is eating large portions of the Mideast. They've become rich. I'm in competition with them"—money would change everything. On the threat of enemies within—"When Mexico sends its people, they're not sending their best. They're not sending you. They're not sending you. . . . They're sending people that have lots of problems and they're bringing those problems with us. They're bringing drugs, they're bringing crime, they're rapists"— his real estate expertise would save the nation. "I would build a great wall. And nobody builds walls better than me, believe me. And I'll build them very inexpensively. I will build a great great wall on our southern border and I'll have Mexico pay for that wall."

Novelists had foreseen the rise of a man like this. *It Can't Happen Here*, Sinclair Lewis's 1935 bestseller, told of the hate-mongering senator Buzz Windrip—"vulgar, almost illiterate, a public liar easily detected"—who wins the 1936 presidential election by fueling fear against immigrants and proceeds to invade Mexico. *The Dead Zone*, Stephen King's 1979 thriller, depicted a "cynical carnival pitchman" and real estate swindler rising to political power on a wave of populist fervor and taking aim at the White House. But those were fictions.

Few took Donald Trump too seriously at the start. The idea that he could be president was unnerving. He was a con man and a grifter. Trump had invented himself as a financial genius, though he had inherited his fortune, and what riches he hadn't squandered through folly he had sustained through fraud. He polished his gold-plated persona on television and in the tabloids. He often said that he had invented the phrase "fake news"—"one of the greatest of all terms I've come up with"—and he had been generating it to tout himself and trash his rivals since the 1970s.

In 2009, Trump had discovered Twitter. He had trolled the president of the United States throughout 2011 and 2012, spewing the conspiracy theory that Obama was born in Africa, not a real American, an illegitimate president, an impostor. In June 2013, he had voiced a yearning for a political tryst with a certain KGB veteran: "Do you think Putin will be going to The Miss Universe Pageant in November in Moscow—if so, will he become my new best friend?" Curiously, he said publicly, and repeatedly, that they already had a relationship. This was by all accounts false. Once in Moscow at the beauty show he owned, he was like a bride left at the altar, asking over and over whether Putin was coming or not. He got a consolation prize: at the Conservative Political Action Conference in March 2014, he had crowed that Putin had sent him "a beautiful present with a beautiful note." This was true. It was a black lacquered box with a sealed

letter inside. What the letter said is a secret unrevealed. A few days
later, he tweeted: "I believe Putin will continue to re-build the Russian Empire." In May, he deepened the mystery of this courtship: "I
spoke indirectly—and directly—with President Putin, who could not
have been nicer." The two had never met. If anything had transpired
between them, it was, as Winston Churchill had said of Stalin's Russia, a riddle, wrapped in a mystery, inside an enigma.

In Saint Petersburg and Moscow, the leaders of the Russian attack
on American democracy studied Trump closely, devising a political
warfare strategy that dovetailed with his candidacy. Twenty-five
days into his presidential campaign, on July 11, 2015, Trump spoke at
FreedomFest, a libertarian convention in Las Vegas. In the audience
was Maria Butina, a flame-haired Russian intelligence agent sent to
infiltrate the National Rifle Association and influence right-wing
activists. She put a question directly to him, planted by her superiors in Moscow. Would Trump continue the punitive economic and
political sanctions Obama had imposed on Russia after the invasion
of Ukraine? "I know Putin," he said, another lie easily detected. "I
would get along very nicely with Putin. . . . I don't think you'd need
the sanctions." This was vitally important information for the Kremlin. The sanctions had sparked a collapse of the Russian ruble, which
had prevented the nation's energy industries, the only vital organs of
its economy, from rolling over their debt. By some estimates, they
had taken a quarter to a third of the Russian economy down in the
course of a year. People's salaries decreased, poverty increased, and
political opposition to Putin grew in the face of his fierce repression.

A few weeks after the Las Vegas encounter, one of Putin's leading
propagandists went to work on Trump's behalf. Konstantin Rykov had
made millions and won election to the Russian Parliament through his
mastery of the internet. He was also the Kremlin's chief foreign policy
troll on Twitter. He created a website—Trump2016.ru—giving the
world a stream of support for Trump's nascent campaign. Trump took
notice. "Russia and the world has already started to respect us again!"

he tweeted. Putin himself would soon weigh in, calling Trump "color-ful" and "talented" and "absolutely the leader in the presidential race." Trump expanded on those views. "When people call you 'brilliant' it's always good," he said, "especially when the person heads up Russia."

He was distinguishing himself from the field of Republican can-didates by praising Putin and insisting that NATO was "obsolete." He called the alliance a bunch of deadbeats; nations from England to Estonia were "ripping off the United States," not paying their fair share for the defense of the free world: "Either they have to pay up . . . or they have to get out. And if it breaks up NATO, it breaks up NATO." All this was catnip for the Russians, who knew their chosen candidate was negotiating in secret with Putin's cronies to build a Trump Tower in Moscow, a venture from which he would have pocketed $50 million or more, and where he planned to offer Putin a sumptuous penthouse for free.

Putin's spies and the trolls at the IRA had entered the presidential race in full force on the heels of Trump's announcement. Their cam-paign was "a vastly more complex and strategic assault on the United States than was initially understood," the Senate Intelligence Com-mittee reported in October 2019. The IRA reached tens of millions of voters. It connected with at least 126 million Americans on Face-book, 20 million people on Instagram, and 1.4 million on Twitter. This generated 76 million interactions on Facebook and 187 million engagements on Instagram; its Twitter accounts were retweeted by Trump, his sons, and his closest aides, among countless others, includ-ing some forty American journalists. The IRA's posts and ripostes to support Trump—2,563 on Facebook, 13,106 on Instagram, 430,185 on Twitter—far exceeded its messages against his rivals. It uploaded more than a thousand videos to YouTube. It spent roughly $15 million all told, and it paid about one hundred Americans who organized forty different political protests across the United States. By midsum-mer of 2015, the IRA's shock troops, an invisible division of thousands of fake personae posing as Americans, were at war on their chosen candidate's behalf. Among the most common words in their Twitter profiles were *God, Christian*, and *Trump*.

The IRA army fought on three fronts: Right, Left, and Black.

The Right front strongly favored Trump, savaging his Republican opponents, working every wedge issue from immigration to Islamic jihad to racist hate for a black president, stoking up rage, urging conservative and right-wing voters to get behind Trump's juggernaut. It launched a Kremlin narrative in July predicting that Trump was going to have a very sensible policy regarding Russia. A strong message in broken English soon followed: "@stop_refugees: Trump said that he is honored by Putin had called him an absolute leader, and expresses his support for Russian president. . . . If we can't work with Russia, that's not a good thing, Trump said. Well to my mind we need Russia on our side, not on the opposite, what's your point? #usdaily #news #hotnews #newspaper #coffee #reading #local #cnn #foxnews #nbc #nytimes #morning #politics #usa #america #americannews #followme #trump #russia #putin." This post represented the work of the IRA's "Hashtag Gamers," who created and promoted commentary on hot topics. Its hottest tags included "#Trump2016" and "#MAGA."

The Left front had orders from the top to help defeat Hillary Clinton, whom Putin had loathed for years. She had formally announced that she was running for the White House in April 2015, via a YouTube video. Her success in pursuit of the presidency depended on the loyalties of both mainstream and left-leaning Democrats—Obama voters, young voters, and specifically black voters, many of whom were wary of her fund-raising affinities with Wall Street and corporate America. The IRA had a plan for that. It worked overtime not simply to attack Clinton, but to suppress voter turnout, promote an election boycott, and boost a fringe candidate, the Green Party's Jill Stein.

Stein, a Harvard-educated doctor, was unlike any presidential hopeful to proceed her. She practically ran on the United Russia ticket.

She had announced her candidacy on RT's American network, and Putin's team clearly liked her critiques of American democracy and foreign policy. She had asserted in July 2015 that "we helped foment a coup against a democratically elected government" in Ukraine, "where ultra-nationalists and ex-Nazis came to power," an exact echo of the Kremlin's position. She was Putin's honored guest at a televised banquet celebrating RT's tenth anniversary. At the same table, smiling for the cameras, sat a remarkable contingent: Putin, Stein, a former KGB chieftain, Putin's top propagandist, and retired lieutenant general Michael Flynn, who joined the Trump campaign six weeks after the banquet. Flynn was a hothead, fired for insubordination as director of the Defense Intelligence Agency, infamous for using his analysts to chase down conspiracy theories. RT had paid him $45,000 for his appearance. His colleagues had warned him that taking Kremlin gold would fatally compromise him, and they also thought that he didn't care. (Flynn's twenty-seven-day stint as Trump's White House national security adviser ended after he lied to the FBI about his conversations with the Russians.)

Stein said her campaign paid for her trip to Moscow, but RT paid her back. It ran more than one hundred stories on its American channel supporting her bid for the White House, amplifying her positions—"a vote for Hillary Clinton is a vote for war"—which reliably corresponded with the party line of the Internet Research Agency. "She's a Russian asset—I mean, totally," Clinton said three years after the election, an intriguing and incendiary charge. The fact that Stein marched in lockstep with the Kremlin's foreign policies went all but unnoticed at the time, as did the possibility that she might matter more than most fringe candidates in American political history. On Election Day, she won 1,457,216 ballots. The IRA had told Americans that "A Vote for Jill Stein Is Not a Wasted Vote," and that turned out to be true: the votes for Stein in Michigan, Pennsylvania, and Wisconsin—the three states that determined the winner in the Electoral College—exceeded Trump's margin of victory.

The IRA's Black front was by many measures its biggest. "No single group of Americans was targeted by IRA information operatives more than African-Americans," the Senate Intelligence Committee found in 2019. "By far, race and related issues were the preferred target of the information warfare campaign designed to divide the country." The IRA's messages to the black community sometimes lobbied for Stein, but far more often argued for boycotting the election entirely. The voter suppression drive aimed at dozens of cities, especially communities where the killings of black citizens by white police officers created flash points for the Black Lives Matter movement. The Black front made an overwhelming effort to keep African Americans away from the ballot boxes with messages like "Our Votes Don't Matter," "Don't Vote for Hillary Clinton," and "Don't Vote at All." Its "Woke Blacks" Instagram account argued that "a particular hype and hatred for Trump is misleading the people and forcing Blacks to vote Killary. We cannot resort to the lesser of two devils."

One of its Facebook pages, "Blacktivist," generated 11.2 million engagements. Ninety-six percent of its YouTube content dealt with race. The most inflammatory video recalled the forged letters from the Ku Klux Klan to African and Asian athletes attending the 1984 Olympics in Los Angeles. The YouTube video was titled "HILLARY RECEIVED $20,000 DONATION FROM KKK TOWARDS HER CAMPAIGN." The IRA recruited assets in the black community, with posts seeking contacts with African American preachers from the Black Baptist Church, followers to attend political rallies, and photographers to document protests. Through a media mirage, a Facebook page called "Black Matters," it reached out to writers, activists, and lawyers, seeking real Americans to give cover to the Russian political warfare campaign.

The Right front scored a direct hit on the American psyche with "Heart of Texas," a Facebook page featuring pictures of longhorn cattle, pushing harsh gun-rights and anti-immigrant memes, and amassing more than a quarter of a million followers, 4.9 million shares, and

5.4 million likes. The Russians used it to drop gasoline on a brush fire of fear burning among conspiracy-minded Texans. The Pentagon had sparked that fear. It had announced that Green Berets and Navy Seals would join a two-month unconventional war exercise code-named Jade Helm 15 ranging across seven states from Texas to California, starting on July 15, 2015. In short order, "Heart of Texas," along with the IRA's Instagram, Twitter, and YouTube accounts, claimed Jade Helm was, by turns, a psyops plan to enable a Chinese occupation of Texas, a United Nations scheme to seize citizens' guns, a commando onslaught to round up conservative Republicans in advance of Obama's imminent imposition of martial law, or, as a Defense Intelligence Agency analyst noted, "a military plan to impose martial law and disarm citizens in the wake of an apocalyptic meteor strike predicted to occur the same day Jade Helm 15 concluded." The idea that Jade Helm was a nefarious Obama plot to take away the guns of right-wing Texans, or to take over Texas itself, was amplified by the Republican governor of Texas, who mobilized the Texas State Guard to monitor the military, and by the Republican presidential candidate Senator Ted Cruz of Texas, who said he was probing Pentagon officials because the Obama administration could not be trusted. The IRA had gotten into the heads of some powerful politicians—and millions of voters.

"At that point, I'm figuring the Russians are saying, 'We can go big-time,'" Air Force general Michael Hayden, the former director of the CIA and the NSA, said later. "And at that point, I think they made the decision, 'We're going to play in the electoral process.'"

The first presidential primaries were still four months away when the NSA saw the footprints of Cozy Bear again in September 2015. The cybercommand at Fort Meade, Maryland, sent a report to Special Agent Adrian Hawkins at the FBI's headquarters in Washington: the Russians had been sending spear-phishing emails to a multitude of American government agencies, contractors, and think tanks; anyone who clicked on a phishing message would let the Russians into their network to ransack their files and documents. Now they had struck the office that had been the target of the Watergate burglars back in 1972. Hawkins read the report, picked up the telephone, and called the Democratic National Committee.

He asked to speak to the head of the computer-security team. There was no head, and no team, so he was transferred to the help desk. He spoke to a young IT contractor named Yared Tamene, who didn't grasp what Hawkins was telling him, nor fully believe that he was talking to the FBI. "I had no way of differentiating the call I just received from a prank call," Tamene wrote in an internal memo. Hawkins called back repeatedly, leaving messages. Throughout October, Tamene never replied. "I did not return his calls," he explained, "as I had nothing to report." In November, Hawkins finally reached Tamene. He said in no uncertain terms that a DNC computer was "calling home" to Moscow. The IT guy saw the picture now. He sent another memo to his bosses—"the FBI thinks that this calling home behavior could be the result of a state-sponsored attack"—but the DNC's leaders didn't see it at the time. Four long months went by before they confronted reality and considered calling in a cyberse-curity team.

By February 2016, the Russian intelligence services had turned their collective energies to the presidential election in full force. That same month, Paul Manafort proposed to manage Trump's campaign. The two men had first met in 1982, when Trump hired Manafort as a lobbyist, joining a client list that included the likes of General Mobutu, Rupert Murdoch, and the National Rifle Association. In March, Manafort went down to Trump's Mar-a-Lago estate in Flor-ida and offered his services for free, which sounded fine to the candi-date. There wasn't any vetting or due diligence; Trump didn't bother with such details. When the news broke, Victoria Nuland, the State Department's top Russia hand, recoiled in revulsion. "Manafort!" she said to herself. "He's been a Russian stooge for fifteen years."

The Kremlin had high-quality *kompromat* on Manafort. The

money-laundering Russia lobbyist owed many millions to Oleg Deripaska, a billionaire aluminum magnate who counted both the leaders
of the Russian mafia and the Russian nation among his allies. (American diplomatic cables called him "among the 2–3 oligarchs Putin turns
to on a regular basis.") The debt came from a failed plan to buy a cable
network in Ukraine, and Deripaska was suing to the tune of $19 mil-
lion. Manafort had bought a lavish Trump Tower condo in New York
after signing a lucrative political consulting contract with Deripaska in
2005; his political skills, Manafort had written, would "greatly benefit
the Putin Government." He boasted at the time that he was already
pushing policies on behalf of the once and future Ukraine president
Victor Yanukovych "at the highest levels of the U.S. government—
the White House, Capitol Hill, and the State Department." All
told, Manafort had received more than $17 million from Yanu-
kovych—$12.7 million off the books—and he had been laundering
the money for years. He had been under FBI investigation for nearly
two years in connection with those dealings, but the bureau hadn't yet
made a case. His ascent to the top of the Trump campaign must have
been met with delight in Moscow, especially when Manafort helped to
rip a plank out of the Republican Party's political platform—a pledge
of military support for Ukraine in its fight against Russian occupation.
That ploy came at the behest of his longtime business associate, the
Russian intelligence operative Konstantin Kilimnik; Manafort in turn
gave him inside information from Trump headquarters to try to barter
his debt with Deripaska.

Putin's spies possessed a deeper understanding of his corruption
than the FBI did. "To keep *kompromat* on enemies is a pleasure,"
the Russian author and journalist Yulia Latynina had written when
Putin first came to power. "To keep *kompromat* on friends is a must."

The Russians wanted a *polezni durak*—a "useful idiot"—inside
the Trump campaign, someone who would do their work without
knowing he was doing it. They had several to choose from within
Trump's small foreign policy cluster, a collection of oddballs and

wingnuts. On April 26, a newly minted member of that team, a twenty-eight-year-old energy lobbyist named George Papadopoulos, had breakfast in a London hotel with a new acquaintance, a mystery man named Joseph Mifsud. Once chef de cabinet in the Ministry of Foreign Affairs in Malta, Mifsud was a regular at the Valdai Discussion Club—a very Russian version of the elite conferences held in Davos and Aspen—led annually by Putin, whom Mifsud heartily embraced. Mifsud had latched on to Papadopoulos like a limpet upon learning that he worked for Trump. This was, as they say in Russia, no coincidence. Mifsud was a recruited Russian agent and, in the parlance of espionage, he was talent-spotting. He cultivated Papadopoulos, introducing him to a woman he called "Putin's niece" (Putin has no niece) and connecting him by email to a man he said was a high-level official in the Russian Foreign Ministry, most likely an intelligence officer. Papadopoulos, a fish out of water, was gaffed. Mifsud shared a deep secret with him: the Russians had dirt on Clinton. They had her emails. Thousands of them. Papadopoulos was enthralled, and he went to work trying to arrange a meeting between Trump and Putin, a task infinitely beyond his grasp. Then, on May 10, clawing his way up the greasy pole of international intrigue, Papadopoulos had too much to drink in a posh London bar and shared his secret with a diplomat whom he had just met: Alexander Downer, Australia's envoy to the United Kingdom. Downer didn't know quite what to make of it all until later. The CIA and the FBI would hear the story in a few months.

On May 26, Trump clinched the Republican nomination. The next day, he called Putin a strong leader, the twenty-eighth time he had praised him or predicted they would have a great relationship. On June 3, two Russians who had befriended Trump at the Miss Universe pageant in Moscow reached out to tell his son, Donald Trump Jr., that emissaries from the Russian government wanted to deliver damaging information about Clinton. "If it's what you say I love it," the younger Trump replied, "especially later in the summer." On June 7, he set up a meeting at Trump Tower in New York, where Manafort and Jared Kushner, Trump's son-in-law, met the Russian delegation. Thirty-eight meetings and 272 contacts between Team Trump and Team Putin have been documented by the FBI. Thirty-three high-ranking campaign officials and advisers knew of these contacts. Every one of them, Trump included, concealed these liaisons by lying and dissembling when questioned by investigators, journalists, and members of Congress. No innocent explanation for this clandestine conduct exists. The FBI never resolved the question of why they all lied.

On June 8, a Russian military intelligence front called DCLeaks .com, hosted by an online persona named Guccifer 2.0, started dropping stolen Democratic National Committee documents like confetti into the political arena. The IRA went into overdrive, blasting out the message: "Trump is our only hope for a better future!" The Russian attack was now a hydra-headed war, as the IRA's ever-intensifying propaganda campaign—"#Trump4President, #Hillary4Prison"—was supercharged with gigabytes of information stolen by Moscow's spies. John Podesta, Clinton's campaign chairman, had clicked on a spear-phishing message, and Moscow's hackers had stolen his account—more than fifty thousand emails. A Democratic Congressional Campaign Committee worker had opened a link to a fake log-in page, letting the Russians break into the committee's computer network, install malware, and rifle through its files, searching for keywords like *Clinton* and *Trump*. The Russians turned the stolen information into weapons of political warfare. They were ready, and they aimed. On June 12, Julian Assange, the warlock of WikiLeaks, gave an interview to Britain's ITV: "WikiLeaks has a very big year ahead," he said. "We have e-mails related to Hillary Clinton which are pending publication."

The DNC had hired the cybersecurity sleuths from CrowdStrike to find out who was behind the theft. They now had an answer: Cozy Bear and Fancy Bear. But no one knew that the Bears were feeding the

IRA and Assange. WikiLeaks had started in 2006 as a radical force against government secrecy, feared and loathed by those who kept the secrets, but not by those who published them. At some point—certainly after he skipped bail on a charge of rape and sought asylum at Ecuador's embassy in London in 2012—Assange had become an instrument of Russian intelligence. Shortly after he made his threat on British television, he had been visited at the embassy by RT's London bureau chief, who slipped him a USB drive. On July 14, Russian hackers using the Guccifer 2.0 persona sent him encrypted files titled "big archive." On July 15, the selfsame Guccifer issued a public threat: "The main part of the papers, thousands of files and mails, I gave to WikiLeaks. They will publish them soon." And on July 22, Assange tweeted: "Are you ready for Hillary? We begin our series today with 20 thousand emails from the top of the DNC." Soon Russian intelligence officers posing as whistleblowers were sending direct messages to American reporters with passwords to protected sites housing hacked Democratic National Committee documents.

The DNC's leaders had written some acerbic things about Clinton's strongest rival, Senator Bernie Sanders, which set off a storm of outrage among his ardent supporters when the Democratic convention opened in Philadelphia four days later. Thanks to CrowdStrike, the Clinton campaign now knew it was under a skillful and stealthy attack from abroad. The campaign's manager, Robby Mook, told CNN: "Experts are telling us that Russian state actors broke into the DNC, stole these emails, and other experts are now saying that the Russians are releasing these emails for the purpose of actually helping Donald Trump." Trump ridiculed this idea in a tweet—"The new joke in town is that Russia leaked the disastrous DNC e-mails, which should never have been written (stupid), because Putin likes me"—and many in the mainstream media thought Mook might be spinning the surpassingly strange story. The campaign press corps, that million-footed centipede, was transfixed by the existence of

Hillary's emails, not by the fact that the Russians had stolen and released them.

On July 24, the *New York Times* published a prescient piece by the perceptive reporters David Sanger and Nicole Perlroth, which began: "An unusual question is capturing the attention of cyberspecialists, Russia experts and Democratic Party leaders in Philadelphia: Is Vladimir V. Putin trying to meddle in the American presidential election?" Trump tried to shut the story down. He declared at a press conference that "this whole thing with Russia" was "ridiculous." He said: "I have nothing to do with Russia," and repeated that five times. In the next breath, he gave a shout-out to the Kremlin: "Russia, if you're listening, I hope you're able to find the thirty thousand emails that are missing." Russia was listening: five hours later, its hackers attacked a domain used by Clinton's personal office.

In London, the Australian envoy Alexander Downer took note of the political hullabaloo across the pond. It stirred memories of the braggadocious Trump aide Papadopoulos and his excitement over the Russians having dirt on Clinton. His story reached the American embassy at the Court of St. James's. The CIA station chief in London, Gina Haspel, sent word to agency headquarters in Langley, Virginia. Her boss, CIA director John Brennan, was becoming convinced that the answer to the question posed by the *Times* reporters was yes. His colleague, FBI director James Comey, weighed and assayed the emerging evidence after dispatching two agents to debrief Downer. The cybersecurity consensus was clear—the Bears were mauling Clinton. The British and Dutch intelligence services had shared information showing beyond a doubt that the Bears danced to the music of Russian masters. And by now the FBI had read a riveting report by the veteran British spy Christopher Steele, who was working for Washington private eyes hired by the Clinton campaign. The bureau had joined forces with Steele before and knew him as a highly reliable reporter on Russia, his field of expertise. He had shared his work with

a trusted confidant, the FBI's legal attaché in Rome, who had relayed
it to headquarters. The report began:

> Russian regime has been cultivating, supporting and assisting
> TRUMP for at least 5 years. Aim, endorsed by PUTIN, has been to
> encourage splits and divisions in western alliance. . . .
>
>   A former top-level Russian intelligence officer still active inside
> the Kremlin . . . asserted that the TRUMP operation was both sup-
> ported and directed by Russian President Vladimir PUTIN. Its aim
> was to sow discord and disunity both within the US itself, but more
> especially within the Transatlantic alliance which was viewed as
> inimical to Russia's interests. . . .
>
>   A senior Russian financial official said the Trump operation
> should be seen in terms of PUTIN's desire to return to Nineteenth
> Century 'Great Power' politics anchored upon countries' interests
> rather than the ideals-based international order established after
> World War Two.

On July 30, Comey opened an FBI counterintelligence investigation code-named Crossfire Hurricane, a tip of the hat to the Rolling Stones. The agents on the case confronted questions that had
no precedent in history. Was the Republican running for president
of the United States a *polezni durak*, a useful idiot uncomprehend-
ingly propagandizing for Putin's causes? (Yes, without a doubt, the
acting director and deputy director of the CIA from 2010 to 2013,
Mike Morell, opined in the *Times* a week later: "In the intelligence
business, we would say that Mr. Putin had recruited Mr. Trump as
an unwitting agent of the Russian Federation.") But idiocy and wit-
lessness were not federal crimes under the FBI's jurisdiction. The
agents had to think about the unthinkable. This required a leap of
the imagination. Was Trump being run by the Russians? Did they
have *kompromat* on him? Was he an agent of influence? The term
came from the KGB itself, and its nuances had been laid out in the

2014 edition of an American counterintelligence manual: "An agent of some stature who uses his or her position to influence public opinion or decision-making to produce results beneficial to the country whose intelligence service operates the agent."

One man who might have had insights into these matters wasn't talking. Paul Manafort was fired as Trump's campaign manager in mid-August after his corrupt dealings in Ukraine and his secret partnership with the Kremlin oligarch Deripaska were exposed by the *New York Times*. After his indictment for conspiracy and fraud, he lied to the FBI about his political contacts with his crony Kilimnik, known to be a Russian intelligence agent. The judge who sentenced him to seven-and-a-half years wondered aloud if he had lied about those contacts to protect only himself, or his superiors too. She answered her question: we don't know. The stonewalling of men linked to Putin's inner circle—like Manafort and the disgraced national security adviser Mike Flynn—made it impossible to resolve key questions of the counterintelligence case. As the special counsel Robert Mueller concluded: "Those lies materially impaired the investigation of Russian election interference"—and the question of whether any Americans aided and abetted an attack on American democracy.

Manafort's successor at the helm of the campaign was Trump's ideologue in chief, Steve Bannon, the progenitor of a prominent far-right news site, who had once proclaimed himself a bomb-throwing Bolshevik in a cocktail party conversation with a neoconservative historian: "I'm a Leninist," Bannon said. "Lenin wanted to destroy the state, and that's my goal too. I want to bring everything crashing down." Bannon would carry his anarchic influence on Trump into the White House, all the while polishing his pithy theory of American electoral politics: "The Democrats don't matter. The real opposition is the media. And the way to deal with them is to flood the zone with shit."

The Russians were flooding the zone with a fire hose as the fight for the presidency went into full swing. But the American intelligence community, still consumed by counterterrorism after fifteen long years, was watching the reboot of Russian active measures without quite knowing what it was seeing. This failure of imagination was not solely their fault. The entire American political establishment, inside and outside the government, stood stock-still, staring wide-eyed and uncomprehending, like a cow watching a train go by.

Not a soul at the top of the Obama administration mobilized to stop the attack on the election once it was detected. No one was prepared to stop disinformation from spreading at the speed of light. No one comprehended how Russian political warfare had deployed the power of social media to transform the politics of the United States. No one thought to revive the Active Measures Working Group. A technologically savvy member of that dream team might have seen things clearly: two-thirds of the American people now got their news from the internet, and a majority of the electorate was walking half-blind into a free-fire zone of falsehood. In the fall of 2016, the top fake stories on Facebook outperformed the top news stories from the nineteen biggest news outlets in shares, reactions, and comments; the two top stories, both pushed heavily by the IRA, were that Pope Francis had endorsed Donald Trump for president and that WikiLeaks had confirmed Hillary Clinton's sale of weapons to ISIS. Those particular falsehoods reached nine million people. No one in America grasped the scope and the impact of the IRA's fabrications.

With the battle for the White House joined, Trump's pronouncements became a palimpsest of propaganda. He repeated and retweeted themes and conspiracy theories straight from the fertile minds of the IRA's trolls and the farthest reaches of the internet. When Iran executed a nuclear scientist for espionage, Trump told his 10.8 million followers on Twitter: "Many people are saying that the Iranians killed the scientist who helped the United States because of Hillary Clinton's hacked emails." At a raucous rally in Florida, he proclaimed that Obama, the African Muslim masquerading as an American, was "the founder of ISIS. He's the founder. He founded ISIS." He added, with a flourish, "I would say the co-founder would be Crooked Hillary Clinton."

Trump was a past master of old-school propaganda, which called for the construction of an alternate reality. Now he was practicing propaganda as Putin did, which demanded the destruction of reality itself. The philosopher Jason Stanley, author of *How Propaganda Works*, summed up the teachings of this new school. "It's crucial to understand this: transforming politics into a post-truth contest of tribal identity is an explicit goal of modern propaganda." That contest was now like a violent video game, a virtual blood sport in which your side won when the other side died.

Trump, the IRA, and WikiLeaks all made a scalding accusation at the start of August: Clinton was going to steal the presidency. The theme and the memes charging her with a gigantic fraud exploded on social media and across the spectrum of the internet as Russian trolls bombarded Americans with the idea and the images of a rigged ballot. The IRA's Facebook group "Being Patriotic" and its Twitter account @March_for_Trump worked with Trump supporters to stage rallies in Florida, Pennsylvania, and New York. The Russians paid Americans to build a cage on a flatbed truck and portray Clinton inside the cage wearing prison stripes. Trump stoked the fear of a fraudulent vote at his campaign appearances, and the crowds went wild, chanting "Lock her up!" when he went after Crooked Hillary. He said that if Clinton won—which seemed highly likely at the time—it would be the result of a plot to "rig the election at the polling booths, where so many cities are corrupt and voter fraud is all too common." She, like Obama, would be an illegitimate president, empowered by a conspiracy so immense that it staggered the imagination.

At the highest levels of the Obama administration, a realization was slowly dawning. The election really could be rigged—by the

Russians. All concerned knew that the Russians had hacked the vote and posted fraudulent results in the Ukraine election of 2014. All worried that they might do it again in the United States by monkey-wrenching the nation's antiquated voting machinery, altering registration data, erasing voters from the rolls, planting Trojan horses in computers calculating the tally. In theory, they had the capability to do all of that and more.

Early in August, the guardians of American national security, including the secretary of defense, the secretary of state, and the heads of the CIA, the FBI, and the Department of Homeland Security, belatedly began to hold a series of tense meetings in the White House Situation Room. The director of national intelligence, James Clapper, a retired air force lieutenant general, was first among equals at these conclaves. A fifty-five-year veteran of America's military and intelligence services, Clapper had served as director of the Defense Intelligence Agency under Bush 41 and Clinton, as the undersecretary of defense for intelligence under Bush 43 and Obama, and since 2010, as the DNI, the top post in the American intelligence community, overseeing the CIA, the FBI, and the NSA. He was seventy-five, bald as a cue ball, borderline brilliant, and crusty as old bread.

"My dashboard warning lights were all lit," Clapper wrote two years later.

Homeland Security reported that the voter registration database in Illinois had been under cyberattack for weeks, and information on two hundred thousand voters had been stolen. Then it was Arizona. Then Florida. The election systems of at least twenty-one states were targets. The possibility was remote, but the fear was real: election night could turn into chaos. No one would know who had won. Clapper reminded his counterparts that Russians didn't need to go to all that trouble. They already had malware—christened Energetic Bear by American cyberwarriors—implanted at key nodes throughout the American electrical grid. They had used that angle of attack to shut off power to hundreds of thousands of people in Ukraine in the dead of winter only eight months before. They could black out American cities at will as citizens went to vote, or as the polls closed, and the country would be sitting in darkness waiting for results that weren't coming in. What were the odds they would do that? No one knew.

But the Russians weren't only inside the American grid. They had gremlins inside the Trump campaign machine. By early August, Clapper wrote, it was becoming clear that "both the Russians and the Trump campaign were, in parallel, pushing conspiracy theories against Secretary Clinton with three identical themes: she was corrupt, she was physically and mentally unwell, and she had ties to Islamic extremism." The FBI's Crossfire Hurricane investigation had started to track and trace some of the many meetings between members of Team Trump and Team Putin, but far from all of them. The June meeting at Trump Tower—a Russian delegation led by a former KGB officer promising dirt on Clinton to Manafort, Kushner, and Donald Trump Jr.—was still a secret. WikiLeaks, fueled by the relentless cyberespionage of Russian intelligence, was in direct communication with the Trump campaign, and this, too, was a secret, though not for long.

More grievously, the Russians were inside Americans' heads, but no one grasped how deeply. The National Security Agency and the Crossfire Hurricane team had barely glanced at the IRA, the subject of a highly detailed 2015 expose in the *New York Times* that hadn't been heeded, and they still had the dimmest understanding of what it was doing. But by now, the intelligence community began to understand this much: the Kremlin was on the campaign trail.

After the second Situation Room meeting, on August 11, with Obama's approval, the CIA director John Brennan began to brief the Gang of Eight: the Senate and House Republican leaders, Mitch McConnell and Paul Ryan; their Democratic Party counterparts, Harry Reid and Nancy Pelosi; and the heads of the congressional intelligence committees, all of whom had a right to know some deep secrets of state. Brennan gave it to them with the bark off: the Russians were trying to undermine the democratic process, denigrate Clinton, damage her electability and her potential presidency, and catapult Trump into the White House. The election was seventy-five days away by the time Brennan reached Senator Reid at home in Las Vegas on August 25 and asked him to get to the nearest secure telephone, the FBI's field office in Sin City. Reid got the full import of what the CIA director was telling him, slept on it, and then composed a letter to FBI director James Comey. "The prospect of a hostile government actively seeking to undermine our free and fair elections represents one of the gravest threats to our democracy since the Cold War," Reid wrote. "The American people deserve to have a full understanding of the facts from a completed investigation before they vote this November." They were denied those facts.

A few days later, at the start of September, America's national security chiefs met again. The picture was becoming clearer. Relying on an exquisitely rare source, a recruited Russian agent working high up in the Kremlin, the CIA had concluded that Putin was presiding over the attack on American democracy. "We all agreed this kind of effort could only be approved at the highest levels of the Russian government," Clapper wrote. "We knew Putin was personally involved." This insight shifted their world on its axis. What were they going to do about it? Who was going to tell the American people?

It was up to Obama to decide. The deputy national security adviser, Ben Rhodes, shut out from the struggle in the Situation Room, had nonetheless caught wind of what was happening and broached the issue with the president. By his account, Obama said: "They've found the soft spot in our democracy."

The president confronted Putin at a summit in Hangzhou, China, on September 5, staring down at him in anger, telling him to knock it off or else. What *or else* meant was a matter of conjecture at the time, but Obama had a lot of options. He could shutter every Russian consulate in America; they were dens of spies. He could impose sanctions so severe as to make the Russian economy scream. He also had some secret weapons. The CIA could leak the details of Putin's personal wealth, conservatively estimated at $40 billion. The NSA had the capability, through its cybercommand, to freeze and evaporate a sizable portion of that fortune. For the moment, Obama did nothing more than summon the four top members of Congress to the White House upon his return to Washington. His goal was to put out a bipartisan statement, based on Brennan's briefing, to tell the nation at least part of what they knew.

Mitch McConnell refused. The senator was the leader of the modern conservative movement in America, started in 1955 by the public intellectual William F. Buckley, who had an immaculate 1950s pedigree—Yale, Skull and Bones, CIA—and represented a political coalition to the right of President Eisenhower. Buckley had proclaimed it was the duty of conservatives to stand athwart history, yelling *Stop*. This was McConnell's credo. He was the grim reaper of the government. He killed legislation that smacked of bipartisanship, he killed the requisite hearings for Obama's Supreme Court nominee, and now he killed the chance for the American citizenry to hear that their democracy was under attack by Russia. McConnell didn't care what kind of man Trump was, or how he got elected, or whether the Russians were behind him, so long as he won.

At this moment, America was no longer governed by two political parties but by two warring tribes, and with that, the Russians were on their way to glory.

For a month, as September turned to October, the Obama administration tried to craft a statement that could let the electorate know what was happening. The effort was agonizing. Should they name and shame Putin? They wouldn't. Brennan and Comey were loath to tip the Russians about the sources and methods of American intelligence. Should they say the Russians were trying to elect Trump? They couldn't. Obama was leery of appearing to put his thumb on the scales of the vote, and out of an overabundance of caution, he wouldn't put his name on the statement at all. No one seemed able to find the right words; the arguments went around and around in circles, with cabinet officers and intelligence czars quibbling over commas and clauses in the Situation Room. Finally, Clapper turned to his counterpart, Homeland Security secretary Jeh Johnson. He said the two of them had to cut the knot. "Jeh and I felt," he wrote, "not only was saying *something* the right thing to do, but if we did not disclose the information we had, there'd be hell to pay later."

They tried to tell the truth but they didn't tell the whole truth. They took a draft statement into their own hands, and following the instincts of the president and the consensus of their colleagues, they filed off its sharpest points. They kept Putin's name out of it, and they kept Trump's name out, too. The words *disinformation* and *Russian intelligence* did not appear. But all agreed that the message was clear, and they thought it would be electrifying:

> The US Intelligence Community is confident that the Russian Gov-
> ernment directed the recent compromises of e-mails from US per-
> sons and institutions, including from US political organizations. The
> recent disclosures of alleged hacked e-mails on sites like DCLeaks
> .com and WikiLeaks and by the Guccifer 2.0 online persona are con-
> sistent with the methods and motivations of Russian-directed efforts.
> These thefts and disclosures are intended to interfere with the US
> election process. . . . We believe, based on the scope and sensitivity of
> these efforts, that only Russia's senior-most officials could have autho-
> rized these activities.

The statement was set for release on Friday afternoon, October 7. But first came an enormous burst from the IRA's trolls—a tweet every five seconds, nearly eighteen thousand in all on the sixth of October, with a potential reach of twenty million people. The messages overwhelmingly came from the IRA's Left front. They aimed at suppressing the vote against Trump, infuriating Sanders supporters with the accusation that Clinton and the Democratic Party had defrauded their candidate, saying she had stolen the presidential nomination through deceit and cunning. The payload powering this blast was political dynamite—a bombshell of emails stolen by the Bears and stockpiled by the IRA and WikiLeaks—and the tweets were just a taste of it. The full force would explode on Friday.

The breaking news about the Russian attack from the American intelligence community went out at 3 p.m. that day. It was the top story for less than an hour. At 4:03 p.m., it was knocked off America's airwaves when the *Washington Post* showed the world the *Access Hollywood* tape of Trump boasting about sexually assaulting women: "When you're a star, they let you do it. . . . Grab 'em by the pussy. You can do anything." (A few members of the dwindling Republican establishment condemned him; his response was to bring three women who had accused Bill Clinton of sexual misconduct decades before to the next presidential debate.) And a half hour later, at 4:32 p.m., WikiLeaks tweeted: "RELEASE: The Podesta Emails." Stolen by the Russians from the Clinton campaign chairman in March, sifted and weighed for six months, and strategically set forth in installments that day and throughout October, the first of the files revealed the Clintons' buckraking on Wall Street, unlikely to endear the candidate to the Bernie brigade. She didn't have a quick comeback that night or the next.

The Russians had sent millions of minds spinning. The fact that they were inside American heads was beyond understanding. And at that moment their political warfare had triumphed. Their attack on American democracy was not part of the national discussion the next day, or the next week, or the next month. The political discourse was crystallized three weeks before Election Day, at the third and last presidential debate in Las Vegas on October 19, when Trump boasted that Putin had said nice things about him.

"Well, that's because he'd rather have a puppet as president of the United States," Clinton said.

"No puppet," Trump sputtered. "No puppet. You're the puppet." The Russians had strung them up and made them dance.

Too late, long after the election was over, American intelligence began to understand how the Kremlin's political warfare campaign helped elect Putin's chosen candidate as the president of the United States. The failure to foresee the approach of the attackers, the failure to warn Americans in real time, and the failure of imagination that enabled the success of the sabotage mirrored the saga of September 11 and its awful aftermath. No one died in the great active measures campaign of 2016. But it was a glorious triumph for Russia and a grievous wound for American democracy. We were fools to let it happen.

The Crossfire Hurricane team finally busted the Internet Research Agency ten months after Trump won the White House. After breaking into its servers and its files, they found a note, like a message in a bottle, from a Russian soldier on the front lines of political warfare.

On November 9, 2016, a sleepless night was ahead of us. And when around 8 a.m. the most important result of our work arrived, we uncorked a tiny bottle of champagne . . . took one gulp each and looked into each other's eyes. . . . We uttered almost in unison: "We made America great."

AN AGENT OF INFLUENCE

Russian spies had inflicted resounding blows against America in the century since Stalin first came to power. Their goals during and after the cold war were the same: subvert the United States, undermine its power, poison its political discourse. Now Putin had pulled off the most audacious political warfare operation since the Greeks pushed a gigantic wooden horse up to the gates of Troy. Trump would prove to be a priceless asset for the Russians' war on democracy and the rule of law. With his inauguration, they had an agent of influence in the White House, a president who supported Putin's geopolitical interests, who echoed his propaganda, and who tried to cover up the evidence of his act of war against America.

Four months after taking office, Trump sacked FBI director James Comey, trying to scuttle the Crossfire Hurricane investigation into the Russian attack. Then he welcomed Russia's foreign minister and ambassador into the Oval Office and boasted: "I just fired the head of the FBI. He was crazy. . . . I faced great pressure because of Russia. That's taken off." His brazen act of obstruction led the Justice Department to appoint Robert Mueller, the FBI director from

2001 to 2013, to lead the criminal and counterintelligence probes of the campaign and the administration. Upon learning that Mueller was on his trail, Trump slumped back in his chair in the Oval Office and moaned: "Oh, my God. This is terrible. This is the end of my presidency. I'm fucked." He knew, as Mueller later put it, that "a thorough FBI investigation would uncover facts about the campaign and the President personally that the President could have understood to be crimes."

The counterintelligence investigators confronted a national security nightmare: Was Trump in the sway of the Russians?

No known evidence proved he had been bribed with cash or blackmailed by *kompromat*. But he had made himself an attractive target for the Russians for thirty years. He had first visited Moscow in 1987, a greedy and vainglorious businessman seeking to build a luxury hotel across Red Square from the Kremlin in partnership with the Soviet government. He had a Czech wife to whom he was unfaithful. He had dropped hints about running for president. A generation later, Trump was still running for president, still trying to build that hotel, and still cheating on his wife, though not the same one. His real estate deals in New York, Miami, Toronto, Panama, and beyond depended in part on Russian money, as did his resurrection from bankruptcy. Whether the Russians took Trump's measure remains a mystery. But he surely was a mark. He had vulnerabilities that their intelligence officers could exploit: his transactional sex life, his greed, his corruption, and above all his ego, in the view of the CIA veteran Rolf Mowatt-Larssen, who had served four years in Moscow, ending up as station chief. He concluded that Trump's conduct in office was "damning evidence" that the president was, in his estimation, "a Russian agent."

Given Trump's towering vanity, if Putin lavished him with praise and lent him political support, he didn't have to slip him secret marching orders. He only had to influence him and win influence in return. Putin's years in the KGB had made him an expert at "manip-

ulating people, blackmailing people, extorting people," said Fiona
Hill, the Kremlinologist and Putin biographer who served under
Trump for two and a half years as the National Security Council's
director for Russia and Europe. "That's exactly what a case officer
does. They get a weakness, and they blackmail their assets. And Putin
will target world leaders. . . . I firmly believe he was also targeting
President Trump." Putin's overarching goal in his political warfare
against the United States, Hill said, was creating chaos: "to divide us
against each another, degrade our institutions, and destroy the faith
of the American people in our democracy." Under Trump, the divisions and the degradation of American political life deepened with
each tumultuous day of his presidency.

The two men met for the first time on July 7, 2017, at a global
economic forum in Hamburg. Trump confiscated his interpreter's
notes of their meeting, and the concealment continued: no formal
records of his five face-to-face meetings with Putin exist. But he
soon started repeating disinformation put out by Putin himself: the
Ukrainians, not the Russians, had manipulated the election, running
a covert operation to help Hillary Clinton. "They tried to take me
down," Trump said. He obsessed over that conspiracy theory; it was
his white whale. How did he know it was true? "Putin told me," he
confided to a top White House aide.

They stood side by side in Helsinki on July 16, 2018, and a reporter
asked who had perpetrated the election attack. Putin said: "As to the
question of who can or can't be believed and whether anyone can be
believed: no one can be believed." *There is no truth.* Trump echoed
him: he said his intelligence chiefs had told him that "they think it's
Russia. I have President Putin; he just said it's not Russia. I will say
this: I don't see any reason why it would be." *There are no facts.*

The American national security establishment exploded in rage.
Senator John McCain, who represented what remained of the con-
science of the Republican Party under President Trump, called this
display of fealty "one of the most disgraceful performances by an

American president in memory. The damage inflicted by President Trump's naivete, egotism, false equivalence, and sympathy for autocrats is difficult to calculate." John Brennan, the CIA director under Obama, said Trump was "wholly in the pocket of Putin." Representative Will Hurd, a Texas Republican and a veteran CIA officer, wrote: "I've seen Russian intelligence manipulate many people over my professional career and I never would have thought that the US President would become one of the ones getting played by old KGB hands." James Clapper, the former national intelligence czar, noted that Putin "knows how to handle an asset, and that's what he's doing with the president."

The watchdogs barked, but Trump's caravan moved on. By his third year in power, he had accomplished what three-quarters of a century of Russian active measures had left undone. He had damaged American democracy.

He undermined the architecture of American national security. He stripped the State Department of envoys to nations great and small, he shut his eyes to the CIA's reporting when it clashed with his invincible ignorance, and he scorned his Pentagon chiefs on matters of life and death. He defamed distinguished American ambassadors as "human scum," trashed FBI agents as subversive traitors, and vilified CIA officers as Nazi storm troopers. He savaged four-star generals and flag officers, calling them "a bunch of dopes and babies" to their faces. Trump saw them all as the sinister forces of a "Deep State"—a cryptocracy subverting his power, a conspiracy seeking to destroy him.

He ceased America's advocacy for freedom and justice at home and abroad. He disparaged the nation's allies. He embraced dictators like Mohammed bin Salman and Kim Jong-un, who, like Putin, imprisoned and assassinated their opponents without fearing Trump would condemn them. He smiled upon autocratic rulers in failing democracies from India to Brazil. When great throngs of people in Hong Kong and Prague took to the streets demanding their right to liberty, the silence of the White House was absolute. By 2020, the number of electoral democracies had dwindled down to the lowest share of the world's nations since the earliest years of the cold war, and as the scholar Larry Diamond wrote, they were dying not by sudden coups, but slowly, "step by step, through the steady degradation of political pluralism, civil liberties, and the rule of law, until the Rubicon has been crossed as if in a fog, without our knowing the precise moment when it happened."

As Trump sawed away at the Atlantic alliance, the first three nations enfolded into NATO by the United States dropped the democratic façade. Hungary's government became a hotbed of hatred and intolerance, its leader basking in Trump's praise. The Czech Republic was led by a racist xenophobe. Poland's rulers corroded the civil liberties for which its people had suffered and died. "We have not truly constructed anything new in the world," lamented Lech Wałęsa, the living emblem of Solidarity. "And there is a loss we have suffered. The loss is the leadership position of the United States. Which is a very bad situation for the world."

No less than Putin, Trump conducted political warfare against the American government. Attacking the rule of law, freedom of religion, freedom of the press, and the legitimacy of elections, he spewed propaganda and hatred into political discourse. He winked at racists and fascists when they marched in the cause of white nationalism. He used the power of his office for personal profit. He denounced his political foes as criminals and threatened them with prison. And as Mueller racked up indictments and convictions against Russian spies and the president's close associates, Trump spoke like a mob boss, heaping contempt on cooperating witnesses and praising those who practiced the code of silence.

Mueller's report, released on April 18, 2019, showed precisely how the Russians had interfered in the presidential election. It laid out how Trump had lied about his conduct and then lied about his lies, sabotaging and stonewalling the investigations. It chronicled seventy-seven falsehoods Trump and his inner circle told the FBI, Congress, and the American people about their contacts with Russians. It damningly detailed ten episodes in which Trump obstructed justice. Testifying before Congress that summer, Mueller was asked point-blank if he had cleared Trump of criminal wrongdoing. "No," Mueller said. And the president exulted that he had been exonerated.

Two weeks later, on May 3, Trump initiated an unscheduled ninety-minute telephone conversation with Putin. They talked about Ukraine, and not for the first time. Putin had Trump convinced that it was not a "real country," but part of Russia. (He had said the same to President Bush a decade before.) He and his intelligence services had led Trump to believe that Ukraine's corrupt power brokers had concealed their collusion with Hillary Clinton and still sought to subvert him. Under Putin's influence, the president set out on the path to his impeachment. A few days thereafter, he ordered his national security adviser, John Bolton, and his personal lawyer, Rudy Giuliani, to help him dig up dirt on his Democratic rivals from a mythical El Dorado in Ukraine. They didn't deliver.

On July 25, the morning after Mueller testified, Trump telephoned the country's newly elected leader, Volodymyr Zelensky, not a politician by trade but an actor who had played a president on television. Trump now took the starring role in "a fictional narrative . . . perpetrated and propagated by the Russian security services," in the words of Fiona Hill. Trump asked for a favor. He needed the outgoing government in Ukraine nailed for the tinfoil-hat notion that it had hacked the American election to help Clinton. And he wanted the incoming government to lodge a libel against former vice president Joe Biden: a brazen lie that he had quashed a corruption case in Kyiv against his own son. Trump's envoys made the White House quid pro quo explicit to the Ukrainians. Give him what he wants. Put your president on CNN to proclaim corruption probes against Trump's enemies. Then he'll give you what you need.

Trump had put the government of the United States in the grip

of a Kremlin intelligence operation, driven by Russian disinformation, in his bid for four more years in power. He was extorting a foreign leader into fabricating falsehoods about his opponents for his
political benefit. He had blocked $391.5 million in military aid Con-
gress appropriated to help Ukraine defend against the Russian occupation of their country. He kept the arms frozen pending a promise
of *kompromat*. The Pentagon, the State Department, and the NSC
all supported the aid to Ukraine. Trump illegally withheld it.

The favor Trump sought had nothing to do with fighting corruption. He was seeking to shape public opinion. He wanted to create propaganda for the coming election, clandestinely. That too was
illegal. American government officials are barred by law from secret
efforts to "influence United States political processes, public opinion, policies, or media," but that was exactly what the president had
in mind. And it worked. Prominent Republicans, Fox News, and
right-wing talk radio all told the story that Biden was corrupt and
Ukraine had conspired against the president.

"Thank God," Putin said on November 20, "no one is accusing
us of interfering in the U.S. elections anymore. Now they're accusing Ukraine." By then, his cyber-spies were working once again on
Trump's behalf. The GRU was taking aim at Biden; its first attacks
were detected by the American cyber security firm Area 1 before the
end of the year. "The timing of the GRU's campaign in relation to
the 2020 U.S. elections raises the specter that this is an early warning of what we have anticipated since the successful cyberattacks
undertaken during the 2016 U.S. elections," the company reported.
Americans had forewarning, if they were listening: the Russians had
the capability to flood the nation with disinformation, launch cyberattacks on the presidential vote count, or knock out a city's electrical
grid on Election Day, all to serve the cause of chaos and their chosen
candidate. Yet Trump refused to mobilize his administration against
a new wave of Russian influence operations and cybercrimes bene-
fitting him.

By the time of his impeachment, it was clear that Trump might do anything to stay in power. He had happily accepted dirt on his rivals from a foreign power in the last election, he had made clear he would do it again, and now he saw that no one would stop him. He had obstructed justice in the Crossfire Hurricane investigation, and paid no price. He had defied every subpoena and blocked every witness at his impeachment, without penalty. The defendant determined what his jury would hear. Trump was guilty, in the words of Senator Mitt Romney, the Republican presidential candidate in 2012, of "an appalling abuse of public trust" and "a flagrant assault on our electoral rights." He said that "corrupting an election process in a democratic republic is about as abusive and egregious an act against the Constitution—and one's oath—that I can imagine. It's what autocrats do."

And Trump governed as an autocrat after his acquittal in the Senate affirmed that he could lie and cheat to stay in power. In Trump's vision of America, all power resided in the president. Congress could not control him. Courts could not judge him. Laws could not constrain him. He worked through his attorney general to erase the evidence of the Kremlin's political warfare, thus "abetting a Russian covert operation to keep him in office for Moscow's interests, not America's," in the words of the former CIA chief John Brennan. His lies proliferated. His insistence that his official acts were infallible required Americans to reject the evidence of their eyes and ears. As he once told his followers: "Don't believe the crap you see from these people, the fake news. What you're seeing and what you're reading is not what's happening."

Authoritarians demand loyalty above all. Expertise and experience count for nothing; speaking truth to power is fatal. The fawning and bootlicking of his allies and aides and right-wing media acolytes now resembled the high councils of North Korea, where everyone must swear undying fealty to the Dear Leader. He purged the leadership of the American intelligence and national security agencies, replacing them with dishonest and disreputable partisans. He cut off the flow of intelligence reporting to Congress and the American people, increasing the risk of dangerous miscalculation and disastrous surprise.

Trump's response to the threat of the novel coronavirus that arose in China and engulfed America in a toxic cloud was a torrent of lying, denying, and disinformation, evoking the Soviet reaction to Chernobyl, the flailing of a failing state. The president called the warnings of a pandemic a political deception cooked up by the Democratic Party and the press to defeat him, propaganda echoed by his allies in the right-wing media. He insisted for weeks that the virus was under control; he claimed it would miraculously disappear in days to come. He resisted the very idea of testing for the virus, calculating that if the number of confirmed cases rose, the chances for his reelection would fall. And then, two months into the crisis, as the death toll started to soar and the economy began to crash, he said he had always taken the danger seriously and that he had moved swiftly to address it. That lie was worthy of Stalin himself. Autocrats everywhere rewrite history in order to maintain and magnify their power.

The president and Putin's political warriors both kept infecting the body politic with falsehoods, inflaming anger, poisoning discourse, flooding the zone with disinformation about the pandemic and the other panic-button issues of the day. Trump's billion-dollar reelection operation already employed digital disinformation strategies adapted from the Internet Research Agency. The IRA itself was back in business, aiming as always to tear Americans apart. As the 2020 campaign began in earnest, with the Kremlin backing Trump as the chaos candidate, there was no foretelling what he would do to stay in power, how he would react if and when the people put an end to his presidency, whether he would surrender the White House peacefully if defeated, or rule as a despot if he prevailed.

On January 29, 1981, in his first news conference as president,

Ronald Reagan had proclaimed that the Russians played by different rules than Americans: "The only morality they recognize is what will further their cause, meaning they reserve unto themselves the right to commit any crime, to lie, to cheat, in order to attain that," he said. "We operate on a different set of standards." Those standards no longer applied. Trump had made America more like Russia. He had endangered the future of American democracy.

A free society cannot survive if its people are force-fed lies. As Vaclav Havel, a Czech playwright deemed an enemy of the state by the Kremlin and jailed for years as a political prisoner, wrote in 1978: "Because the regime is captive to its own lies, it must falsify everything. It falsifies the past. It falsifies the present, and it falsifies the future. . . . It pretends to persecute no one. It pretends to fear nothing. It pretends to pretend nothing. Individuals need not believe all these mystifications, but they must behave as though they did, or they must at least tolerate them in silence. . . . For this reason, however, they must live within a lie." By virtue of his passionate embrace of the truth, Havel became the president of a free nation. He died in 2011, the year that Donald Trump began to construct a political empire built on lies.

Our democracy depends on truths it has held to be self-evident. We created a government of laws, not men. Our elections are free and fair. No one is above the law. The president is not a king. Trump threatened to prove these ideals false. And if America's politics are founded on falsehoods, the weapons of political warfare will prevail, and a long darkness will descend on the last best hope of what once was known as the free world. Only a free people and a free press stand in the way of its falling.

—March 20, 2020

ACKNOWLEDGMENTS

In 1956, the year I was born, a rookie reporter at the *Goldsboro News-Argus* went to see his boss about a story. The *News-Argus*, circulation eight thousand, was the paper of record in its patch of eastern North Carolina; Goldsboro, the seat of Wayne County, was a small town surrounded by tobacco and cotton, a place where nothing much of moment happened, other than the struggle for civil rights and that time a B-52 broke up in midair and dropped two fully armed thermonuclear weapons a few miles away. The reporter, Gene Roberts, was only twenty-four years old, but he had the weighty responsibility of writing the paper's best-read feature, "Rambling Through Rural Wayne," which on any given day might bear witness to an emotional family reunion or depict a sweet potato that closely resembled General Charles de Gaulle. "The world could be exploding, but the 'Rambling Through Rural Wayne' had to come out," Roberts remembered fifty years later.

Roberts also wrote deeper stories about people's lives, stories people would remember, and on the day that he sat down with his boss, Henry Belk, he was bearing a copy of his latest dispatch. Belk had edited the paper since 1929. He was six-foot-seven, walked with a cane, and wore a battered gray fedora. He tilted back in his big oak armchair, the springs creaking, the warm wind blowing in the window off the town square, while Roberts read the story out loud. The reporters of the *News-Argus* had to read to their ancient editor because he had gone blind. And if a story had ragged holes in the reporting or dull thuds in the writing, the old boy would pound his desk and declaim: *Ah cain't see it. Make me see it!*

Twenty-five years later, Gene Roberts was my editor at the *Phila-delphia Inquirer*. His peculiar genius inspired a generation of reporters. He made us look at all the trees to let our readers see the forest. In 1987, he sent me to see how the CIA's multibillion-dollar weapons pipeline to the Islamic rebels fighting the Soviet occupation in Afghanistan was working. This wasn't a story you could report from a desk in Washington. You had to see it for yourself. The assignment changed my life in a way I didn't foresee. Before I took off, I called up the CIA's public information officer and asked for a country briefing on Afghanistan. He scoffed and hung up. I returned to Washington three months later, and I hadn't been back at my desk for more than a day when my phone rang. "Tim! How are you? How was your trip? How'd you like to come in for that briefing now?"

Off I went to the CIA's headquarters. I walked into the magnificent atrium and looked up at the words from the Gospel of John carved in gold bas-relief: *And ye shall know the truth and the truth will make you free.* I knew then that I wanted to cover the CIA the way other reporters covered the cops and the courts.

Joe Lelyveld hired me at the *New York Times* to do that job. Gene and Joe had both covered the civil rights movement for the *Times* in the deep south in the 1960s. Joe's father was a rabbi who marched, and was bloodied, in that struggle; Gene's father was a minister who published a small paper in North Carolina. Without being preachy about it, both of them had an instinctive sense that journalism was a vocation. Gene went to Vietnam and then ran the national desk at the *Times* during the first Nixon administration. Joe became one of the great foreign correspondents of his generation. He covered the fight against apartheid in South Africa, and his book *Move Your Shadow* remains the greatest chronicle of that epic battle.

By 1994, Joe was the executive editor and Gene the managing editor at the *Times*. I was their national security reporter, parachuting into places like Afghanistan and Sudan every so often, and never was an ink-stained wretch happier to wake up at home in the morning with the paper at the doorstep, wondering what the day might bring.

I owe a debt of gratitude for almost every word I have ever written to these two men, along with a tip of the old fedora to the memory of Henry Belk.

An equal measure of thanks goes to Kathy Robbins, who became my literary agent in 1994. Ever since, she has urged me on, gently coaxing inchoate ideas toward oblivion and forcefully driving good ones forward, reading every draft, and making sure that my work could be published not only in America but around the world. I didn't know how to write a book before I met Kathy, though I'd written one. Five books later, I feel like I am getting the hang of it, and she is a great part of the reason why. Thanks to everyone at the Robbins Office: David Halpern, Janet Oshiro, and Alexandra Sugarman. At CAA stands Matthew Snyder, always at the ready. Rick Pappas knows the law.

Four of those books have been written in part at Yaddo, the colony for artists and writers in Saratoga Springs, New York, where this one got its start. Yaddo is a spring that faileth not, and its presiding genius is the incomparable Elaina Richardson, without whom my life as a writer would be irreparably abridged.

The Folly and the Glory owes its life to everyone who has had a hand in it along the way at the publishing house of Holt. The wisdom of chairman Steve Rubin and executive editor Serena Jones brought it forth from conception to birth. My gratitude goes to all at Holt, and in particular Amy Einhorn, Pat Eisemann, Maggie Richards, Madeline Jones, Chris Sergio, and Caitlin O'Shaughnessy. The manuscript had another reader, someone whom I would trust with my life: my brother Richard.

Something else immeasurably marvelous happened to me in 1994. I had the infinite good fortune to marry Kate Doyle. Among her many virtues is her avocation: as a senior analyst at the National Security Archive, she has worked for nearly thirty years with human rights groups, truth commissions, prosecutors, and judges to obtain files from secret government archives that shed light on state-sanctioned crimes against humanity in Latin America. Kate has kept me honest, picked me up when I have stumbled, given me strength and hope and joy. The greatest joys are our daughters, Emma Doyle and Ruby Doyle, who have shown me unconditional love even when I didn't deserve it. Emma helped research this book, challenged my assumptions, and helped me think things through. Ruby keeps me off my high horse and on the good foot. This book is dedicated first and last to these three strong women, the light of my life.

NOTES

Chapter 1: The Seeds of Future Struggle

5 at least 117 national elections: Dov H. Levin, "When the Great Power Gets a Vote: The Effects of Great Power Electoral Interventions on Election Results," *International Studies Quarterly* 60, no. 2 (June 2016): 189–202, https://doi.org /10.1093/isq/sqv016; and Levin, "Partisan Electoral Interventions by the Great Powers: Introducing the PEIG Dataset," *Conflict Management and Peace Science* 36, no.1 (January 2019): 88–106, https://journals.sagepub.com/doi/abs/10.1177 /0738894216661190.

5 "Imagine a country": Gorbachev interview, PBS, April 23, 2001, https://www.pbs .org/wgbh/commandingheights/shared/minitext/int_mikhailgorbachev.html.

6 "There weren't any foreign policy problems": Baker oral history, Miller Center, January 29, 2000, https://millercenter.org/the-presidency/presidential-oral -histories/james-baker-iii-oral-history-2000-white-house-chief.

6 "Beware the vividness of transient impressions": Powell oral history, Miller Center, December 16, 2011, https://millercenter.org/the-presidency/presidential-oral -histories/colin-powell-oral-history-chairman-joint-chiefs-staff.

6 "What we did not realize": Robert M. Gates, *Duty: Memoirs of a Secretary at War* (New York: Alfred A. Knopf, 2014), 149–50. Gates went on to write that as the millennium approached, "our moment alone in the sun, and the arrogance with which we conducted ourselves in the 1990s and beyond as the sole surviving super-power, caused widespread resentment. And so when the World Trade Center came down on September 11, 2001, many governments and peoples—some publicly, many more privately, welcomed the calamity that had befallen the United States. In their eyes, an arrogant, all-powerful giant had been deservedly humbled."

7 "turned significantly back": Morell interview, *Politico*, December 11, 2017, https://
   www.politico.com/magazine/story/2017/12/11/the-full-transcript-michael
   -morell-216061.

7 "You think we are living in 2016": Krutskikh remarks at Infoforum 2016, https://
   infoforum.ru/conference/2016. No one in the American press appears to have
   noticed the speech for almost a year, until a few days before Trump's inauguration. See David Ignatius, "Russia's Radical New Strategy for Information Warfare," *Washington Post*, January 18, 2017, www.washingtonpost.com/blogs/post
   -partisan/wp/2017/01/18/russias-radical-new-strategy-for-information-warfare
   /?utm_term=.492f34e18be9.

Chapter 2: The Perpetual Rhythm

9 "a man of incredible criminality": George F. Kennan, *Russia and the West Under
   Lenin and Stalin* (Boston: Little, Brown, 1961), 254–55.

10 "He was terribly absorbed": John Lewis Gaddis, *George F. Kennan: An American
   Life* (New York: Penguin, 2012), 212.

10 "No one in Moscow believes": Memorandum by the Counselor of Embassy in the
   Soviet Union (Kennan), "Russia's International Position at the Close of the War
   with Germany," *Foreign Relations of the United States* (hereafter cited as *FRUS*),
   Diplomatic Papers, 1945, Europe, Volume V, Document 643, https://history.state
   .gov/historicaldocuments/frus1945v05/d643.

11 "I felt like the moon": David McCullough, *Truman* (New York: Simon &
   Schuster, 1992), 353.

11 "I thought of Carthage": Truman diary, July 16, 1945, in Robert H. Ferrell, ed.,
   Off the Record: The Private Papers of Harry S Truman (Columbia: University of
   Missouri Press, 1997), 52.

13 "They have asked for it": Walter Isaacson and Evan Thomas, "The Reluctant
   Prophet," *Washington Post*, August 31, 1986, https://www.washingtonpost.com
   /archive/lifestyle/magazine/1986/08/31/the-reluctant-phophet/4b1c0c4a-2f9e
   -4eed-b1da-cd84a4025804/.

13 "so strange to our form of thought": The Chargé in the Soviet Union (Kennan) to the Secretary of State, February 22, 1946, *FRUS*, 1946, Eastern Europe,
   The Soviet Union, Volume VI, Document 475, https://history.state.gov
   /historicaldocuments/frus1946v06/d475.

14 Soviet spies in America: "The Soviets had placed more than 200 agents and
   sources inside the United States government," a startling fact from an authoritative in-house CIA historian. David Robarge, "Moles, Defectors, and Deceptions:
   James Angleton and CIA Counterintelligence," *Journal of Intelligence History* 3,
   no. 2 (Winter 2003): 21–49.

15 "a preponderance of strength": Gaddis, *George F. Kennan: An American Life*, 239–40.

15 "The Sources of Soviet Conduct": *Foreign Affairs*, July 1947, excerpted online at
   https://www.foreignaffairs.com/articles/russian-federation/2016-10-31/sources
   -soviet-conduct-excerpt.

17 "The General": Dean Acheson, *Present at the Creation: My Years in the State
   Department* (New York: W. W. Norton, 1970), 212.

18 "guerrilla warfare corps": Kennan to Forrestal, September 27, 1947, Record Group 165, ABC files, 352:1, National Archives and Records Administration.

18 "to resort to virtual civil war": Policy Planning Staff 13, "Résumé of World Situation," *FRUS*, 1947, General, The United Nations, Volume I, Document 393, https://history.state.gov/historicaldocuments/frus1947v01/d393.

19 "covert psychological operations": Souers to Hillenkoetter, NSC 4-A, Subject: Psychological Operations, December 17, 1947, *FRUS*, 1945–1950, Emergence of the Intelligence Establishment, Document 257, https://history.state.gov /historicaldocuments/frus1945-50Intel/d257.

19 "start World War III": Willems to Chamberlin, March 30, 1948, reproduced in Thomas Boghardt, "By All Feasible Means," https://www.wilsoncenter.org/blog -post/all-feasible-means#_ftn1; Truman to Forrestal, March 10, 1948, *FRUS*, 1948, Western Europe, Volume III, Document 477, https://history.state.gov /historicaldocuments/frus1948v03/d477.

19 a formal approval of operations already underway: NSC 1/3, *FRUS*, 1948, Western Europe, Volume III, Document 475, https://history.state.gov /historicaldocuments/frus1948v03/d475.

20 "The inauguration of organized political warfare": Policy Planning Staff Memorandum, May 4, 1948, *FRUS*, 1945–1950, Emergence of the Intelligence Establishment, Document 269, https://history.state.gov/historicaldocuments/frus1945 -50Intel/d269.

23 "reduce the power": Kennan, "U.S. Objectives Towards Russia," August 20, 1948, NSC meeting files, Box 204, Harry S. Truman Library.

24 "the gradual retraction": Report to the President by the National Security Council, "U.S. Objectives with Respect to the USSR to Counter Soviet Threats to U.S. Security," November 23, 1948, *FRUS*, 1948, General; the United Nations, Volume I, Part 2, Document 60, https://history.state.gov/historicaldocuments/frus1948v01p2/d60.

24 "As the international situation develops": Kennan to Wisner, January 6, 1949, *FRUS*, 1945–1950, Emergence of the Intelligence Establishment, Document 308, https://history.state.gov/historicaldocuments/frus1945-50Intel/d308.

24 "the original architects": Wisner memo, June 1, 1949, *FRUS*, 1945–1950, Emergence of the Intelligence Establishment, Document 310, https://history.state.gov /historicaldocuments/frus1945-50Intel/d310.

25 It was the first concrete plan: Policy Planning Staff Paper, "U.S. Policy Toward the Soviet Satellite States in Eastern Europe," August 25, 1949, *FRUS*, 1949, Eastern Europe; The Soviet Union, Volume V, Document 10, https://history.state.gov /historicaldocuments/frus1949v05/d10.

26 "atomic weapons can hardly be used": Simon Sebag Montefiore, *Stalin: The Court of the Red Tsar* (New York: Alfred A. Knopf, 2004), 601.

26 "No one wants to use it": John Lewis Gaddis, *The Long Peace: Inquiries into the History of the Cold War* (New York: Oxford University Press, 1987), 113.

Chapter 3: Truth Is Not Enough

28 "I see nothing": Eisenhower quoted in the *New York Times*, August 15, 1945, 3.

29 "I personally think": "Notes on a Meeting at the White House," January 31, 1951,

FRUS, 1951, European Security and the German Question, Volume III, Part 1, Document 248, https://history.state.gov/historicaldocuments/frus1951v03p1/d248.

30 "The most pressing thing": Eisenhower letter to Truman, December 16, 1950, Dwight D. Eisenhower Presidential Library.

30 "In a very real sense": Jean Edward Smith, *Eisenhower in War and Peace* (New York: Random House, 2012), 499.

30 "If I do what I want": Truman to Eisenhower, in McCullough, *Truman*, 888.

31 "Hanging over all our plans and actions": Bohlen memo, March 7, 1953, Box 23, Record Group 59, Policy Planning Staff file "USSR 1953," State Department.

33 "Every gun that is made": "The Chance for Peace," Eisenhower address to American Society of Newspaper Editors, April 16, 1953, https://www.presidency.ucsb.edu/documents/address-the-chance-for-peace-delivered-before-the-american-society-newspaper-editors.

34 "It is of critical importance": NSC 136/1, November 20, 1952, *FRUS*, 1952–1954, Iran, 1951–1954, Second Edition (hereafter *FRUS* Iran), Document 147, https://history.state.gov/historicaldocuments/frus1951-54IranEd2/d147. This document and the following documentation on the Iran coup in this chapter were declassified in 2018, giving rich new detail on the CIA's operation to restore the shah.

34 a ten-thousand-man guerrilla force: Progress Report to the National Security Council, March 20, 1953, *FRUS* Iran, Document 180, https://history.state.gov/historicaldocuments/frus1951-54IranEd2/d180.

34 "a network with numerous press, political, and clerical contacts": Memorandum Prepared in the Directorate of Plans, Central Intelligence Agency, "Capabilities of CIA Clandestine Services in Iran," March 3, 1953, *FRUS* Iran, Document 170, https://history.state.gov/historicaldocuments/frus1951-54IranEd2/d170.

34 "Associated with the Nazi efforts": Waller to Roosevelt, "Factors Involved in the Overthrow of Mossadeq," April 16, 1953, *FRUS* Iran, Document 192, https://history.state.gov/historicaldocuments/frus1951-54IranEd2/d192.

34 "The communists": Memorandum of Discussion at the 135th Meeting of the National Security Council, March 4, 1953, *FRUS* Iran, Document 171, https://history.state.gov/historicaldocuments/frus1951-54IranEd2/d171.

35 $5,330,000: The dollar figure, declassified in 2018, appears in a CIA after-action report, "Campaign to Install Pro-Western Government in Iran," March 8, 1954, *FRUS* Iran, Document 363, https://history.state.gov/historicaldocuments/frus1951-54IranEd2/d363.

35 "It was cleared directly": Telephone conversation between Allen Dulles and John Foster Dulles, July 24, 1953, *FRUS*, 1952–1954, Iran, 1951–1954, Volume X, Document 335, https://history.state.gov/historicaldocuments/frus1952-54v10/d335.

35 "Mossadegh, learning of the plan": CIA memorandum, "Campaign to Install Pro-Western Government in Iran," March 8, 1954, *FRUS* Iran, Document 363, https://history.state.gov/historicaldocuments/frus1951-54IranEd2/d363.

35 "genuine peoples [*sic*] uprising": Roosevelt to CIA headquarters, August 20, 1953, *FRUS* Iran, Document 289, https://history.state.gov/historicaldocuments/frus1951-54IranEd2/d289.

35 "This demonstration": Henderson to State Department, August 20, 1953, *FRUS* Iran, Document 283, https://history.state.gov/historicaldocuments/frus1951 -54IranEd2/d283.

36 "The time has come": Record of meeting at CIA headquarters, August 28, 1953, *FRUS* Iran, Document 307, https://history.state.gov/historicaldocuments/frus1951 -54IranEd2/d307.

36 "the restoration": Eisenhower diary, October 8, 1953, *FRUS* Iran, Document 328, https://history.state.gov/historicaldocuments/frus1951-54IranEd2/d328.

36 "The Shah and the Prime Minister": Project Outline Prepared in the Central Intelligence Agency, June 15, 1954, *FRUS* Iran, Document 368, https://history .state.gov/historicaldocuments/frus1951-54IranEd2/d368.

36 "The principal new features": National Intelligence Estimate, "Probable Developments in Iran Through 1955," December 7, 1954, *FRUS* Iran, Document 375, https://history.state.gov/historicaldocuments/frus1951-54IranEd2/d375.

36 "The Shah is now our boy": Record of meeting at CIA headquarters, August 28, 1953, *FRUS* Iran, Document 307, https://history.state.gov/historicaldocuments /frus1951-54IranEd2/d307.

37 "unified and dynamic": This and the following citations are from the top secret "Report to the President by the President's Committee on International Information Activities," June 30, 1953, *FRUS*, 1952–1954, National Security Affairs, Volume II, Part 2, Document 370, https://history.state.gov/historicaldocuments/frus1952 -54v02p2/d370.

37 "anything from the singing of a beautiful hymn": Memorandum by the President to the Secretary of State, October 24, 1953, *FRUS*, 1952–1954, Western Europe and Canada, Volume VI, Part 1, Document 307, https://history.state.gov /historicaldocuments/frus1952-54v06p1/d307.

39 "Death to Communism": Ronald D. Landa, "Almost Successful Recipe: The United States and East European Unrest Prior to the 1956 Hungarian Revolution," draft historical study, Office of the Secretary of Defense, 2012 (declassified 2017), https://nsarchive2.gwu.edu//dc.html?doc=3473778-Document-01 -Almost-Successful-Recipe-The-United.

40 "covertly stimulate," "encourage elimination of key puppet officials," "train and equip underground organizations," "nourish resistance," and "convince the free world": NSC 158, United States Objectives and Actions to Exploit the Unrest in the Satellite States, June 29, 1953, https://nsarchive2.gwu.edu/NSAEBB /NSAEBB50/doc74.pdf.

40 ""fuzzy thinking": Helms memo to Wisner, CIA, August 6, 1953, cited in Landa, "Almost Successful Recipe," 53.

41 "undoubtedly unless U.S. military forces": Bross memo to Dulles, CIA, January 13, 1954, cited in Landa, "Almost Successful Recipe," 66.

41 "It looked to him" and "The United States": Memorandum of Discussion at the 163d Meeting of the National Security Council, September 24, 1953, *FRUS*, 1952– 1954, National Security Affairs, Volume II, Part 1, Document 91, https://history .state.gov/historicaldocuments/frus1952-54v02p1/d91.

42 "We are facing an implacable enemy": Report on the Covert Activities of the Central Intelligence Agency, September 30, 1954, *FRUS*, 1950–1955, The Intelligence Community, 1950–1955, Document 192, https://history.state.gov/historicaldocuments/frus1950-55Intel/d192.

44 "Create and exploit": National Security Council Directive, NSC 5412/2, December 28, 1955, *FRUS*, 1950–1955, The Intelligence Community, 1950–1955, Document 250, https://history.state.gov/historicaldocuments/frus1950-55Intel/d250.

44 "Khrushchev, it was said": John Rettie, "The Day Khrushchev Denounced Stalin," BBC World Service, February 18, 2006, http://news.bbc.co.uk/2/hi/programmes/from_our_own_correspondent/4723942.stm.

44 "the possibility that Khrushchev had been drunk": Memorandum of Discussion at the 280th Meeting of the National Security Council, Washington, March 22, 1956, *FRUS*, 1955–1957, Soviet Union, Eastern Mediterranean, Volume XXIV, Document 34, https://history.state.gov/historicaldocuments/frus1955-57v24/d34.

45 "If it's authentic": Manor told the story of obtaining Khrushchev's "secret speech" to the Israeli journalist Yossi Melman fifty years after the fact. Melman, "Trade Secrets," Haaretz.com, September 3, 2006.

45 "KHRUSHCHEV TALK ON STALIN": Harrison E. Salisbury *New York Times*, June 5, 1956, 1.

46 "Virtually every Hungarian": Telegram from the Legation in Hungary to the Department of State, Budapest, October 24, 1956, *FRUS*, 1955–1957, Eastern Europe, Volume XXV (hereafter *FRUS* Eastern Europe), Document 103, https://history.state.gov/historicaldocuments/frus1955-57v25/d103.

46 "the revolt in Hungary": Memorandum of Discussion at the 301st Meeting of the National Security Council, Washington, October 26, 1956, *FRUS* Eastern Europe, Document 116, https://history.state.gov/historicaldocuments/frus1955-57v25/d116.

46 "If they could have some kind of existence": Memorandum of a Telephone Conversation Between the President and the Secretary of State, October 26, 1956, *FRUS* Eastern Europe, Document 121, https://history.state.gov/historicaldocuments/frus1955-57v25/d121.

47 "The heroic people of Hungary": Address by the Secretary of State Before the Dallas Council on World Affairs, October 27, 1956, *FRUS* Eastern Europe, Document 128, https://history.state.gov/historicaldocuments/frus1955-57v25/d128.

47 "incited the Hungarians to action": Telegram from the Embassy in Austria to the Department of State, Vienna, October 28, 1956, *FRUS* Eastern Europe, Document 129, https://history.state.gov/historicaldocuments/frus1955-57v25/d129.

47 "All restraints have gone off": Radio Free Europe transcripts, October 28, 1956, in Csaba Békés, Malcolm Byrne, and János M. Rainer, eds., *The 1956 Hungarian Revolution: A History in Documents* (Budapest: Central European University Press, 2002).

47 "In dramatic overnight change": Telegram from the Legation in Hungary to the Department of State, Budapest, October 31, 1956, *FRUS* Eastern Europe, Document 148, https://history.state.gov/historicaldocuments/frus1955-57v25/d148.

47 "A new Hungary": Dwight D. Eisenhower, Radio and Television Report to the American People on the Developments in Eastern Europe and the Middle East,

October 31, 1956, https://www.presidency.ucsb.edu/documents/radio-and
-television-report-the-american-people-the-developments-eastern-europe-and-the.
48 "What had occurred there was a miracle": Memorandum of Discussion at the 302d
Meeting of the National Security Council, Washington, November 1, 1956, *FRUS*
Eastern Europe, Document 152, https://history.state.gov/historicaldocuments
/frus1955-57v25/d152.

The profound failure of the CIA to see the events in Hungary clearly, and the
death blow that those events delivered to the Eisenhower administration's dreams
of liberation, compelled the president to ask Ambassador David Bruce and former
secretary of defense Robert Lovett to look into what really went on at the CIA.
Both men had been in the tight circle of cognoscenti at the inauguration of political
warfare in 1948. Bruce was a close friend to Dulles and Wisner; his personal journals
show that he had met with them for drinks or dinner dozens of times in the passing
years. Lovett served on the president's newly created board of intelligence consultants. "Bruce was very much disturbed," Lovett reflected. "He approached it from the
standpoint of 'what right have we to go barging around into other countries buying
newspapers and handing money to opposition parties or supporting a candidate for
this, that or the other office?'" Both men knew too well of the CIA's shortcomings in
its primary mission of gathering intelligence against America's main enemy.

Their report to Eisenhower on December 20, 1956, was scathing. It made five
crucial points. Covert operations mounted by Dulles and Wisner, which consumed 80 percent of the CIA's $800 million annual budget, often were unvetted
and uncontrolled by the National Security Council. CIA station chiefs abroad
often kept American ambassadors in the dark about what they were doing and
what they had done. Dulles did the same with the president and the NSC; the
Soviets sometimes knew more about what the CIA was doing than the White
House did. Covert action could collide with the stated aims of American foreign
policy. And this could someday lead to a calamity:

> The CIA, busy, monied and privileged, likes its "King-making" respon-
> sibility (the intrigue is fascinating—considerable self-satisfaction, some-
> times with applause, derives from successes—no charge is made for
> "failures"—and the whole business is very much simpler than collecting
> covert intelligence on the USSR through the usual CIA methods!). . . .
> There are always, of course, on record the twin, well-worn purposes of
> "frustrating the Soviets" and keeping others "pro-western" oriented.
> Under these, almost any psychological warfare and paramilitary action
> can be, and is being, justified. . . .
> CIA support, and its maneuvering of local news media, labor groups,
> political figures and parties, and other activities, are sometimes com-
> pletely unknown to or only hazily recognized by [American ambassa-
> dors]. . . . One obvious, inevitable result is to divide US foreign policy
> resources and to incline the foreigner, often the former "opposition" now
> come to power (and who *knows* with whom he is dealing) to play one
> U.S. agency against the other. . . .

Should not someone, somewhere in an authoritative position in our government on a continuing basis, be counting the immediate costs of disappointments (Jordan, Syria, Egypt, et al.), long-range wisdom of activities which have entailed our virtual abandonment of the international "golden rule," and which, if successful to the degree claimed for them, are responsible in a great measure for stirring up the turmoil and raising the doubts about us that exist in many countries of the world today? What of the effects on our present alliances? Where will we be tomorrow?

We are sure that the supporters of the 1948 decision to launch this government on a positive psychological warfare and paramilitary program could not possibly have foreseen the ramifications of the operations which have resulted from it. No one, other than those in the CIA immediately concerned with their day to day operation, has any detailed knowledge of what is going on.

The report was buried; no copy of its full text seems to have survived. These passages are taken from the president's foreign intelligence board's files, but no evidence exists that they were heeded. The questions it raised were not addressed for twenty years.

49 "What can we do": Memorandum of Discussion at the 303d Meeting of the National Security Council, Washington, November 8, 1956, *FRUS* Eastern Europe, Document 175, https://history.state.gov/historicaldocuments/frus1955-57v25/d175.

50 "Russia's rulers": Special Message to the Congress on the Situation in the Middle East, January 5, 1957, https://www.presidency.ucsb.edu/documents/special-message-the-congress-the-situation-the-middle-east.

50 "If you go and live with these Arabs": Memorandum of Discussion at the 410th Meeting of the National Security Council, Washington, June 18, 1959, *FRUS*, 1958–1960, East Asia-Pacific Region; Cambodia; Laos, Volume XVI, Document 36, https://history.state.gov/historicaldocuments/frus1958-60v16/d36.

51 Eisenhower authorized . . . a coup: The operation is detailed in my book *Legacy of Ashes: The History of the CIA* (New York: Random House, 2007).

52 "the decisive factor": Richard M. Nixon, "The Emergence of Africa: Report to President Eisenhower," *State Department Bulletin*, April 22, 1957.

54 "Some of these were sniper shots": Alma Fryxell, "Psywar by Forgery," CIA, n.d., https://www.cia.gov/library/center-for-the-study-of-intelligence/kent-csi/vol5no1/html/v05i1a03p_0001.html.

54 "thereby contributing directly to the breakup of the NATO alliance": CIA, "The Soviet and Communist Bloc Defamation Campaign," September 1965, https://www.cia.gov/library/readingroom/docs/CIA-RDP67B00446R000500070011-8.pdf.

56 "Dick Bissell was my oldest friend" and "a normal relationship": Carl Bernstein, "The CIA and the Media," *Rolling Stone*, October 20, 1977, http://www.carlbernstein.com/magazine_cia_and_media.php. See also John M. Crewdson et al., "C.I.A.: Secret Shaper of Public Opinion," *New York Times*, December 25–27, 1977.

57 "afraid of nuclear war": Memorandum of Conversation, Camp David, September 26 and 27, 1959, *FRUS*, 1958–1960, Volume X, Part 1, Eastern Europe

Region; Soviet Union; Cyprus; Document 133, https://history.state.gov /historicaldocuments/frus1958-60v10p1/d133.

57 "where the barometer pointed": Memorandum of Conversation, Camp David, September 27, 1959, *FRUS*, 1958–1960, Berlin Crisis, 1959–1960; Germany; Austria, Volume IX, Document 14, https://history.state.gov/historicaldocuments /frus1958-60v09/d14.

58 "I didn't realize how high a price": Michael R. Beschloss, *Mayday: Eisenhower, Khrushchev, and the U-2 Affair* (New York: Harper & Row, 1986), 372.

58 "the stupid U-2 mess": George B. Kistiakowsky, *A Scientist at the White House* (Cambridge, MA: Harvard University Press, 1976), 358.

Chapter 4: The Last Hope for the West

61 "We are opposed": President John F. Kennedy, Address Before the American Newspaper Publishers Association, April 27, 1961, https://www.jfklibrary .org/archives/other-resources/john-f-kennedy-speeches/american-newspaper -publishers-association-19610427.

62 assassination plots: The CIA mounted assassination plots against Castro at the behest of the White House. On August 10, 1962, the new director of central intelligence, John McCone, an Eisenhower man selected by JFK, met in Secretary of State Dean Rusk's conference room with Bobby Kennedy and Defense Secretary Robert McNamara. McCone remembered that they discussed a proposal "to liquidate top people in the Castro regime," in particular Fidel and his brother Raúl, Cuba's defense minister. McCone objected on moral and ethical grounds. The Kennedys evidently did not. *FRUS*, 1961–1963, Volume X, Cuba, January 1961–September 1962, 923, https://history.state.gov/historicaldocuments /frus1961-63v10/pg_923.

62 "create circumstances": Christopher Andrew and Vasili Mitrokhin, *The Sword and the Shield: The Mitrokhin Archive and the Secret History of the KGB* (New York: Basic Books, 2000), 180–81.

63 "the heart of the Cold War struggle": Carlucci oral history, Foreign Affairs Oral History.

64 "the first voice really to shout": Roberts oral history, FAOH.

64 "I don't think anybody": McIlvaine oral history, FAOH.

65 "Before independence equals after independence": Stephen R. Weissman, *American Foreign Policy in the Congo, 1960–1964* (Ithaca, NY: Cornell University Press, 1974), 55.

66 "The Prime Minister said" and "Just not a rational being": Conversation Between the Secretary and Prime Minister Lumumba, July 27, 1960, *FRUS*, 1958–1960, Africa, Volume XIV, Document 152, https://history.state.gov/historicaldocuments /frus1958-60v14/d152.

66 "The United States must be prepared": Memorandum of Discussion at the 454th Meeting of the National Security Council, August 1, 1960, *FRUS*, 1958–1960, Africa, Volume XIV, Document 156, https://history.state.gov/historicaldocuments /frus1958-60v14/d156.

66 "In the last 12 months": Memorandum of Conference with President Eisenhower, August 1, 1960, *FRUS*, 1958–1960, Africa, Volume XIV, Document 157, https://history.state.gov/historicaldocuments/frus1958-60v14/d157.

68 "We had a very clear mission": Author interview with Larry Devlin, March 2008.

68 "Lumumba moving left": Telegram from the Station in the Congo to the Central Intelligence Agency, Léopoldville, August 11, 1960, *FRUS*, 1964–1968, Volume XXIII, Congo, 1960–1968 (hereafter *FRUS* Congo), Document 8, https://history.state.gov/historicaldocuments/frus1964-68v23/d8.

68 "Whether or not": Editorial note summarizing telegram 0772 to the Central Intelligence Agency, Léopoldville, August 18, 1960, *FRUS* Congo, Document 10, https://history.state.gov/historicaldocuments/frus1964-68v23/d10.

68 an extraordinary meeting of the National Security Council: Editorial note summarizing the NSC meeting of August 18, 1960, *FRUS* Congo, Document 11, https://history.state.gov/historicaldocuments/frus1964-68v23/d11.

69 "the inevitable result": Telegram from the Central Intelligence Agency to the Station in the Congo, August 27, 1960, *FRUS* Congo, Document 14, https://history.state.gov/historicaldocuments/frus1964-68v23/d14.

69 "a three-page plan": Telegram from the Station in the Congo to the Central Intelligence Agency, Léopoldville, September 8, 1960, *FRUS* Congo, Document 17, https://history.state.gov/historicaldocuments/frus1964-68v23/d17.

70 "political action potential": Editorial note summarizing telegram 0927 from the Station in Léopoldville to the Central Intelligence Agency, September 13, 1960, *FRUS* Congo, Document 19, https://history.state.gov/historicaldocuments/frus1964-68v23/d19.

71 "crash operation": Editorial note summarizing telegram 0963 from the Station in Léopoldville, September 18, 1960, *FRUS* Congo, Document 23, https://history.state.gov/historicaldocuments/frus1964-68v23/d23.

71 "The Mobutu military dictatorship": "An Analytical Chronology of the Congo Crisis," January 25, 1961, Papers of John F. Kennedy, President's Office Files, Kennedy Library, https://www.jfklibrary.org/asset-viewer/archives/JFKPOF/114/JFKPOF-114-015.

71 "Lumumba was not yet disposed of": Editorial note summarizing the 460th meeting of the National Security Council on September 21, 1960, *FRUS*, 1958–1960, Africa, Volume XIV, Document 223, https://history.state.gov/historicaldocuments/frus1958-60v14/d223.

72 "Jesus H. Christ!": Author interview with Larry Devlin, March 2008.

72 Bissell dispatched two more men: The plot and the roles of the would-be assassins are in *Alleged Assassination Plots Involving Foreign Leaders: An Interim Report of the Select Committee to Study Governmental Operations with Respect to Intelligence Activities*, United States Senate (New York: W. W. Norton, 1976), 64.

73 "With respect to Congo": Telegram from the Embassy in the Soviet Union to the Department of State, Moscow, April 1, 1961, *FRUS*, 1961–1963, Volume V, Soviet Union, Document 51, https://history.state.gov/historicaldocuments/frus1961-63v05/d51. The Kremlin completely misperceived what was happening

in the Congo. Khrushchev blamed the UN and Dag Hammarskjöld for Mobutu's coup and his expulsion of Soviet "advisers." The Soviets blamed Lumumba's
death on them as well. A Soviet government statement of February 14, 1961, read:
"The murder of Patrice Lumumba and his comrades-in-arms in the dungeons of
Katanga is the culmination of Hammarskjöld's criminal activities. It is clear to
every honest person throughout the world that the blood of Patrice Lumumba is
on the hands of this henchman of the colonialists and cannot be removed."

73 "Agree political realities": Telegram from the Station in the Congo to the Central
Intelligence Agency, Léopoldville, November 3, 1960, *FRUS* Congo, Document
40, https://history.state.gov/historicaldocuments/frus1964-68v23/d40.

74 "As you requested last week": Editorial note summarizing a memorandum for
President Kennedy from Special Assistant for National Security Affairs McGeorge
Bundy, June 10, 1961, *FRUS*, 1961–1963, Volume XX, Congo Crisis, Document 71,
https://history.state.gov/historicaldocuments/frus1961-63v20/d71.

75 A KGB beachhead in Stanleyville: Natalia Telepneva, "Cold War on the Cheap:
Soviet and Czechoslovak Intelligence in the Congo, 1960–1963," in Philip Mue-
hlenbeck and Natalia Telepneva, eds., *Warsaw Pact Intervention in the Third
World: Aid and Influence in the Cold War*, International Library of Twentieth
Century History (London: I.B. Tauris, 2018), 123–48.

76 "enhance the political image": Memorandum for the Special Group, Covert
Action in the Congo, November 16, 1961, *FRUS* Congo, Document 100, https://
history.state.gov/historicaldocuments/frus1964-68v23/d100.

This memorandum, a rarity, documents presidential approval of the CIA's
covert financial support for foreign leaders. JFK and Bundy evidently viewed these
payoffs as a distasteful necessity, a cost of doing business abroad. In 1964, as the
White House was weighing a fresh CIA request for $3.3 million in political funds
for Mobutu and his political cronies, Secretary of State Rusk asked if there was a
better way to do business than black bags stuffed with cash. Devlin found one: a
business transaction handled by a Washington lobbyist. CIA's chiefs noted that the
idea had the merit of keeping everyone's skirts clean. Bundy blessed it. The remarkable thing about this—the secretary of state and the national security adviser devot-
ing close attention to the details of cash-on-the-barrelhead electoral corruption
abroad—was that it was unremarkable in the context of American political warfare.

77 "A multitude of nearly insoluble problems": Editorial note summarizing telegram 6298 from Léopoldville to the Central Intelligence Agency, March 14, 1963,
FRUS Congo, Document 137, https://history.state.gov/historicaldocuments
/frus1964-68v23/d137. The summary gives the flavor of Devlin's daily struggles:

The Chief of Station reported that the Congo Government was in serious political trouble caused by lack of political organization and know-
how, [*text not declassified*], and a multitude of nearly insoluble problems
which had plagued the Congo since independence. When he warned
[*text not declassified*] that the U.S. Government did not want to pour
money into a lost cause, [*text not declassified*] said it would probably take
at least a year for the [*text not declassified*] to create a political organization

of the type required to eliminate or reduce constant vote-buying. The Chief of Station noted that the United States had a choice between terminating support for the moderates, which would probably result in their fall, or continuing to provide support over the coming year, [*text not declassified*]. He pointed out that, although frustrating, the [*text not declassified*] operation had maintained a government which was as pro-American as any that could be expected in Africa at that time.

78 "CIA was very big and conspicuous": Hoffacker oral history, FAOH.

78 "If you give me equipment": Memorandum of Conversation [between President Kennedy and General Mobutu], Washington, May 31, 1963, *FRUS*, 1961–1963, Volume XX, Congo Crisis, Document 423, https://history.state.gov /historicaldocuments/frus1961-63v20/d423. The memo concludes: "As the President walked out to say goodbye to General Mobutu he said that there was nobody in the world that had done more than the General to maintain freedom against the Communists and that whenever there was any crisis in the Congo, Mobutu's name was mentioned."

79 "Siberian exile": Voronin's KGB colleague in the Congo station, Oleg Nazhestkin, published a personal history of the spy service's work, titled "The Years of the Congolese Crisis, 1960–1963: A Secret Service Man's Memoirs," and his account of the arrest, imprisonment, and expulsion appears in Sergey Mazov, *A Distant Front in the Cold War: The USSR in West Africa and the Congo, 1956–1964* (Palo Alto, CA: Stanford University Press, 2010), 178–81.

80 "that CIA do everything possible covertly": CIA director John McCone Memorandum for the Record, Discussion with Secretary of State Dean Rusk, Washington, January 8, 1965, *FRUS* Congo, Document 383, https://history.state.gov /historicaldocuments/frus1964-68v23/d383.

80 The stalwart diplomat: Kirsten Lundberg and Charles Cogan, "Containing the Chaos: the US-UN Intervention in the Congo 1960–1965," Harvard Kennedy School case study, 1999.

81 "Tshombe had little external support": Lundberg and Cogan, "Containing the Chaos."

82 "I knew it was foolhardy to stay": Hoyt oral history, FAOH. The Stanleyville hostages were held three months while the CIA and the Joint Chiefs read and rejected rescue plans from the air, over land, and by water. One of the ideas was to drop seventeen Cubans upriver from Stanleyville on rafts; the team was in country, led by William "Rip" Robertson, who had run major paramilitary operations for the CIA in the Korean War and in the 1954 coup in Guatemala, and who had barely survived the doomed landing at the Bay of Pigs. Then someone remembered the town was just downriver from Stanley Falls—seven cataracts dropping a total of two hundred feet. "It would have been the raft trip of the century," consul Mike Hoyt said.

82 "Stanleyville is in rebel hands": Memorandum from William H. Brubeck of the National Security Council Staff to President Johnson, August 6, 1964, *FRUS* Congo, Document 199, https://history.state.gov/historicaldocuments/frus1964-68v23/d199.

82 "Commie field day in the Congo": Telegram from the Station in the Congo to the Central Intelligence Agency, Léopoldville, August 10, 1964, *FRUS* Congo, Document 208, https://history.state.gov/historicaldocuments/frus1964-68v23/d208.

82 "The Congolese Army is totally ineffective": Paper Prepared in the Central Intelligence Agency, August 13, 1964, *FRUS* Congo, Document 219, https://history.state.gov/historicaldocuments/frus1964-68v23/d219.

83 "we may well soon find ourselves": Telegram from the Embassy in the Congo to the Department of State, Léopoldville, August 19, 1964, *FRUS* Congo, Document 227, https://history.state.gov/historicaldocuments/frus1964-68v23/d227.

83 another Vietnam: Che Guevara had sought to export the Cuban revolution into the heart of Africa. On December 11, 1964, after the battle of Stanleyville, he addressed the United Nations General Assembly. "Those who used the name of the United Nations to commit the murder of Lumumba are today, in the name of the defense of the white race, murdering thousands of Congolese," Che proclaimed. "All free men of the world must be prepared to avenge the crime." He embarked on a ten-nation tour of Africa, met the Katangan rebel Laurent Kabila in Dar es Salaam, and traveled to Beijing to enlist Chou en-Lai's support for a revolution. He soon launched a major guerrilla assault alongside Kabila. Che's army of Cubans and Congolese fought in a vast expanse of jungles and mountains rising from the shores of Lake Tanganyika—the world's longest freshwater lake, running 420 miles from north to south on Congo's eastern border. Devlin, whose air force still ran regular bombing missions against Mobutu's foes, now needed a navy. At CIA headquarters, Thomas Clines, the deputy head of the clandestine division's maritime branch, and Edwin Wilson, who ran a CIA front company called Maritime Consultants, obtained Swift boats—patrol craft armed with mortars and heavy machine guns. They cut them up, flew them in, and reassembled them for battle. (Both men later became international arms dealers, often working with the CIA, and both wound up in prison, Wilson serving twenty-two years.) Devlin sought and won authority from the White House to crew the Swift boats under command of the mercenary "Mad Mike" Hoare. In a classic battle of the cold war, the CIA's Cubans fought Che's Cubans to the death. They routed him and crushed his dreams of glory. The CIA hunted Che down two years later in Bolivia and ended his battles forever.

84 "Mobutu turned to Devlin": Telegram from the Station in the Congo to the Central Intelligence Agency, Léopoldville, November 19, 1965, *FRUS* Congo, Document 446, https://history.state.gov/historicaldocuments/frus1964-68v23/d446.

84 "Mobutu stressed": Telegram from the Station in the Congo to the Central Intelligence Agency, Léopoldville, November 22, 1965, *FRUS* Congo, Document 448, https://history.state.gov/historicaldocuments/frus1964-68v23/d448.

85 *Crisis in Congo*: Memorandum from Robert W. Komer of the National Security Council Staff to the President's Special Assistant for National Security Affairs (Bundy), November 22, 1965, *FRUS* Congo, Document 447, https://history.state.gov/historicaldocuments/frus1964-68v23/d447.

85 "We can back Mobutu": Memorandum from Harold H. Saunders of the National

Security Council Staff to Robert W. Komer of the National Security Council Staff, Washington, November 23, 1965, *FRUS* Congo, Document 449, https:// history.state.gov/historicaldocuments/frus1964-68v23/d449.

85 "the last hope for the West in the Congo": Telegram from the Station in the Congo to the Central Intelligence Agency, Léopoldville, November 25, 1965, *FRUS* Congo, Document 454, https://history.state.gov/historicaldocuments /frus1964-68v23/d454.

86 "In those years": Author interview with Larry Devlin, March 2008.

87 "a brilliant schemer and plotter": Oakley oral history, FAOH.

88 "President Mobutu is arguably unique": CIA, National Intelligence Estimate, "Zaire: Prospects for the Mobutu Regime," November 7, 1986, https://www.cia .gov/library/readingroom/docs/CIA-RDP90T00155R001200090006-6.pdf.

88 "There was great fear": Grove oral history, FAOH.

89 "I think that, looking back": Harrop oral history, FAOH.

Chapter 5: The Voice of America

91 "My children": Steven Casey, *Cautious Crusade: Franklin D. Roosevelt, American Public Opinion, and the War Against Nazi Germany* (New York: Oxford University Press, 2001), 114.

92 "Communism does not fit the Poles": Stanislaw Mikolajczyk, *The Pattern of Soviet Domination* (London: Sampson Low, Marston, 1948), 112.

93 "a monumental disaster": Author interview with John McMahon, October 2004.

94 "I need not": Memorandum from Robert P. Joyce of the Policy Planning Staff to the Deputy Under Secretary of State (Matthews), Washington, December 31, 1952, *FRUS*, 1950–1955, The Intelligence Community, 1950–1955, Document 142, https://history.state.gov/historicaldocuments/frus1950-55Intel/d142.

94 "I was struck from the very beginning": Brzezinski eulogy for Henze, July 17, 2011, https://pressroom.rferl.org/a/in-memoriam-henze-eulogy-brzezinski/27770941 .html.

95 poison factory, creating chaos, "The struggle," "Why don't we advocate sabotage?" "stupid," and "hare-brained": A. Ross Johnson, *Radio Free Europe and Radio Liberty: The CIA Years and Beyond* (Washington, DC: Woodrow Wilson Center Press, 2010), 47–54.

95 "During the first broadcasts": Cummings quoted in Roland Elliott Brown, "From Propaganda to Journalism: How Radio Free Europe Pierced the Iron Curtain," posted on the website "Journalism Is Not a Crime," June 26, 2017, https:// journalismisnotacrime.com/en/features/1898/.

96 It belonged to Josef Swiatlo: The Swiatlo story is detailed in L. W. Gluchowski, "The Defection of Jozef Swiatlo and the Search for Jewish Scapegoats in the Polish United Workers' Party, 1953–1954," Columbia University Electronic Journal of Modern Central European History, https://ece.columbia.edu/files/ece /images/gluchowski-1.pdf.

96 "If there was turmoil": Ted Shackley, *Spymaster: My Life in the CIA* (Dulles, VA: Potomac Books, 2005), 79–85.

97 "the most successful case": A. Ross Johnson, "Origins of the Swiatlo Broadcasts on RFE," Expanded Text of Remarks Presented at the Conference "'Radio Wolna Europa w walce z komunizmem,'" Warsaw, November 6–7, 2009.

97 "You know, this place is going to blow sky high": Johnson oral history, FAOH.

98 "it wouldn't be an unmixed evil": Minutes of 290th NSC meeting, July 12, 1956, https://nsarchive2.gwu.edu/NSAEBB/NSAEBB76/doc2.pdf.

98 "Polish regime thoroughly shaken": Telegram from the Embassy in Poland to the Department of State, Warsaw, September 21, 1956, *FRUS* Eastern Europe, Document 89, https://history.state.gov/historicaldocuments/frus1955-57v25/d89.

99 "the distortions of the fundamental principles of socialism": Editorial note, *FRUS* Eastern Europe, Document 95, https://history.state.gov/historicaldocuments /frus1955-57v25/d95.

99 "A people, like the Poles": Editorial note, *FRUS* Eastern Europe, Document 99, https://history.state.gov/historicaldocuments/frus1955-57v25/d99.

99 "need have no fear": Memorandum of a Telephone Conversation Between the President and the Secretary of State, October 26, 1956, *FRUS* Eastern Europe, Document 120, https://history.state.gov/historicaldocuments/frus1955-57v25 /d120.

99 "to persist in the political attitudes": Memorandum from the Director of Central Intelligence (Dulles) to the Secretary of State, April 15, 1957, *FRUS* Eastern Europe, Document 246, https://history.state.gov/historicaldocuments/frus1955 -57v25/d246.

100 "How much the Poles are getting away with": Memorandum by George F. Kennan, "Impressions of Poland, July, 1958," *FRUS* 1958–1960, Eastern Europe; Finland; Greece; Turkey, Volume X, Part 2, Document 50, https://history.state .gov/historicaldocuments/frus1958-60v10p2/d50.

100 "The Voice of America": Fischer oral history, FAOH.

101 "We found ourselves using music as an instrument of propaganda": Terence M. Ripmaster, *Willis Conover: Broadcasting Jazz to the World* (Lincoln, NE: iUniverse, 2007), 23.

101 "the single most effective instrument": Ripmaster, *Willis Conover*, 27.

102 "once they've agreed on that": Conover oral history, FAOH.

102 "a musical reflection": John S. Wilson, "Who Is Conover? Only We Ask," *New York Times*, September 13, 1959.

102 "RFE is not advocating ideas": conversation between Gomulka and Vice President Nixon, Warsaw, August 3, 1959, *FRUS* 1958–1960, Eastern Europe; Finland; Greece; Turkey, Volume X, Part 2, Document 74, https://history.state.gov /historicaldocuments/frus1958-60v10p2/d74.

103 "Radio Free Europe": Memorandum of Discussion at the 362d Meeting of the National Security Council, Washington, April 14, 1958, *FRUS* 1958–1960, Eastern Europe; Finland; Greece; Turkey, Volume X, Part 2, Document 45, https:// history.state.gov/historicaldocuments/frus1958-60v10p2/d45.

103 "We have been doing our best": Notes of the Legislative Leadership Meeting, August 16, 1960, *FRUS* 1958–1960, Foreign Economic Policy, Volume IV,

Document 264, https://history.state.gov/historicaldocuments/frus1958 -60v04/d264.

104 "centers of ideological-political sabotage": Paweł Machcewicz, *Poland's War on Radio Free Europe, 1950–1989* (Palo Alto, CA: Stanford University Press, 2015), 118–19.

104 "Look at what it will mean": Conversation Between President Nixon and His Chief of Staff (Haldeman), Washington, March 22, 1972, *FRUS*, 1969–1976, Volume XXIX, Eastern Europe; Eastern Mediterranean, 1969–1972, Document 156, https://history.state.gov/historicaldocuments/frus1969-76v29/d156.

105 "We are unable": Minutes of a National Security Council Meeting, Washington, January 13, 1977, *FRUS*, 1969–1976, Volume XXXVIII, Part 2, Organization and Management of Foreign Policy; Public Diplomacy, 1973–1976, Document 83, https://history.state.gov/historicaldocuments/frus1969-76v38p2/d83.

106 "The activity of dissidents": Paper Prepared in the Central Intelligence Agency for the Special Activities Working Group, Washington, February 4, 1977, *FRUS* 1977–1980, Volume XX, Eastern Europe, 1977–1980, Document 3, https:// history.state.gov/historicaldocuments/frus1977-80v20/d3.

106 "The situation in Poland": Intelligence Memorandum Prepared in the Central Intelligence Agency, "Dissident Activity in East Europe: An Overview," April 1, 1977, *FRUS* 1977–1980, Volume XX, Eastern Europe, 1977–1980, Document 5, https://history.state.gov/historicaldocuments/frus1977-80v20/d5.

107 "I don't believe I *ever* saw Irving": Braden quoted in Frances Stonor Saunders, *The Cultural Cold War: The CIA and the World of Arts and Letters* (New York: New Press, 2013), 87.

107 "A blow-up there": Intelligence Memorandum Prepared in the Central Intelligence Agency, "Dissident Activity in East Europe: An Overview."

107 "A program such as this": Memorandum from Paul Henze of the National Security Council Staff to the President's Assistant for National Security Affairs (Brzezinski), "CIA's Soviet and East European Book and Publications Program," Washington, January 23, 1979, *FRUS* 1977–1980, Volume XX, Eastern Europe, 1977–1980, Document 29, https://history.state.gov/historicaldocuments/frus1977-80v20/d29.

108 "watching the nightly news": Virden oral history, FAOH.

109 "Two years ago": Minutes of the August 23, 1980, meeting of the Polish Politburo, in Machcewicz, *Poland's War on Radio Free Europe*, 233.

109 "It was thanks to Free Europe": Machcewicz, *Poland's War on Radio Free Europe*, 232.

110 "What is going on in Poland": Editorial note, *FRUS* 1977–1980, Volume XX, Eastern Europe, 1977–1980, Document 38, https://history.state.gov /historicaldocuments/frus1977-80v20/d38.

110 "a ripple effect": Douglas J. MacEachin, *U.S. Intelligence and the Polish Crisis, 1980–1981* (Washington, DC: CIA Center for the Study of Intelligence, 2000), 14, https://www.cia.gov/library/readingroom/docs/2000-01-01.pdf; Robert M. Gates, *From the Shadows: The Ultimate Insider's Story of Five Presidents and How They Won the Cold War* (New York: Simon & Schuster, 1996), 163; "Recent

Military Activities in and Around Poland," MacEachin, *U.S. Intelligence and the Polish Crisis*, 34.

111 Colonel Ryszard Kuklinski: For a blow-by-blow account of the colonel's role, see Mark Kramer, "Colonel Kuklinski and the Polish Crisis, 1980–81," *Cold War International History Project (CWIHP) Bulletin* 11, 48–59, https://www.wilsoncenter.org/sites/default/files/CWIHP_Bulletin_11.pdf.

111 "I believe the Soviets": MacEachin, *U.S. Intelligence and the Polish Crisis*, 32; Gates, *From the Shadows*, 166.

111 fifteen divisions . . . "decision to invade": MacEachin, *U.S. Intelligence and the Polish Crisis*, 36–38

112 "a global shadow of tension": Gates, *From the Shadows*, 231.

113 "We Poles realize": Benjamin Weiser, *A Secret Life: The Polish Officer, His Covert Mission, and the Price He Paid to Save His Country* (New York: PublicAffairs, 2004), 239.

113 "In my view": Gates, *From the Shadows*, 233.

114 "the human failings": MacEachin, *U.S. Intelligence and the Polish Crisis*, 193. See also Tina Rosenberg, *The Haunted Land: Facing Europe's Ghosts After Communism* (New York: Vintage, 1996), 205–8.

115 "The recent events in Poland": Message from President Reagan to Soviet General Secretary Brezhnev, Washington, undated, *FRUS*, 1981–1988, Volume III, Soviet Union, January 1981–January 1983, Document 122, https://history.state.gov/historicaldocuments/frus1981-88v03/d122.

116 "a very robust program": Simons oral history, FAOH.

116 "We developed channels": Kirkland oral history, FAOH.

116 at least $4 million: figure was cited by one of the American participants, Eric Chenoweth, in "AFL-CIO Support for Solidarity: Moral, Political, Financial," Presentation to the Conference on AFL-CIO Foreign Policy, Ghent, Belgium, October 6–8, 2011, https://www.idee.org/Chenoweth_AFLCIO%20Support%20for%20Solidarity_111513.pdf.

116 "The printing presses we got from the West": Kulerski quoted in Arch Puddington, *Lane Kirkland: Champion of American Labor* (Hoboken, NJ: John Wiley & Sons, 2005), 185.

117 sentenced him to death in absentia: Najder's work is documented in Gregory F. Domber, *Empowering Revolution: America, Poland, and the End of the Cold War* (Chapel Hill: University of North Carolina Press, 2014), 110–12.

118 "The President brought up to the Pope": Melady oral history, FAOH.

118 "contain and reverse": NSDD 32, "U.S. National Security Strategy," May 20, 1982, https://fas.org/irp/offdocs/nsdd/nsdd-32.pdf.

118 "show relative independence": NSDD 54, "United States Policy Toward Eastern Europe," September 2, 1982, https://fas.org/irp/offdocs/nsdd/nsdd-54.pdf.

119 CIA operation code-named QR/HELPFUL: The QR/HELPFUL cryptonym and some operational details about CIA support for Solidarity were first published in September 2018 in Seth G. Jones, *A Covert Action: Reagan, the CIA, and*

the Cold War Struggle in Poland (New York: W. W. Norton, 2018). Details also
appear in Gates, *From the Shadows*; and Domber, *Empowering Revolution*. A full
record awaits the declassification of White House, State, and CIA documents.
The most reliable account was published in 2012 by a longtime official CIA historian: Benjamin B. Fischer, "Solidarity, the CIA, and Western Technology," *International Journal of Intelligence and CounterIntelligence* 25, no. 3 (2012): 427–69.
My account relies on these sources and on interviews conducted on background
with former senior CIA officials.

119 "In the case of *Solidarność*": Shultz oral history, Miller Center, December 18,
2002, https://millercenter.org/the-presidency/presidential-oral-histories/george
-p-shultz-oral-history-secretary-state.

119 sophisticated printing and broadcasting capabilities: Fischer, "Solidarity, the CIA,
and Western Technology"; John P. C. Matthews, "The West's Secret Marshall
Plan for the Mind," *International Journal of Intelligence and CounterIntelligence*
16, no. 3 (Fall 2003): 409–27, http://cryptome.org/cia-minden.htm#matthews;

120 1.3 million leaflets: Gregory Wolk, "To Limit, To Eradicate, or To Control?
The SB and the 'Second Circulation,' 1981–1989/90, in Gwido Zlatkes, Paweł
Sowiński, and Ann M. Frenkel, eds., *Duplicator Underground: The Independent
Publishing Industry in Communist Poland, 1976–89* (Bloomington, IN: Slavica
Publishers, 2016), 265.

121 a network of mobile clandestine television transmitters: Bob Gates wrote in 1996
that the CIA "provided a good deal of money and equipment to the Polish underground for this—actually to take over the airwaves for a brief time." Gates, *From
the Shadows*, 451.

121 "We could hear the sirens": Michael T. Kaufman, *Mad Dreams, Saving Graces:
Poland: A Nation in Conspiracy* (New York: Random House, 1989), 85.

123 "to remember how shocking": Rosenberg, *The Haunted Land*, 235.

123 "hostile elements" and "if you look at the 'experience' of Poland": Quoted in
Mark Kramer, "The Collapse of East European Communism and the Repercus-
sions within the Soviet Union (Part 2)," *Journal of Cold War Studies* 6, no. 4 (Fall
2004): 3–64, https://muse.jhu.edu/article/174712/pdf.

124 "All right, the Germans": Vladimir Putin et al., *First Person: An Astonishingly
Frank Self-Portrait by Russia's President* (New York: PublicAffairs, 2000), 78–79.

Chapter 6: A Very Dirty Game

127 "Leningrad was a much tougher KGB town": Merry oral history, FAOH.

129 the KGB's First Chief Directorate: Thomas Boghardt, "Soviet Bloc Intelligence
and Its AIDS Disinformation Campaign," *Studies in Intelligence* 53, no. 4 (December 2009), https://www.cia.gov/library/center-for-the-study-of-intelligence
/csi-publications/csi-studies/studies/vol53no4/pdf/U-%20Boghardt-AIDS
-Made%20in%20the%20USA-17Dec.pdf.

129 "The heart and soul of Soviet intelligence": Oleg Kalugin, "Inside the KGB: An
interview with retired KGB Maj. Gen. Oleg Kalugin," CNN, January 1998.

131 Where the KGB truly excelled: United States Information Agency "Soviet Active

Measures in the Era of Glasnost: A Report to Congress," March 1988, http:// insidethecoldwar.org/sites/default/files/documents/Soviet%20Active%20 Measures%20in%20the%20Era%20of%20Glasnot%20March%201988.pdf.

131 "He was tall, thin, and stooped": David Robarge, "Moles, Defectors, and Deceptions: James Angleton and CIA Counterintelligence," *Journal of Intelligence History* 3, no. 2 (Winter 2003).

133 "The bulk of information": Memorandum from Vice President Rockefeller to President Ford, "Report by James J. Angleton, former chief of counterintelligence for the CIA," Washington, undated, *FRUS*, 1969–1976, Volume XXXVIII, Part 2, Organization and Management of Foreign Policy; Public Diplomacy, 1973–1976, Document 41, https://history.state.gov/historicaldocuments /frus1969-76v38p2/d41.

134 "Given the importance of propaganda": McMahon testimony, Hearing on Soviet Covert Action, February 6, 1980, House of Representatives, Permanent Select Committee on Intelligence, Subcommittee on Oversight.

135 Active Measures working group: For an overview of the Active Measures Working Group, see Fletcher Schoen and Christopher J. Lamb, *Deception, Disinformation, and Strategic Communications: How One Interagency Group Made a Major Difference*, Institute for National Strategic Studies, Strategic Perspectives, no. 11 (Washington, DC: National Defense University Press, June 2012), https://ndupress.ndu .edu/Portals/68/Documents/stratperspective/inss/Strategic-Perspectives-11.pdf.

136 "This was new": Kux oral history, FAOH.

137 "In late 1979": "Soviet 'Active Measures': Forgery, Disinformation, Political Operations" (State Department Special Report No. 88, October 1981), http:// insidethecoldwar.org/sites/default/files/documents/Soviet%20Active%20 Measures%20Forgery,%20Disinformation,%20Political%20Operations%20 October%201981.pdf. In its first two years, the group also published "Soviet Active Measures: An Update" (July 1982); "Moscow's Radio Peace and Progress" (August 1982); "Communist Clandestine Broadcasting" (December 1982); "Soviet Active Measures: Focus on Forgeries" (April 1983); "The World Peace Council's Peace Assemblies" (May 1983); and "World Federation of Trade Unions: Soviet Foreign Policy Tool" (August 1983). By 1986, the CIA was publishing its own quarterly report, *Worldwide Active Measures and Propaganda Alert*, which went to a very select readership: the president, the vice president, the secretaries of state and defense, the National Security Council, and the top brass at the Pentagon, the State Department, the FBI, and the National Security Agency. It was not a substantial improvement on the reporting by the Active Measures Working Group.

139 "The Administration is harboring": Memorandum from John Lenczowski to John M. Poindexter, "Subject: Statement on Soviet Intervention in the U.S. Electoral Process," August 16, 1984, NSC Executive Secretariat Records, Ronald Reagan Library.

140 "competent bodies": "Soviet Active Measures: Focus on Forgeries," Foreign Affairs Note, State Department, Washington, DC, April 1983, http://insidethecoldwar .org/sites/default/files/documents/Department%20of%20State%20Note%20

Soviet%20Active%20Measures%20Focus%20on%20Forgeries%20April%201983
.pdf.

141 "AFRICAN MONKEYS!": "Active Measures: A Report on the Substance and
Process of Anti-U.S. Disinformation and Propaganda Campaigns," State Depart-
ment, August 1986, http://insidethecoldwar.org/sites/default/files/documents
/Soviet%20Active%20Measures%20Substance%20and%20Process%20of%20
Anti-US%20Disinformation%20August%201986.pdf.

142 "no enthusiasm": Tim Weiner, "C.I.A. Official Tells of Botching Ames Case,"
New York Times, September 30, 1994, https://www.nytimes.com/1994/09/30/us
/cia-official-tells-of-botching-of-ames-case.html?searchResultPosition=1.

144 "turn Soviet active measures": "SUBJECT: Soviet Political Action Working
Group: December 15 Meeting," NSC, December 30, 1983.

144 "a covert CIA operation": "Launching the Private Network," draft report, House Foreign Affairs Committee, undated but likely mid-1988, https://consortiumnews
.com/wp-content/uploads/2014/12/lostchapter.pdf.

144 "senior CIA officials": "State Department and Intelligence Community Involvement in Domestic Activities Related to the Iran/Contra Affair," staff report,
House Foreign Affairs Committee, September 7, 1988, https://nsarchive2.gwu
.edu/NSAEBB/NSAEBB40/04302.pdf.

146 "Operation 'DENVER'": The East German and Bulgarian memos were first published in translation on July 22, 2019, by the Wilson Center, with an accompa-
nying article that corrected the widely held belief that the operation had been
code-named INFEKTION. See Douglas Selvage and Christopher Nehring,
"Operation 'Denver': KGB and Stasi Disinformation Regarding AIDS," Wilson
Center, https://www.wilsoncenter.org/blog-post/operation-denver-kgb-and
-stasi-disinformation-regarding-aids.

147 "To be honest": Author interview with Bailey.

150 "So, we go forward!" Memorandum of Conversation, Moscow, October 23, 1987,
FRUS, 1981–1988, Volume VI, Soviet Union, October 1986–January 1989, Document 84, https://history.state.gov/historicaldocuments/frus1981-88v06/d84.

152 "that there would be not only arms reduction": Memorandum of Conversation,
Working Luncheon with General Secretary Mikhail Gorbachev, Washington,
December 10, 1987, *FRUS*, 1981–1988, Volume VI, Soviet Union, October
1986–January 1989, Document 115, https://history.state.gov/historicaldocuments
/frus1981-88v06/d115.

152 "Our enhanced program": Paper Prepared in the Central Intelligence Agency,
Washington, November 13, 1987, *FRUS*, 1981–1988, Volume VI, Soviet Union, October 1986–January 1989, Document 93, https://history.state.gov/historicaldocuments
/frus1981-88v06/d93.

152 "Russian-language propaganda pamphlet": Minutes of a National Security Planning Group Meeting, "Review of Covert Action Programs," July 11, 1988, *FRUS*,
1981–1988, Volume VI, Soviet Union, October 1986–January 1989, Document
166, https://history.state.gov/historicaldocuments/frus1981-88v06/d166.

Chapter 7: "The Deceitful Dream of a Golden Age"

156 "At a time": Gates oral history, Miller Center, July 23–24, 2000 https://millercenter.org/the-presidency/presidential-oral-histories/robert-m-gates-deputy-director-central.

156 "expanding NATO": George F. Kennan, "A Fateful Error," *New York Times*, February 5, 1997, https://www.nytimes.com/1997/02/05/opinion/a-fateful-error.html.

156 "Why are you sowing": Elaine Sciolino, "Yeltsin Says NATO Is Trying to Split Continent Again," *New York Times*, December 6, 1994, https://www.nytimes.com/1994/12/06/world/yeltsin-says-nato-is-trying-to-split-continent-again.html?searchResultPosition=1.

156 "We were assured": Medvedev quoted in Uwe Klussmann, Matthias Schepp, and Klaus Wiegrefe, "NATO's Eastward Expansion: Did the West Break Its Promise to Moscow?" *Der Spiegel*, November 26, 2009, http://www.spiegel.de/international/world/nato-s-eastward-expansion-did-the-west-break-itspromise-to-moscow-a-663315.html.

156 "wanted a complete victory": Putin interview quoted in Radio Free Europe/Radio Liberty dispatch, January 11, 2016, https://www.rferl.org/a/russia-putin-eu-sanctions-absurd/27481012.html.

156 "a serious provocation": Putin's Prepared Remarks at 43rd Munich Conference on Security Policy, February 12, 2007, http://www.washingtonpost.com/wp-dyn/content/article/2007/02/12/AR2007021200555.html.

157 "The strength of NATO": "Bush-Kohl Telephone Conversation on the Situation in Eastern Europe," October 23, 1989, George H. W. Bush Presidential Library, https://digitalarchive.wilsoncenter.org/document/116230.

157 "the Soviet Union's worst nightmare": Brent Scowcroft to the president, "The Soviets and the German Question," November 29, 1989, "German Unification" folder, box 91116, Scowcroft Files, GBPL. Key documents from the George Bush Presidential Library cited in this chapter, unavailable online as this book went to press, were published in Joshua R. Itzkowitz Shifrinson, "Deal or No Deal? The End of the Cold War and the U.S. Offer to Limit NATO Expansion," *International Security* 40, no. 4 (Spring 2016): 7–44. See also Mary Elise Sarotte, "Perpetuating U.S. Preeminence: The 1990 Deals to 'Bribe the Soviets Out' and Move NATO In," *International Security* 35, no. 1 (Summer 2010): 110–37.

157 "We beat the Germans twice, and now they're back": Carsten Volkery, "'The Germans Are Back!'" *Der Spiegel*, September 11, 2009, https://www.spiegel.de/international/europe/the-iron-lady-s-views-on-german-reunification-the-germans-are-back-a-648364.html.

158 "Every other leader": Gates oral history, Miller Center.

158 "Life is forcing us": Gorbachev's Speech to the United Nations, December 8, 1988, https://apnews.com/1abea48aacda1a9dd520c380a8bc6be6.

158 "Talking eye to eye": "Record of Conversation Between Mikhail Gorbachev and George H. W. Bush at Malta Summit," December 2, 1989, notes of A. S. Chernyaev, Gorbachev Foundation Archive, Moscow. Published in Gorbachev,

Gody trudnykh resheniy [Years of Difficult Decisions] (Moscow: Alfa-print, 1993), https://digitalarchive.wilsoncenter.org/document/117223.

159 "We fought alongside with you": Mary Elise Sarotte, "Not One Inch Eastward? Bush, Baker, Kohl, Genscher, Gorbachev, and the Origin of Russian Resentment Toward NATO Enlargement in February 1990," *Diplomatic History* 34, no. 1 (January 2010): 119–40. Sarotte fought for, and won, the declassification of key documents cited in this chapter, and she is the leading scholar on the question of NATO expansion. Key conversations between the Bush administration and Gorbachev are in a 2017 National Security Archive briefing book, "NATO Expansion: What Gorbachev Heard," https://nsarchive2.gwu.edu//dc.html?doc=4325680-Document-06-Record-of-conversation-between.

159 "categorical assurances": Philip Zelikow, "NATO Expansion Wasn't Ruled Out," *New York Times*, August 10, 1995, https://www.nytimes.com/1995/08/10/opinion/IHT-nato-expansion-wasnt-ruled-out.html.

160 Their conversation: Memorandum of Conversation, George H. W. Bush Presidential Library, February 24, 1990, https://bush41library.tamu.edu/files/memcons-telcons/1990-02-24--Kohl.pdf.

160 "Beyond containment lies democracy": Baker address to the World Affairs Council of Dallas, March 30, 1990.

161 "I wanted to emphasize": Baker to Gorbachev, May 18, 1990, National Security Archive, https://nsarchive2.gwu.edu//dc.html?doc=4325695-Document-18-Record-of-conversation-between.

161 "we are not": Bush to Gorbachev, May 31, 1990, National Security Archive, https://nsarchive2.gwu.edu//dc.html?doc=4325698-Document-21-Record-of-conversation-between.

161 like he had fallen into a trap: Sarotte, "Not One Inch Eastward?"

161 "For months": Scowcroft oral history, Miller Center, November 12–13, 1999 https://millercenter.org/the-presidency/presidential-oral-histories/brent-scowcroft-oral-history.

163 "As the sun went down the first day": Merry oral history, FAOH.

163 "The one phone": Merrill oral history, FAOH.

164 "They were taking down the huge statue": Merry oral history, FAOH.

164 "a great metaphor": Merry oral history, FAOH.

166 "a war of murderous naivete" and "I think Mother Teresa": Lake quoted in Jason DeParle, "The Man Inside Bill Clinton's Foreign Policy," *New York Times*, August 20, 1995, https://www.nytimes.com/1995/08/20/magazine/the-man-inside-bill-clinton-s-foreign-policy.html.

166 "democratic enlargement": Anthony Lake, "From Containment to Enlargement" (speech delivered at the Johns Hopkins School of Advanced International Studies, Washington, DC, September 21, 1993), https://www.mtholyoke.edu/acad/intrel/lakedoc.html.

167 "The challenge for NATO over the next generation": Undersecretary of State Lynn Davis, "Strategy for NATO's Expansion and Transformation," State Depart-

ment, September 7, 1993, https://nsarchive2.gwu.edu//dc.html?doc=4390816
-Document-02-Strategy-for-NATO-s-Expansion-and.

168 "We were barely away from the dock": Strobe Talbott, *The Russia Hand: A Memoir of Presidential Diplomacy* (New York: Random House, 2002), 64.

168 "the spirit": Yeltsin Letter on NATO Expansion, September 15, 1993, https://nsarchive2.gwu.edu//dc.html?doc=4390818-Document-04-Retranslation-of-Yeltsin-letter-on.

168 "If Russia went south": Lake 2004 oral history, Miller Center, November 6, 2004 https://millercenter.org/the-presidency/presidential-oral-histories/anthony-lake-oral-history-2004-national-security-advisor.

169 "Boy, do I ever miss the cold war!": Talbott, *The Russia Hand*, 91.

170 "neuralgic to the Russians": James Collins to Warren Christopher, October 20, 1993, https://nsarchive2.gwu.edu//dc.html?doc=4390820-Document-06-Your-October-21-23-visit-to-Moscow.

170 "full participation in the future": Christopher's meeting with Yeltsin, October 22, 1993, https://nsarchive2.gwu.edu//dc.html?doc=4390822-Document-08-Secretary-Christopher-s-meeting-with.

171 "Now the question": The President's News Conference with Visegrad Leaders in Prague, January 12, 1994, https://www.presidency.ucsb.edu/documents/the-presidents-news-conference-with-visegrad-leaders-prague. "Russia is not a near-term threat," Clinton personally told the Czech leader Vaclav Havel the day before. "But if historical trends do reassert themselves, we will have organized ourselves so that we could move quickly not only to NATO membership but other security relations that can serve as a deterrent."

171 "The contrast was quite stark": Merry oral history, FAOH.

172 "NATO expansion will, when it occurs": Talbott to Christopher, September 12, 1994; "Our current position": Talbott to Christopher, December 9, 1994; "It's Russia that must move": Talbott to Christopher, March 24, 1995, cited in Mary Elise Sarotte, "How to Enlarge NATO: The Debate Inside the Clinton Administration, 1993–95," *International Security* 44, no. 1 (Summer 2019), https://doi.org/10.1162/ISEC_a_00353.

173 "Have we not already seen": Alexander Hamilton, Federalist No. 6, November 14, 1787, https://avalon.law.yale.edu/18th_century/fed06.asp.

174 "the big mess," "Pizza! Pizza!" and "We're going to move forward": Talbott, *The Russia Hand*, 133–36.

174 "will be interpreted": Yeltsin letter to Clinton, November 29, 1994, https://nsarchive2.gwu.edu//dc.html?doc=4390827-Document-13-Official-informal-No-248-Boris-Bill.

175 "the first chance ever": "President's Dinner with President Yeltsin," State Department cable, 1994-Moscow-01457, January 14, 1994, cited in Sarotte, "How to Enlarge NATO," 7–41.

176 "I wanted us to use air strikes": Zimmermann oral history, FAOH.

176 "And so it continued": Talbott, *The Russia Hand*, 77.

176 "As NATO expands": Norman Kempster, Dean E. Murphy, "Broader NATO May Bring 'Cold Peace,' Yeltsin Warns," *Los Angeles Times*, December 6, 1994, https:// www.latimes.com/archives/la-xpm-1994-12-06-mn-5629-story.html. Even as Yeltsin spoke, Russian warplanes were attacking the breakaway Russian republic of Chechnya in the Northern Caucasus, and a week later a full-bore ground invasion began. Yeltsin had authorized the invasion after trying and failing to mount a coup against the renegade Chechen president. The Russian defense minister, Pavel Grachev, had assured Yeltsin that the military could crush the Chechen resistance in a day or two. The lie would have impressed Stalin with its audacity. Grachev's deputy resigned in protest at the stupidity and brutality of the attack, as did the deputy commander of Russia's ground forces, who called it a crime for Yeltsin to send the army against his own people. By the time Russia sued for peace, nineteen months later, at least fifty thousand were dead, perhaps twice that number by some estimates, and by far, most of them were civilians.

176 "Europe, even before": James M. Goldgeier, "Promises Made, Promises Broken? What Yeltsin Was Told About NATO in 1993 and Why It Matters," *War on the Rocks*, July 12, 2016, https://warontherocks.com/2016/07/promises-made -promises-broken-what-yeltsin-was-told-about-nato-in-1993-and-why-it-matters/.

177 "We had to be careful": Talbott quoted in James M. Goldgeier and Michael McFaul, *Power and Purpose: U.S. Policy Toward Russia After the Cold War* (Washington, DC: Brookings Institution Press, 2003), 148.

177 "For me to agree": Summary Report on One-on-One Meeting Between Presidents Clinton and Yeltsin, Saint Catherine's Hall, the Kremlin, May 10, 1995, https://nsarchive2.gwu.edu//dc.html?doc=4390833-Document-19-Summary -report-on-One-on-One-meeting.

178 "to perhaps add a little": Memorandum of Telephone Conversation: "The President's Discussion with President Yeltsin on the Russian Election, Bilateral Relations, START II Ratification and NATO," February 21, 1996, William J. Clinton Presidential Library, in National Security Archive briefing book, "The Clinton-Yeltsin Relationship in Their Own Words," October 2, 2018, https:// nsarchive.gwu.edu/briefing-book/russia-programs/2018-10-02/clinton-yeltsin -relationship-their-own-words.

178 "Bill, for my election campaign": Memorandum of Telephone Conversation with Russian President Yeltsin on CTBT, Chechnya, Economics, CFE and Russian Election, May 7, 1996, ibid.

179 three times longer than the Great Depression: Robert David English, "Russia, Trump, and a New Détente," *Foreign Affairs*, March 10, 2017.

180 "our position with regard to NATO expansion": Evgeny Primakov, "Materials on the Subject of NATO for Use in Conversations and Public Statements," January 31, 1997, https://nsarchive2.gwu.edu//dc.html?doc=4390839-Document-25 -Excerpts-from-Evgeny-Primakov-Memo.

181 "for Europe's east": Jane Perlez, "Poland, Hungary and the Czechs Join NATO," *New York Times*, March 13, 1999, https://www.nytimes.com/1999/03/13/world /expanding-alliance-the-overview-poland-hungary-and-the-czechs-join-nato.html.

182 "We have to launch": Memorandum of Telephone Conversation with President Yeltsin, National Security Archive, March 24, 1998, https://nsarchive2 .gwu.edu//dc.html?doc=4950575-Document-16-Memorandum-of-Telephone -Conversation.

183 "it sometimes seemed to Russian generals": Talbott, *The Russia Hand*, 411–12.

184 "I would like to tell you about him": Memorandum of Telephone Conversation with President Yeltsin, National Security Archive, September 8, 1999, https:// nsarchive2.gwu.edu//dc.html?doc=4950576-Document-17-Memorandum-of -Telephone-Conversation.

185 "Putin, of course": Memorandum of Conversation, Meeting with Russian President Yeltsin, Istanbul, November 19, 1999, 565–66, https://clinton .presidentiallibraries.us/items/show/57569.

185 "Boris, I believe": Memorandum of Telephone Conversation with President Yeltsin, National Security Archive, December 31, 1999, https://nsarchive2 .gwu.edu//dc.html?doc=4950577-Document-18-Memorandum-of-Telephone -Conversation.

Chapter 8: This Untamed Fire

188 democracy fell into a long global recession: As a leading scholar of democracy studies wrote in 2015: "The world has been in a mild but protracted democratic recession since about 2006. Beyond the lack of improvement or modest erosion of global levels of democracy and freedom, there have been several other causes for concern. First, there has been a significant and, in fact, accelerating rate of democratic breakdown. Second, the quality or stability of democracy has been declining in a number of large and strategically important emerging-market countries, which I call 'swing states.' Third, authoritarianism has been deepening, including in big and strategically important countries. And fourth, the established democracies, beginning with the United States, increasingly seem to be performing poorly and to lack the will and self-confidence to promote democracy effectively abroad." Larry Diamond, "Facing Up to the Democratic Recession," *Journal of Democracy* 26, no. 1 (January 2015), https://www.journalofdemocracy.org/wp-content /uploads/2015/01/Diamond-26-1_0.pdf. A comprehensive and convincing survey of data supporting this conclusion is in Michael A. Weber, "Global Trends in Democracy: Background, U.S. Policy, and Issues for Congress," Congressional Research Service, United States Congress, October 17, 2018, https://fas.org/sgp /crs/row/R45344.pdf.

189 "new democracies": Bush address at Warsaw University, June 15, 2001, https:// www.presidency.ucsb.edu/documents/address-warsaw-university.

189 "looked the man in the eye" and 'Look, this is a military organization": Bush news conference with Putin, Kranj, June 16, 2001, https://www.presidency.ucsb .edu/documents/the-presidents-news-conference-with-president-vladimir-putin -russia-kranj.

190 "We were devoid of a fundamental understanding of Afghanistan": Douglas Lute, Lessons Learned Record of Interview, in Craig Whitlock, Leslie Shapiro, and

Armand Emamdjomeh, "The Afghanistan Papers: A Secret History of the War," *Washington Post*, December 6, 2019, https://www.washingtonpost.com/graphics /2019/investigations/afghanistan-papers/documents-database/?document=lute _doug_ll_01_d5_02202015.

192 "everything of interest to us, all the time": Tim Weiner, "Pentagon Envisioning a Costly Internet for War," *New York Times*, November 13, 2004, https://www .nytimes.com/2004/11/13/technology/pentagon-envisioning-a-costly-internet -for-war.html?searchResultPosition=1.

193 "For the first time in the history of warfare": General Yuri Baluyevskiy, cited in Linda Robinson, Todd C. Helmus, Raphael S. Cohen, Alireza Nader, Andrew Radin, Madeline Magnuson, and Katya Migacheva, *Modern Political Warfare: Current Practices and Possible Responses* (Santa Monica, CA: RAND Corporation, 2018), 49, https://www.rand.org/pubs/research_reports/RR1772.html.

193 "Information has become": Makhmut Akhmetovich Gareev and Vladimir Slipchenko, *Future War* (Fort Leavenworth, KS: Foreign Military Studies Office, 2007), cited in T. S. Allen and A. J. Moore, "Victory without Casualties: Russia's Information Operations," *Parameters* 48, no. 1 (Spring 2018), https://ssi.armywarcollege .edu/parameters-vol-48-no-1-spring-2018.

"Victory without Casualties" is a seminal work. At the time of its publication, Captain Allen was the intelligence officer of Able Squadron, Asymmetric Warfare Group, aligned with EUCOM and AFRICOM. Master Sergeant Moore was troop sergeant major of 2 Troop, Able Squadron, Asymmetric Warfare Group. He had been continuously deployed in Afghanistan and Iraq with the 75th Ranger Regiment and 173rd Airborne Brigade since October 2001.

193 "The systematic broadcasting": Makhmut Akhmetovich Gareyev, *If War Comes Tomorrow? The Contours of Future Armed Conflict*, ed. Jacob W. Kipp (London: Frank Cass, 1998), 51–52, cited in Allen and Moore, "Victory without Casualties."

193 "the mechanism of foreign political propaganda": Panarin quoted in Paul A. Goble, "Defining Victory and Defeat: The Information War between Russia and Georgia," in Svante E. Cornell and S. Frederick Starr, eds., *The Guns of August 2008: Russia's War in Georgia* (London and New York: Routledge, 2015), 194.

Panarin had made his name by predicting that a civil war driven by economic and social conflagrations would someday shatter the United States into five republics—California and the rest of the West going to China, Texas and the South to Mexico, the Midwest to Canada, the Atlantic states to the European Union, Hawaii to China or Japan, and Alaska to Russia, which had once owned it. That might sound insane, but it was really only mirror-imaging, reflecting the impact upon the Russian mind of the forces that had broken up the Soviet Union and its spheres of influence in the world.

194 "the Information KGB": Jolanta Darczewska, "The Anatomy of Russian Information Warfare" (Warsaw: Centre for Eastern Studies, 2014), https://www.osw.waw .pl/sites/default/files/the_anatomy_of_russian_information_warfare.pdf.

This vital analysis gives a deeper flavor of Panarin's work: "In his book 'Information World War II—War against Russia,' Panarin claimed that all the so-called 'colour' revolutions in the CIS area and the 'Arab Spring' were a product of social control technology and information aggression from the United States. In his opinion, the protest movement on Bolotnaya Square in Moscow after the recent [2012] parliamentary and presidential elections was also a manifestation of this aggression: de facto a result of the Western operation codenamed 'Anti-Putin' controlled from abroad. In the context of the 'velvet revolutions', he defines the basic terms used in information warfare technology for Russian purposes. In practice these are operations of influence, such as: social control, i.e. influencing society; social manoeuvring, i.e. intentional control of the public aimed at gaining certain benefits; information manipulation, i.e. using authentic information in a way that gives rise to false implications; disinformation, i.e. spreading manipulated or fabricated information or a combination thereof; the fabrication of information, i.e. creating false information, and lobbying, blackmail and extortion of desired information."

194 "directors of the information war": Marcel H. Van Herpen, *Putin's Propaganda Machine: Soft Power and Russian Foreign Policy* (Lanham, MD: Rowman & Littlefield, 2015), 8.

195 "undermine political, economic, and social systems": *Conceptual Views Regarding the Activities of the Armed Forces of the Russian Federation in Information Space* (Moscow: Russian Ministry of Defense, 2011), quoted in Timothy L. Thomas, "Russia's 21st Century Information War: Working to Undermine and Destabilize Populations," *Defence Strategic Communications* 1, no. 1 (Winter 2015): 12.

195 "CIA project": Masha Lipman, "Putin's Fear of the Internet," *New Yorker*, April 25, 2014, https://www.newyorker.com/news/news-desk/putins-fear-of-the-internet.

195 "At all turns": Fiona Hill and Clifford G. Gaddy, *Mr. Putin: Operative in the Kremlin* (Washington, DC: Brookings Institution Press, 2015), 343.

198 "dictatorship of international affairs": "Putin Accuses U.S. of Double Standard," *Washington Post*, December 4, 2004, https://www.washingtonpost.com/archive/politics/2004/12/04/world-in-brief/90debod9-6bed-4edc-82f4-6c40075c8f34/.

199 "It is the policy of the United States": Bush, Second Inaugural Address, January 20, 2005, https://www.presidency.ucsb.edu/documents/inaugural-address-13.

Remarkably, the idea of inserting the phrase "ending tyranny" in the speech came from the cold-war historian John Lewis Gaddis, George Kennan's biographer, in a session with the president's speechwriters ten days before the inaugural.

199 "democracies have ever been spectacles of turbulence and contention": James Madison, Federalist No. 10, November 23, 1787, https://avalon.law.yale.edu/18th_century/fed10.asp.

200 "Kick ass!": Jean Edward Smith, *Bush* (New York: Simon & Schuster, 2016), 398.

200 "The day is coming": Secretary of State Condoleezza Rice, Remarks at the American University in Cairo, Egypt, June 20, 2005, https://2001-2009.state.gov/secretary/rm/2005/48328.htm.

200 "We don't know yet how best to promote democracy": David Finkel, "U.S. Ideals Meet Reality in Yemen," *Washington Post*, December 18, 2005, https://www.washingtonpost.com/archive/politics/2005/12/18/us-ideals-meet-reality-in-yemen/c507277c-ef84-41a1-9171-0d1ec2604a63/.

200 "We didn't know": Edelman oral history, Miller Center, June 2, 2017, https://
millercenter.org/the-presidency/presidential-oral-histories/eric-edelman-oral
-history.

200 "Not only was the strategy": Rice oral history, SMU Center for Presidential
History, July 20, 2015, https://www.smu.edu/-/media/Site/CPH/Collective
-Memory-Project/The-Surge/Rice-Condoleezza--FINAL--20199.pdf?la=en.

201 "bordering on despair": Negroponte oral history, Miller Center, September 14,
2012 https://millercenter.org/the-presidency/presidential-oral-histories/john
-negroponte-oral-history.

201 "to move forward, not backward, along freedom's path": National Security Strategy of
the United States, March 2006, https://www.comw.org/qdr/fulltext/nss2006.pdf.

201 "leading a growing community": Bush statement on the National Security
Strategy, March 16, 2006, https://georgewbush-whitehouse.archives.gov/nsc/nss
/2006/intro.html.

202 "A group of FSB operatives": "The Making of a neo-KGB State," *Economist*, August
23, 2007, https://www.economist.com/briefing/2007/08/23/the-making-of-a
-neo-kgb-state.

202 "The Kremlin began cultivating relationships": See "Putin's Asymmetric Assault
on Democracy in Russia and Europe: Implications for U.S. National Security,"
a minority staff report prepared for the Senate Foreign Relations Committee,
January 10, 2018, https://www.foreign.senate.gov/imo/media/doc/FinalRR.pdf.
As the report pointed out, Putin's political warfare attracted all manner of people on both fringes of the spectrum, and Russia also covertly supported fringe
political parties of ex-communists, as well as a handful of environmental groups,
and attracted American evangelicals and neo-Nazis before and during the Trump
administration. It is worth quoting here at length:

> The Kremlin has also adopted a new practice in cultivating relationships
> with some of the more mainstream far-right parties in Europe, by estab-
> lishing "cooperation agreements" between the dominant United Russia
> party and parties in Austria (Freedom Party), Hungary (Jobbik), Italy
> (Northern League), France (National Front), and Germany (AfD). These
> cooperation agreements include plans for regular meetings and "collab-
> oration where suitable on economic, business and political projects."
> Kremlin-linked banks, funds, and oligarchs even lent nearly $13 million
> in 2014 to France's far-right National Front party to finance its election
> campaign. And the German newspaper *Bild* reported that the Russian
> government clandestinely funded the AfD ahead of 2017 parliamentary
> elections—perhaps without the AfD's knowledge—by using middlemen
> to sell its gold at below-market prices. In addition to monetary resources,
> the Kremlin has reportedly also offered organizational, political, and
> media expertise and assistance to far-right European parties.
>
> Different Kremlin narratives attract different groups from left and
> right. Scholars Peter Pomerantsev and Michael Weiss describe how
> "European right-nationalists are seduced by the [Kremlin's] anti-EU

message; members of the far-left are brought in by tales of fighting US hegemony; [and] U.S. religious conservatives are convinced by the Kremlin's stance against homosexuality." The Congressional Research Service reports that many of the far-right European parties linked to the Kremlin are "anti-establishment and anti-EU, and they often share some combination of extreme nationalism; a commitment to 'law and order' and traditional family values; and anti-immigrant, anti-Semitic, or anti-Islamic sentiments. . . . [They included] delegates from Germany's neo-Nazi NPD party, Bulgaria's far-right Ataka party, the far-left KKK party in Greece, and the pro-Kremlin Latvian Russian Union party."

[In March 2015], the leaders of some of Europe's most controversial and fringe right-wing political organizations—as well as some from similar groups in the United States—met in Saint Petersburg for the first International Russian Conservative Forum. The event was organized by Russia's nationalistic Rodina ("Motherland") party, and its objective was clearly stated: to unite European and Russian conservative forces "in the context of European sanctions against Russia and the United States' pressure on European countries and Russia." Speakers reportedly urged white Christians to reproduce, referred to gays as perverts, and said that murdered Russian opposition activists were resting in hell. They also decried same-sex marriage, globalization, radical Islam, immigration, and New York financiers, while consistently praising Russia's President Vladimir Putin for upholding and protecting conservative and masculine values. A British nationalist speaker showed a picture of a shirtless Putin riding a bear, and declared: "Obama and America, they are like females. They are feminized men. But you have been blessed by a man who is a man, and we envy that." James Taylor, an American who runs a white nationalist website, spoke at the event, where he called the United States "the greatest enemy of tradition everywhere."

In the United States, many extreme right-wing groups, including white nationalists, look up to Putin—a self-proclaimed champion of tradition and conservative values. At a protest in Charlottesville, Virginia, against the removal of a statue of Confederate general Robert E. Lee, white nationalists repeatedly chanted "Russia is our friend." Andrew Anglin, the publisher of the Daily Stormer, the world's biggest neo-Nazi website, apparently spent much of 2015 and 2016 running his website from inside of Russia, from where his content was promoted by a suspected Russian bot network. In addition, the Kremlin has cultivated ties with organizations that promote gun rights and oppose same-sex marriage. For example, Kremlin-linked officials have also cultivated ties with groups in the United States like the National Rifle Association (NRA). Alexander Torshin, a former senator in Putin's United Russia party who allegedly helped launder money through Spain for Russian mobsters, developed a relationship with David Keene when the latter was the NRA's President. In 2015, the NRA sent a delegation to Moscow to meet with Dmitry Rogozin, a Putin ally and deputy prime minister who fell under U.S. sanctions in 2014 for his role in the crisis in Ukraine. U.S. evangelicals, including Franklin Graham, have also supported Putin's suppression of LGBT rights in Russia, saying that Putin "has taken a stand to protect his nation's children from the damaging effects of any gay and lesbian agenda."

203 twenty-seven nations: A 2017 report by the German Marshall Fund named Belarus, Bulgaria, Canada, Cyprus, the Czech Republic, Denmark, Estonia, Finland, France, Georgia, Germany, Hungary, Italy, Latvia, Lithuania, Macedonia, Moldova, Montenegro, Norway, Poland, Portugal, Spain, Sweden, Turkey, the United Kingdom, Ukraine, and the United States as targets of Russian warfare attacks since 2004. Oren Dorell, "Alleged Russian Political Meddling Documented in 27 Countries Since 2004," *USA Today*, September 7, 2017, https://www.usatoday.com/story/news/world/2017/09/07/alleged-russian -political-meddling-documented-27-countries-since-2004/619056001/.

Chapter 9: The First Casualties

204 "WORLD'S FIRST VIRTUAL ATTACK AGAINST NATION STATE": U.S. Embassy in Tallinn, June 4, 2007, https://wikileaks.org/plusd/cables /07TALLINN366_a.html.

205 "It was quite a day": Smith oral history, FAOH.

206 "take Estonnet the fuck down :)": Joshua Davis, "Hackers Take Down the Most Wired Country in Europe," *Wired*, August 21, 2007, https://www.wired.com /2007/08/ff-estonia/.

207 "They've basically been brought to their knees": Schmidt quoted in Larry Greenemeier, "Estonian Attacks Raise Concern over Cyber 'Nuclear Winter,'" *InformationWeek*, May 24, 2007.

207 "Those who are trying today": "Putin Warns Against 'Belittling' War Effort," Radio Free Europe/Radio Liberty, May 9, 2007, https://www.rferl.org/a/1076356 .html.

207 "The potential exists": Lynn quoted in Jim Garamone, "Lynn: NATO Must Get Ahead of Cyber Threat," American Forces Press Service, January 25, 2011, http:// www.archive.defense.gov/news/newsarticle.aspx?id=62572, and cited in Stephen Herzog, "Revisiting the Estonian Cyber Attacks: Digital Threats and Multinational Responses," *Journal of Strategic Security* 4, no. 2 (Summer 2011).

207 "What they do to us": Ilves quoted in Sheera Frenkel, "The New Handbook for Cyberwar Is Being Written by Russia," BuzzFeed News, March 19, 2017.

208 "Information Security Doctrine": Russia's "Information Security Doctrine" and General Vorobyev's shock doctrine are explicated in Ulrik Franke, *War by Non-Military Means: Understanding Russian Information Warfare* (Stockholm: Swedish Defence Research Agency, 2015), 16–23.

208 "a world in which there is one master": Putin speech at the Munich Conference

on Security Policy, February 10, 2007, http://en.kremlin.ru/events/president/transcripts/24034.

209 "Trying to bring Georgia and Ukraine into NATO": Gates, *Duty*, 157–58.

209 "NATO was created": Putin press statement and answers to journalists' questions, Bucharest, April 4, 2008, http://en.kremlin.ru/events/president/transcripts/24903.

211 "Putin Accuses Georgia of Genocide": RT, August 9, 2008, https://www.rt.com/news/putin-accuses-georgia-of-genocide. After the battle, Putin's information warfare grew to include a charge that the Lugar Center, a sophisticated public health lab in Tbilisi named after a United States senator, was a secret Pentagon bioweapons factory conducting diabolical experiments on the people of Georgia.

211 "They burned our girls": Arkady Ostrovsky, *The Invention of Russia: From Gorbachev's Freedom to Putin's War* (New York: Viking, 2015), 296.

212 "dismiss the critic": Edward Lucas and Ben Nimmo, "Information Warfare: What Is It and How to Win It?" Center for European Policy Analysis, November 2015.

212 "Bet you're thinking": Goble, "Defining Victory and Defeat," 181.

212 "a new form of warfare": Modern War Institute, "Analyzing the Russian Way of War: Evidence from the 2008 Conflict with Georgia," March 20, 2018, https://mwi.usma.edu/wp-content/uploads/2018/03/Analyzing-the-Russian-Way-of-War.pdf.

213 "Russian television doesn't suggest": Mikhail Zygar, "Why Putin Prefers Trump," *Politico*, July 27, 2016, https://www.politico.com/magazine/story/2016/07/donald-trump-vladimir-putin-2016-214110.

215 "irresponsible": Ben Rhodes, *The World as It Is: A Memoir of the Obama White House* (New York: Random House, 2018), 12.

215 "all elements of our power": "Senate Confirmation Hearing: Hillary Clinton," *New York Times*, January 13, 2009, https://www.nytimes.com/2009/01/13/us/politics/13text-clinton.html.

215 "It too often became surge surge surge": Koh quoted in James Traub, "The Hillary Clinton Doctrine," *Foreign Policy*, November 6, 2015, https://foreignpolicy.com/2015/11/06/hillary-clinton-doctrine-obama-interventionist-tough-minded-president/.

216 "our clumsy and failed putsch": Gates, *Duty*, 359.

216 "I am going to tell the ministers": Gates oral history, Miller Center.

216 "This is the president": Reuters, "Hillary Clinton, Campaigning, Ponders Putin's Soul," January 6, 2008, https://www.reuters.com/article/us-usa-politics-putin/hillaryclinton-campaigning-ponders-putins-soul-idUSN0633656720080107.

216 "We worked hard": Reuters, "Clinton, Lavrov Push Wrong Reset Button on Ties," March 6, 2009, https://www.reuters.com/article/idUSN06402140.

217 "Just as we're getting on track" and "at the bottom of the huge funnel": Gates, *Duty*, 410–13.

219 Putin watched that tape and "Medvedev takes the stage": Ioffe interview for *Frontline*, "The Putin Files," https://www.pbs.org/wgbh/frontline/interview/julia-ioffe/#highlight-2289-2302.

220 "Russian voters deserve": David J. Kramer, "Now Hear This, Moscow," *Foreign*

Policy, December 8, 2011, https://foreignpolicy.com/2011/12/08/now-hear-this
-moscow/.

220 "She set the tone": David M. Herszenhorn and Ellen Barry, "Putin Con-
tends Clinton Incited Unrest over Vote," *New York Times*, December 8, 2011,
https://www.nytimes.com/2011/12/09/world/europe/putin-accuses-clinton-of
-instigating-russian-protests.html.

220 "The Kremlin successfully erodes": Peter Pomerantsev and Michael Weiss,
"The Menace of Unreality: How the Kremlin Weaponizes Information, Culture and Money," Institute of Modern Russia, 2014, https://imrussia.org/media
/pdf/Research/Michael_Weiss_and_Peter_Pomerantsev__The_Menace_of
_Unreality.pdf.

221 "break the monopoly of Anglo-Saxon global information streams": Putin interview with Margarita Simonyan, RT, June 12, 2013.

221 "a real-world equivalent": Ambassador Daniel B. Baer, U.S. permanent representative to the OSCE, "Mind the GONGOs: How Government Organized NGOs
Troll Europe's Largest Human Rights Conference," U.S. Mission to the Organization for Security and Cooperation in Europe, September 30, 2016.

221 a shadowy organization called the Internet Research Agency: Philip N. Howard,
Bharath Ganesh, Dimitra Liotsiou, John Kelly, and Camille François, "The IRA,
Social Media and Political Polarization in the United States, 2012–2018," Compu-
tational Propaganda Research Project, Oxford Internet Institute, December 2018,
https://comprop.oii.ox.ac.uk/wp-content/uploads/sites/93/2018/12/The-IRA
-Social-Media-and-Political-Polarization.pdf.

222 "The Gerasimov Doctrine": Mark Galeotti, "In Moscow's Shadows," blog post,
July 6, 2014, https://inmoscowsshadows.wordpress.com/2014/07/06/the
-gerasimov-doctrine-and-russian-non-linear-war/.

223 "the threat or the use of force": Steven Pifer, *The Eagle and the Trident: U.S.-
Ukraine Relations in Turbulent Times* (Washington, DC: Brookings Institution
Press, 2017), 70.

224 "You don't understand, George": Angela E. Stent, *The Limits of Partnership: U.S.-
Russian Relations in the Twenty-First Century* (Princeton, NJ: Princeton University Press, 2014), 168. As Putin reminded the Russian parliament in a March
2014 speech: "In 1954, a decision was made to transfer the Crimean region to
Ukraine. . . . This was the personal initiative of the Communist Party head Nikita
Khrushchev. What stood behind this decision of his—a desire to win the support
of the Ukrainian political establishment or to atone for the mass repressions of
the 1930's in Ukraine—is for historians to figure out."

226 "fuck the EU": BBC, "Ukraine Crisis: Transcript of Leaked Nuland-Pyatt Call,"
February 7, 2014, https://www.bbc.com/news/world-europe-26079957.

226 "They hadn't put a phone call on the street": Nuland interview for *Frontline*, "The
Putin Files," https://www.pbs.org/wgbh/frontline/interview/victoria-nuland
/#highlight-3137-3166.

226 "Operation Armageddon": Brian Prince, "'Operation Armageddon' Cyber
Espionage Campaign Aimed at Ukraine: Lookingglass," *SecurityWeek*, April 28,

2015, https://www.securityweek.com/operation-armageddon-cyber-espionage
-campaign-aimed-ukraine-lookingglass.

227 The Russians cut Ukraine's fiber-optic cables": Jen Weedon, "Beyond 'Cyber War': Russia's Use of Strategic Cyber Espionage and Information Operations in Ukraine," in Kenneth Geers, ed., *Cyber War in Perspective: Russian Aggression Against Ukraine* (Tallinn: NATO CCD COE Publications, 2015), https://ccdcoe.org/uploads/2018/10/Ch08_CyberWarinPerspective_Weedon.pdf.

228 "If Ukraine succeeds": Opening Statement of Ambassador William B. Taylor Jr. to the Congressional Impeachment Inquiry, October 22, 2019, https://www.nytimes.com/interactive/2019/10/22/us/politics/william-taylor-ukraine-testimony.html?module=inline.

228 "a government sponsor—specifically, a government based in Moscow": FireEye, "APT28: A Window into Russia's Cyber Espionage Operations?" October 27, 2014, https://www.fireeye.com/content/dam/fireeye-www/global/en/current-threats/pdfs/rpt-apt28.pdf.

229 "I saw people": Kulkarni quoted in Molly Schwartz, "The Man Who Taught the Kremlin How to Win the Internet," Public Radio International, May 7, 2018, https://www.pri.org/stories/2018-05-07/man-who-taught-kremlin-how-win-internet.

229 "the most amazing information warfare blitzkrieg": John Vandiver, "SACEUR: Allies Must Prepare for Russia 'Hybrid War,'" *Stars and Stripes*, September 4, 2014, https://www.stripes.com/news/saceur-allies-must-prepare-for-russia-hybrid-war-1.301464.

230 "We had a massive information gap": Nuland interview, "The Putin Files."

230 "hand-to-hand combat": Joseph Marks, "NSA Engaged in Massive Battle with Russian Hackers in 2014," Nextgov, April 3, 2017, https://www.nextgov.com/cybersecurity/2017/04/nsa-engaged-massive-battle-russian-hackers-2014/136683/.

230 "Russia is a regional power": Scott Wilson, "Obama Dismisses Russia as 'Regional Power' Acting out of Weakness," *Washington Post*, March 25, 2014, https://www.washingtonpost.com/world/national-security/obama-dismisses-russia-as-regional-power-acting-out-of-weakness/2014/03/25/1e5a678e-b439-11e3-b899-20667de76985_story.html.

Chapter 10: Democracy in America

232 "to write that white is black": Anton Troianovski, "A Former Russian Troll Speaks: 'It Was Like Being in Orwell's World,'" *Washington Post*, February 17, 2018, https://www.washingtonpost.com/news/worldviews/wp/2018/02/17/a-former-russian-troll-speaks-it-was-like-being-in-orwells-world/.

233 "purple states": indictment, *United States v. Internet Research Agency et al.*, February 16, 2018, https://www.justice.gov/file/1035477/download.

233 "Our task": "An ex-St. Petersburg 'troll' speaks out," Dozhd, October 15, 2017, cited in *Report of the Select Committee on Intelligence United States Senate on Russian Active Measures Campaigns and Interference in the 2016 U.S. Election, Volume 2: Russia's Use of Social Media*, October 9, 2019, https://www.intelligence.senate

.gov/sites/default/files/documents/Report_Volume2.pdf. (In 2014, Dozhd [TV Rain], an opposition channel, was dropped by cable providers and evicted from its Moscow studio space.)

233 "blur the lines": Renee DiResta, Kris Shaffer, Becky Ruppel, David Sullivan, Robert Matney, Ryan Fox, Jonathan Albright, and Ben Johnson, "The Tactics and Tropes of the Internet Research Agency," New Knowledge, December 17, 2018, https://cdn2.hubspot.net/hubfs/4326998/ira-report-rebrand_FinalJ14.pdf.

234 "Perhaps the most worrisome dimension": Diamond, "Facing Up to the Democratic Recession."

234 "really rich": Adam B. Lerner, "The 10 Best Lines from Donald Trump's Announcement Speech," Politico, June 16, 2015, https://www.politico.com/story/2015/06/donald-trump-2016-announcement-10-best-lines-119066.

235 "Do you think Putin": Trump tweet, June 18, 2013, https://www.lawfareblog.com/donald-trumps-statements-putinrussiafake-news-media.

235 black lacquered box: Michael Isikoff and David Corn, Russian Roulette: The Inside Story of Putin's War on America and the Election of Donald Trump (New York: Twelve, 2018), 14–18.

236 "I believe Putin": Trump tweet, March 22, 2014, https://www.lawfareblog.com/donald-trumps-statements-putinrussiafake-news-media.

236 "I spoke indirectly": Trump at National Press Club, May 27, 2014, C-Span, https://www.c-span.org/video/?c4616416/trump-i-spoke-indirectly-directly-present-putin-nicer.

236 "I know Putin," "Russia and the world," "colorful," and "When people call you 'brilliant'": Philip Bump, "The Subtle Evolution of Trump's Views on Putin and Russia, Washington Post, July 17, 2018, https://www.washingtonpost.com/news/politics/wp/2018/07/17/the-subtle-evolution-of-trumps-views-on-putin-and-russia/.

237 "ripping off the United States": Ashley Parker, "Donald Trump Says NATO Is 'Obsolete,' UN Is 'Political Game,'" New York Times, April 2, 2016, https://www.nytimes.com/politics/first-draft/2016/04/02/donald-trump-tells-crowd-hed-be-fine-if-nato-broke-up/.

237 "a vastly more complex": Report of the Select Committee on Intelligence United States Senate on Russian Active Measures Campaigns and Interference in the 2016 U.S. Election, Volume 2: Russia's Use of Social Media.

237 The IRA reached tens of millions of voters: Howard et al., "The IRA, Social Media and Political Polarization in the United States."

238 "@stop_refugees": DiResta et al., "The Tactics and Tropes of the Internet Research Agency."

238 "Hashtag Gamers": Darren L. Linvill and Patrick L. Warren, "Touched by the Trolls: How and Why a Coordinated Information Operation Interacts with Outsiders" (Clemson University, October 6, 2019), http://pwarren.people.clemson.edu/Touched_Linvill_Warren_Oct6_2019.pdf.

239 "we helped foment a coup": Stein interview on 2016 presidential race by OnTheIssues.org, July 6, 2015, https://www.ontheissues.org/Archive/OnTheIssues_Presidential_Jill_Stein.htm.

239 "a vote for Hillary Clinton is a vote for war": Stein tweet, October 12, 2016, https://twitter.com/drjillstein/status/786366228378050561?lang=en.

239 "She's a Russian asset": Aaron Blake, "Hillary Clinton Suggests Putin Has Kompromat on Trump, Russia Will Back Tulsi Gabbard Third-Party Bid," *Washington Post*, October 18, 2019, https://www.washingtonpost.com/politics/2019/10/18/hillary-clinton-suggests-putin-has-kompromat-trump-russians-will-back-tulsi-gabbard-third-party-bid/.

240 "No single group": *Report of the Select Committee on Intelligence United States Senate on Russian Active Measures Campaigns and Interference in the 2016 U.S. Election, Volume 2: Russia's Use of Social Media.*

240 "a particular hype": indictment, *United States v. Internet Research Agency et al.*

240 "HILLARY RECEIVED $20,000 DONATION FROM KKK" and "Black Matters": DiResta et al., "The Tactics and Tropes of the Internet Research Agency."

240 a quarter of a million: Howard et al., "The IRA, Social Media and Political Polarization in the United States."

The "Heart of Texas" Facebook page promoted a protest against Muslims in front of the Islamic Da'wah Center in Houston in May 2016. The IRA then launched a counterprotest, set for the same time at the same place, through its "United Muslims for America" Facebook page, which had more than 325,000 followers. The two sides met and confronted one another in a screaming rage. The cost for creating this brawl was $200. The IRA paid for its Facebook promotions through phony PayPal accounts using social security numbers and dates of birth stolen from Americans and supplied by Russian cybercriminals protected by the Kremlin's intelligence services.

241 "a military plan": Glenda Jakubowski, "What's Not to Like? Social Media as Information Operations Force Multiplier," *Joint Force Quarterly* 94 (3rd Quarter, July 2019), https://ndupress.ndu.edu/Portals/68/Documents/jfq/jfq-94/jfq-94_8-17_Jakubowski.pdf?ver=2019-07-25-162024-817.

241 "At that point": R. G. Ratcliffe, "Russians Sowed Divisions in Texas Politics, Says U.S. Senate Report," *Texas Monthly*, December 20, 2018, https://www.texasmonthly.com/news/russians-sowed-divisions-texas-politics-says-u-s-senate-report/.

242 "I had no way": Eric Lipton, David E. Sanger, and Scott Shane, "The Perfect Weapon: How Russian Cyberpower Invaded the U.S.," *New York Times*, December 13, 2016, https://www.nytimes.com/2016/12/13/us/politics/russia-hack-election-dnc.html.

242 "Manafort!": Nuland cited in Isikoff and Corn, *Russian Roulette*, 94.

243 "among the 2–3 oligarchs," "greatly benefit," and "at the highest levels": Associated Press, "Before Trump Job, Manafort Worked to Aid Putin," March 22, 2017, https://apnews.com/122ae0b5848345faa88108a03de40c5a.

243 "To keep *kompromat*": Yulia Latynina, *Okhota na Izubria* (Moscow: Olma Press, 1999).

246 "big archive": Marshall Cohen, Kay Guerrero, and Arturo Torres, "Security Reports Reveal How Assange Turned an Embassy into a Command Post for Elec-

tion Meddling," CNN, July 15, 2019, https://www.cnn.com/2019/07/15/politics /assange-embassy-exclusive-documents/index.html.

246 "Experts are telling us": Mook interview with Jake Tapper, CNN, July 24, 2016, https://www.youtube.com/watch?v=uDpdOifwVJE.

246 "The new joke": Trump tweet, July 25, 2016, https://www.lawfareblog.com /donald-trumps-statements-putinrussiafake-news-media.

248 "In the intelligence business": Michael J. Morell, "I Ran the C.I.A. Now I'm Endorsing Hillary Clinton," *New York Times*, August 5, 2016, https://www .nytimes.com/2016/08/05/opinion/campaign-stops/i-ran-the-cia-now-im -endorsing-hillary-clinton.html.

249 "An agent of some stature": "Terms & Definitions of Interest for DoD Counterintelligence Professionals," Office of Counterintelligence, Defense CI and HUMINT Center, Defense Intelligence Agency, July 1, 2014, https://www.hsdl .org/?abstract&did=699056.

249 "Those lies": Robert S. Mueller III, *Report on the Investigation into Russian Interference in the 2016 Presidential Election*, Volume 1, Justice Department, March 2019, 9.

249 "I'm a Leninist": Ronald Radosh, "Steve Bannon, Trump's Top Guy, Told Me He Was 'a Leninist,'" *Daily Beast*, April 13, 2017, https://www.thedailybeast.com /steve-bannon-trumps-top-guy-told-me-he-was-a-leninist.

249 "flood the zone with shit": David Remnick, "Trump vs. The Times: Inside an Off-the-Record Meeting," *New Yorker*, July 30, 2018, https://www.newyorker .com/news/news-desk/trump-vs-the-times-inside-an-off-the-record -meeting.

Remnick pointed out how Trump's attack on journalists as "the enemy of the people" and purveyors of "fake news" was in keeping with the language of autocrats around the world:

> Last year, the Chinese state news agency denied a report that police had tortured Xie Yang, a human-rights activist, as "essentially fake news." The Syrian President, Bashar al-Assad, denied an Amnesty International report on the thousands of people who died in a military prison between 2011 and 2015 by telling Yahoo News, "You can forge anything these days. We are living in a fake-news era." U Kyaw San Hla, a top security official in Rakhine State, in Myanmar, denied ethnic cleansing in the country, insisting, "There is no such thing as Rohingya. It is fake news." (Two Reuters journalists who exposed the killings of ten Rohingya are currently on trial in Myanmar and face up to fourteen years in prison.) In Venezuela, President Nicolás Maduro went on the Russian state channel RT and declared that "Venezuela is being exposed to bullying by the world media besieging us.... This is what we call 'fake news' today, isn't it?" After the Cambodian government put journalists in prison, expelled Radio Free Asia, and closed dozens of radio stations and the *Cambodia Daily*, Prime Minister Hun Sen went on the offensive against critical coverage in the West, saying, "I would like to send a

message to the President that your attack on CNN is right. American media is very bad."

Trump seemed to relish telling the *Times* executives that not only had he invented the phrase "fake news" but that some countries had banned "fake news."

250 the top fake stories: Craig Silverman, "This Analysis Shows How Viral Fake Election News Stories Outperformed Real News on Facebook," Buzzfeed, November 16, 2016, https://www.buzzfeednews.com/article/craigsilverman/viral-fake-election-news-outperformed-real-news-on-facebook. Silverman wrote: "During these critical months of the campaign, 20 top-performing false election stories from hoax sites and hyper-partisan blogs generated 8,711,000 shares, reactions and comments on Facebook.... Within the same time period, the 20 best performing election stories from 19 major news websites generated a total of 7,367,000 shares, reactions and comments on Facebook."

250 "Many people are saying": Tara Golshan, "Trump's Fake Controversy About Clinton's Emails Getting an Iranian Scientist Killed, Explained," *Vox*, August 9, 2016, https://www.vox.com/2016/8/9/12410882/clinton-emails-trump-iranian-scientist-executed-amiri.

251 "the founder of ISIS": Nick Corasaniti, "Donald Trump Calls Obama 'Founder of ISIS' and Says It Honors Him," *New York Times*, August 10, 2016, https://www.nytimes.com/2016/08/10/us/politics/trump-rally.html.

251 "It's crucial": Stanley quoted in Sean Illing, "How Propaganda Works in the Digital Age," *Vox*, October 18, 2019, https://www.vox.com/policy-and-politics/2019/10/18/20898584/fox-news-trump-propaganda-jason-stanley.

251 "rig the election": Jeremy Diamond, "Trump: I'm Afraid the Election's Going to Be Rigged," CNN, August 2, 2016, https://www.cnn.com/2016/08/01/politics/donald-trump-election-2016-rigged/index.html.

252 "My dashboard warning lights": James R. Clapper with Trey Brown, *Facts and Fears: Hard Truths from a Life in Intelligence* (New York: Viking, 2018), 348ff.

254 "The prospect of a hostile government": Reid letter to Comey, August 27, 2016, https://archive.org/stream/ReidLetterToComey08272016/2016-08-27--Reid%20Letter%20oto%20Comey_djvu.txt.

254 "They've found the soft spot": Rhodes, *The World as It Is*, 398.

256 "The US Intelligence Community": Joint Statement from the Department of Homeland Security and Office of the Director of National Intelligence on Election Security, October 7, 2016, https://www.dhs.gov/news/2016/10/07/joint-statement-department-homeland-security-and-office-director-national.

Afterword: An Agent of Influence

259 "I just fired the head of the FBI": Matt Apuzzo, Maggie Haberman, and Matthew Rosenberg, "Trump Told Russians that Firing 'Nut Job' Comey Eased Pressure from Investigation," *New York Times*, May 19, 2017, https://www.nytimes.com/2017/05/19/us/politics/trump-russia-comey.html.

260 "Oh, my God" and "a thorough FBI investigation": *Report on the Investigation into Russian Interference in the 2016 Presidential Election*, vol. 1, 76, 78.

260 "damning evidence": author interview with Rolf Mowatt-Larssen, January 2020.

260 "manipulating people": Fiona Hill deposition, House impeachment inquiry, October 14, 2019, https://www.justsecurity.org/wp-content/uploads/2019/11/ukraine-clearinghouse-hill_transcript-2019.10.14.pdf.

261 "to divide us": Fiona Hill testimony, House impeachment inquiry, *Washington Post*, November 21, 2019, https://www.washingtonpost.com/politics/2019/11/21/transcript-fiona-hill-david-holmes-testimony-front-house-intelligence-committee.

    Representative Jamie Raskin of Maryland asked Hill: "Why do you believe that Putin was targeting Donald Trump from his days as a businessman?" She answered: "Because that's exactly what President Putin and others were doing. Again, he was part of a directorate in the KGB in Leningrad. That's what they did. . . . The more that people are looking for business opportunities, the more that they're doing something that is illegal or certainly shady and nefarious, the more that Putin can step forward and the people around him to exploit this."

261 "tried to take me down": "Read Kurt Volker's Prepared Opening Statement From the Impeachment Hearing," *New York Times*, November 19, 2019, https://www.nytimes.com/2019/11/19/us/politics/volker-statement-testimony.html.

261 "Putin told me": Shane Harris, Josh Dawsey, and Carol D. Leonnig, "Former White House Officials Say They Feared Putin Influenced the President's Views on Ukraine and 2016 Campaign," *Washington Post*, December 19, 2019, https://www.washingtonpost.com/national-security/former-white-house-officials-say-they-feared-putin-influenced-the-presidents-views-on-ukraine-and-2016-campaign/2019/12/19/a0fdbf6-20e9-11ea-bed5-880264cc91a9_story.html.

261 "As to the question": Masha Gessen, "How Putin and Trump Each Lied in Helsinki," *New Yorker*, July 17, 2018. The translation is Gessen's. https://www.newyorker.com/news/our-columnists/how-putin-and-trump-each-lied-in-helsinki.

    Why did Trump kowtow at Helsinki? "I think . . . that there is indeed compromising information that Vladimir Putin has on Donald Trump," said the CIA's former operations director for Russia, Steven Hall. He surmised that the Russians had loaned Trump a fortune when no other bank would touch him, bailing him out in secret, and that Putin had held that *kompromat* over his head for years. Anderson Cooper interview with Steven Hall, *Anderson Cooper 310 Degrees*, CNN, July 19, 2018, http://transcripts.cnn.com/TRANSCRIPTS/1807/19/acd.01.html.

    "There's two people I think Putin pays: Rohrabacher and Trump," the House Republican leader Kevin McCarthy said to his colleagues in Congress in a private conversation on June 15, 2016. Dana Rohrabacher was a Californian Republican known as a fervent defender of Putin and Russia. Trump was about to become the Republican nominee for president. Adam Entous, "House Majority Leader to Colleagues in 2016: 'I Think Putin Pays' Trump," *Washington Post*, May 17, 2017, https://www.washingtonpost.com/world/national-security/house-majority

-leader-to-colleagues-in-2016-i-think-putin-pays-trump/2017/05/17/515f6f8a
-3aff-11e7-8854-21f359183e8c_story.html.

261 "they think it's Russia": Julie Hirschfeld Davis, "Trump, at Putin's Side, Questions U.S. Intelligence on 2016 Election," *New York Times*, July 16, 2018, https://www.nytimes.com/2018/07/16/world/europe/trump-putin-election
-intelligence.html.

What Trump said in Helsinki only made sense if understood in the full context of the conspiracy theory—that a server with damning Hillary Clinton emails somehow had been spirited away to Ukraine—whose pursuit sped his impeachment: "You have groups that are wondering why the FBI never took the server—haven't they taken the server. Why was the FBI told to leave the office of the Democratic National Committee? I've been wondering that—I've been asking that for months and months and I've been tweeting it out and calling it out on social media. Where is the server? I want to know where is the server and what is the server saying? With that being said, all I can do is ask the question. My people came to me, [Director of National Intelligence] Dan Coats came to me and some others, they said they think it's Russia. I have President Putin; he just said it's not Russia. I will say this: I don't see any reason why it would be. But I really do want to see the server. . . . What happened to the servers of the Pakistani gentleman that worked on the DNC? Where are those servers? They're missing; where are they?"

261 "one of the most disgraceful": Amber Phillips, "'Disgraceful' and 'Tragic': John McCain's Excoriation of Trump on Russia, Annotated," *Washington Post*, July 16, 2018, https://www.washingtonpost.com/news/the-fix/wp/2018/07/16
/disgraceful-and-tragic-john-mccains-excoriation-of-trump-on-russia-annotated.

262 "wholly in the pocket of Putin": John O. Brennan tweet, July 16, 2018, https://
twitter.com/johnbrennan/status/1018885971104985093.

262 "I've seen Russian intelligence": Will Hurd quoted in Justin Wise, "GOP Lawmaker: Trump Is 'Getting Played By' a Former KGB Agent," July 16, 2018, https://
hurd.house.gov/media-center/in-the-news/gop-lawmaker-trump-getting-played
-former-kgb-agent.

262 "knows how to handle an asset": Jim Sciutto interview with James Clapper, *The Lead with Jake Tapper*, CNN, December 18, 2017, http://transcripts.cnn.com
/TRANSCRIPTS/1712/18/cg.01.html.

262 "human scum": Susan B. Glasser, "On 'Human Scum' and Trump in the Danger Zone," *New Yorker*, October 24, 2019, https://www.newyorker.com/news/letter
-from-trumps-washington/on-human-scum-and-trump-in-the-danger-zone.

262 "a bunch of dopes and babies": Philip Rucker and Carol Leonnig, *A Very Stable Genius: Donald J. Trump's Testing of America* (New York: Penguin, 2020), 157.

263 "step by step": Larry Diamond, "Breaking Out of the Democratic Slump," *Journal of Democracy* 31 no. 1 (January 2020) 36–50, doi:10.1353/jod.2020.0003.

263 "We have not truly constructed": Michael Hirsh interview with Lech Wałęsa, "Why Democracy Is Failing: 'There Is No Leadership,'" *Foreign Policy*, November 14, 2019, https://foreignpolicy.com/2019/11/14/lech-walesa-poland-why
-democracy-failing-there-is-no-leadership.

264 "real country": Greg Jaffe and Josh Dawsey, "A Presidential Loathing for Ukraine is at the Heart of the Impeachment Inquiry," *Washington Post*, November 2, 2019, https://www.washingtonpost.com/national-security/a-presidential-loathing-for -ukraine-is-at-the-heart-of-the-impeachment-inquiry/2019/11/02/8280ee60 -fcc5-11e9-ac8c-8eced29ca6ef_story.html.

264 "a fictional narrative": Fiona Hill testimony, House impeachment inquiry, *Washington Post*, November 21, 2019, https://www.washingtonpost.com/politics/2019 /11/21/transcript-fiona-hill-david-holmes-testimony-front-house-intelligence -committee.

The fictional narrative that Ukraine, not Russia, hacked the Democrats may have first reached Trump via his now-imprisoned campaign manager, Paul Manafort, who got it from his business partner, Konstantin Kilimnik, who had deep ties to Russian intelligence. It was also parroted by Trump's now-convicted campaign aide Roger Stone. Among those promoting the fiction in the fall of 2019 were Devin Nunes, the ranking Republican on the House Intelligence Committee, and Tom Cotton, a Republican member of the Senate Intelligence Committee.

265 "influence United States political processes": After Oliver North, Walt Raymond, and the NSC's Soviet Active Measures Working Group created fake news for a domestic audience, as detailed in chapter 6, Congress passed and President George H. W. Bush signed a law barring the American government from mounting secret operations to "influence United States political processes, public opinion, policies, or media." The law was the 1991 Intelligence Authorization Act: https://www.congress.gov/bill/102nd-congress/senate-bill/1325.

265 "Thank God": Putin remarks at VTB Capital Investment Forum, RIA News, November 20, 2019, https://ria.ru/20191120/1561164253.html.

265 "The timing of the GRU's campaign": Area 1 Security, "Phishing Burisma Holdings," undated January 2020, https://cdn.area1security.com/reports/Area-1 -Security-PhishingBurismaHoldings.pdf.

266 It's what autocrats do": McKay Coppins, "How Mitt Romney Decided Trump Is Guilty," *Atlantic*, February 5, 2020, https://www.theatlantic.com/politics/archive /2020/02/romney-impeach-trump/606127.

266 "abetting a Russian covert operation": Brennan tweet, February 20, 2020, https:// twitter.com/johnbrennan/status/1230647803254333440.

266 "Don't believe the crap" Emily Cochrane, "Trump Talks Likes (Tariffs) and Dislikes (Media) in V.F.W. Speech," *The New York Times*, July 24, 2018, https://www .nytimes.com/2018/07/24/us/politics/trump-vfw-veterans.html.

268 "The only morality they recognize": Reagan news conference, January 29, 1981, https://www.presidency.ucsb.edu/documents/the-presidents-news-conference -992.

268 "Because the regime is captive": Vaclav Havel, "The Power of the Powerless," trans. Paul Wilson, October 1978, https://hac.bard.edu/amor-mundi/the-power-of -the-powerless-vaclav-havel-2011-12-23.

INDEX

Rice, Condoleezza, 200–201
Rickard, Donald, 80
Roberts, Owen, 64
Rockefeller, D., 194
Rockefeller, Nelson, 54–55
Romania, 181, 197
Romney, Mitt, 266
Roosevelt, Franklin D., 11
Roosevelt, Kim, 33, 35–37
Rose Revolution, 196–97, 198, 201, 222
Rosenberg, Tina, 123
Roundtable group, 122–23
Rowan, Carl, 82–83
RT, 193–94, 210, 221, 239
Rumsfeld, Donald, 105, 191, 192
Rusk, Dean, 73–74, 80, 82
Russia
    cyberattack on Estonia by, 204, 206–7
    Estonia and, 205
    Italian elections and, 18
    NATO expansion and, 180
    political warfare capabilities of, 2
    privatization scheme in, 178–79
    sanctions on, 236
    See also Soviet Union; individual leaders
Ryan, Paul, 253
Rykov, Konstantin, 236

Saakashvili, Mikheil, 196, 210
Salisbury, Harrison, 45–46
Salman, Mohammed bin, 262
Sanchez, Ricardo, 200
Sanders, Bernie, 246
Sandinistas, 144–45
Sanger, David, 247
Sarotte, Mary Elise, 172
Sartre, Jean-Paul, 131
Savimbi, Jonas, 87
Savinov, B. A., 64
Schmidt, Howard, 207
Scowcroft, Brent, 157, 161–62
secret police, history of, 3
Senate Intelligence Committee, 233, 237, 240
September 11 attacks, 190
Serov, Ivan, 48, 53
Service A (KGB), 129, 136
Shackley, Ted, 93, 96
Shah Reza Pahlavi, 34, 35, 36–37
Shalikashvili, John, 167
Shelepin, Alexander, 53, 62
Shevardnadze, Eduard, 149, 152, 161, 196
Shoigu, Sergei, 227

Shultz, George, 119, 149–52
siloviki, 202
Simba, 81–82, 83
Simons, Thomas W., Jr., 116
Skuratov, Yuri, 184–85
sleepers, in United States, 217
Slipchenko, Vladimir, 193
Slovakia, 181, 197
Slovenia, 181, 197
Smith, Keith, 205
Smith, William French, 141
Snowden, Edward, 142
social media, 235–37, 250
Société Générale, 65, 87
Solidarity movement (Solidarność), 107, 110, 113–24, 140, 157
Solidarity TV, 121
Soros, George, 196
"Sources of Soviet Conduct, The" (Kennan), 15–16
South Ossetia, 210–11
"Soviet Active Measures," 135
"Soviet Active Measures: Forgery, Disinformation, Political Operations," 137
Soviet Intelligence Activities: A Report on Active Measures and Propaganda, 1986–87, 150–51
Soviet Political Action Working Group, 143–44
Soviet Union
    Africa and, 80
    atomic bomb and, 26
    attempted coup in, 163–64
    collapse of, 5, 155, 163–65, 195, 223
    Congo and, 66–69, 71, 73, 75–76, 79
    espionage and, 14
    forced unity of, 29
    Hungarian uprising and, 47–49
    hydrogen bomb and, 41
    Iran and, 34–35
    perestroika and, 122
    Poland and, 112
    reunification of Germany and, 158–60
    Third World and, 62
    US push back on, 23–25
    See also Russia; individual leaders
spear-phishing emails, 241–42
Special Group, 76, 85
Special Warfare School, Fort Bragg, 78
spetsnaz, 210
spies. See espionage/spying

ABOUT THE AUTHOR

TIM WEINER has won the Pulitzer Prize and the National Book Award for his reporting and writing on national security and intelligence. He covered the CIA, the war in Afghanistan, and crises and conflicts in fourteen nations for *The New York Times*. Weiner has taught history and writing at Princeton and Columbia. *The Folly and the Glory* is his sixth book.